AGAINST THE ODDS

the high-risk student in the community college

AGAINST THE ODDS

william moore, jr.

 Jossey-Bass Inc., Publishers

615 Montgomery Street • San Francisco • 1970

AGAINST THE ODDS
The High-Risk Student in the Community College
by William Moore, Jr.

Copyright © 1970 by Jossey-Bass, Inc., Publishers

Copyright under Pan American and Universal
Copyright Conventions. All rights reserved.
No part of this book may be reproduced in any
form—except for brief quotation (not to exceed
1,000 words) in a review or scholarly book—
without written permission from the publishers.
Address all inquiries to:

Jossey-Bass, Inc., Publishers
615 Montgomery Street
San Francisco, California 94111

Library of Congress Catalog Card Number 74–118720

International Standard Book Number ISBN 0–87589–067–9

Manufactured in the United States of America
        Composed and printed by Hamilton Printing Company
        Bound by Chas. H. Bohn & Co., Inc.

JACKET DESIGN BY WILLI BAUM, SAN FRANCISCO

FIRST EDITION

Code 7018

THE JOSSEY-BASS SERIES IN HIGHER EDUCATION

General Editors

JOSEPH AXELROD, *San Francisco State College*

MERVIN B. FREEDMAN, *San Francisco State College and Wright Institute, Berkeley*

To—
the men and women of the General Curriculum staff
of Forest Park Community College who work hard,
think straight, and feel deeply about the low achiever,
and who never write a student off until he has had another
chance—this book is fondly dedicated

Preface

*T*his book was conceived in anger. For several years it incubated in hostility while I watched thousands of students labeled *high-risk* [1] get an inadequate education (or no education) in an institution purported to be innovative enough to serve all students. Although thousands of so-called *able* students make the same claim, the focus of this effort is on the marginal student. I wrote this book for three reasons. The first reason has to do with the plight of the high-risk student. Entrance examinations and other selection techniques are screening out *more*—not fewer—students from the community college. The dropout rate of low achievers in the open-door college continues to increase, while the number of these students who get into the regular college (as opposed to a remedial program) continues to decrease. *Against the Odds* asks why. I wrote it after observing the humiliation of the marginal student who is poorly evaluated but indiscriminately assigned to remedial courses. It is a response to the student's contempt for English

---

[1] The term *high-risk* has other preferred euphemisms: educationally disadvantaged, marginal, remedial, low-achieving.

101 and to his disgust for Western Civilization, not because these subjects are contemptible or disgusting in themselves but because they have been prostituted to prevent the education of low achievers—not to enhance it.

Any audit of the scorn projected by the student reveals not only his distaste for poor and inadequate instruction but also his discontent with administrators who continue to *reward* the poor teacher instead of condemning him or, at least, attempting to help him improve. By *reward,* the student means providing increases in salary, tenure, promotions, satisfactory evaluations, and so on, in the absence of improved performance. Furthermore, the student recognizes that he gets miserable counseling. He is keenly aware that the curriculum he uses was developed in another time, in another place, for other reasons, and for a different mind style. Finally, the high-risk student, perhaps even more than his teachers, knows that if he is to be assisted in the community college, a whole new professional attitude and a genuine commitment from faculties and administrators will have to emerge. The great paradox in all of this is that educators have attempted to convince the student that *he* is the problem. Until fairly recently, they have been rather successful in the attempt. Student frustration is the first provocation for writing *Against the Odds.*

There are, to be sure, hard-working, involved, open-minded, and committed educators who are enraged because the educational establishment does not respond in a concrete way to the needs of the marginal students. They know what can be done. For almost two decades I saw dedicated people help low achievers. Their areas spanned the continuum from kindergarten through the university. These involved men and women were in the forefront and were successfully instructing educationally disadvantaged students long before the various federal education acts subsidized education for doing what it should have been doing in the first place. The outstanding quality about these instructors who are effective in working with high-risk students is that they see the students first as people. They do not condescend by accepting the student; rather, they appreciate him. They are practitioners who feel that people are what education is all about. They are pedagogues who listen when students speak. Their standards are high but not only in terms of academic goals. The improvement of instruction is not a cliche but a goal with them. It is an objective which they internalize and define on human, academic, and operational levels. The human level has to do with the interaction between the instructor and his student, where the sheer impact of one personality on the other brings out the best qualities in both the teacher and the learner. Each is richer for having known the other. Each discovers something which will help him learn but which transcends books, courses, classes, and other educational apparatus. Each is more concerned about the status of the other. The academic level of the improvement of instruction involves finding the best of all possible ways for taking a student from one point on an academic continuum to another. In short, the student should show an improvement. The increase in skills, however, does not always have to meet predetermined goals quantitatively if the skills learned have been truly mastered, and if in the learning process of acquiring one body of knowledge the student, through his interactions with others, gains additional educational fringe benefits. The third level of the improvement of instruction is the operational and feedback level. In other words, can the student do what the school prepared him to do? If so, can he do it well? Is he looking for new ways to do it better? The good instructor finds out; he seeks and gets feedback.

Although the instructors who are effective with high-risk students are dedicated, they are also people who are angry with the traditional educational system, which has not been willing to reverse the trend or overcome the inertia, whichever is more appropriate, so we can better serve the high-risk student. These angry people are too few in number. They are the creative rebels who rock the boat and make waves. They are young and old, black and white, veterans and neophytes. They are the instructors whom students like and respect. They are the persistent antagonists who will not let the status quo continue. They can be found in Florida and New York, Missouri and California, Illinois and Oregon. They have sighed and screamed, acquiesced and protested, asked and demanded that the educational world be told, indeed convinced, that high-risk students can be educated. Their commitment, their request, and their anger constitute the second reason for writing *Against the Odds*.

There is a third reason. I was a high-risk student. According to all of the evaluative predictors, I should never have gotten a college education. My aunt once told me that I would never finish high school; the high school counselor said I probably would not get to college; the college advisor said that I was not master's degree material; and my friends told me the Ph.D. was out of the question. Fortunately, I did not know it. Since completing my schooling, I have spent eighteen of my nineteen years in education working with children and young adults from slum schools who were not supposed to be able to learn. Yet, many more of them learned than were predicted to learn. The fifteen of those years spent in the famous Banneker School District in St. Louis, Missouri, as a teacher, reading clinician, and administrator convinced me that low achievers can be helped if those charged with instructing them are committed. I am angry when educators fail to serve them. This, then, explains the third reason for writing *Against the Odds*.

Seattle
March, 1970

WILLIAM MOORE, JR.

Contents

AGAINST THE ODDS

✿✿✿✿✿✿✿✿✿✿✿✿✿✿✿✿✿✿✿✿✿✿✿✿✿✿✿✿✿✿✿✿✿✿✿✿

the high-risk student in the community college

So, then, to every man his chance—to every man
regardless of his birth, his shining, golden opportunity—
to every man the right to love, to live, to work, to be himself,
and to become whatever thing his manhood
and his vision can combine to make him—
this, seeker, is the promise of America.

Thomas Wolfe
You Can't Go Home Again

Prologue

The
Odds

*T*he high-risk student comes to the community college and faces overwhelming odds, the least of which are the academic hurdles he must surmount. No other student in higher education is subjected to the deliberate professional neglect that is shown the remedial student. There are no books written about him and virtually no research. The innovations heralded in education are not to be found in the method, content, idiom, objectives, and sphere of activity related to the marginal student. No part of the community college facility is normally constructed with the low-achieving student in mind. This student is an afterthought. He is one of the academic squatters with no specific section of the institution permanently assigned to him. Educators treat him as the villain rather than the victim.

One of the significant confrontations of the marginal student is his encounter with the opinion of his teachers. The collective attitude of the majority of his instructors is that he cannot learn. He perceives their attitude through the persistent, intangible, and undefined gut-feedback one gets when he knows he is not wanted. Because of this sensitivity, hundreds of his questions go unasked. Thousands go unanswered. He is

1

a victim of the dictum: You have to be one to teach one. Many
accept poor teaching for him as legitimate. The marginal student makes mistakes and sees his professors look the other way
because they know neither how nor what to teach him. Some
instructors who feel that the student cannot do the work do not
challenge him. Some become his pals and let him get by; they
feed the student's ego and neglect his mind. Often this treatment is understood by the student. It is one of the mutual de-
ceptions between student and instructor frequently found in
a remedial learning situation. Other teachers challenge him beyond his capabilities, seeking to prove that he has no place in
college. In either case, it is a fair statement that as a whole,
those charged with assisting the student devote little more than
a backyard effort to the task. Few speak his language and understand his feelings. Fewer still tolerate his learning style. The
term *remedial* is spoken like a dirty word by many, including
his college-age peers who are in the academic hierarchies above
him. Curriculum for this student is considered a kind of intra-
mural education that nobody takes seriously. These are the
minor pillories the high-risk student is subjected to. The shift
from the maximum lip service given to his needs to the minimum concrete action in priorities, programs, and practice is
all but convulsive. Thus, the odds are against him.

The high-risk student is asked to study books he cannot
read; write themes which are of no interest to him about subjects that are irrelevant; assigned to a curriculum that is nothing more than a patchwork of remedial measures not specifically
designed to meet his needs. This student is asked to change
his habits and to refute what he believes without having his
beliefs replaced by other ideas he considers important to him.
He has little opportunity to lead. Few people know of his positive attributes or his talents and fewer still ask him to make a
contribution. Everything he does well is a surprise—never an
expectancy. At the college level the high-risk student is considered an academic caricature because his achievement scores
have been skewed in the direction of low performance. Obviously this student is no stranger to failure. In fact, failure for
him is often a psychological expectancy. This is true whether

he looks back or ahead. In short, the odds are that the remedial student will not be any better off academically after his college experience than he was before he had the experience unless educators change the existing rules of the game or the student does what he had not been able to do in the past—that is, learn to play the educator's game. This game is difficult for the student because he has not been able, on his own, to conceptualize, memorize, absorb, or believe much of the well-defined academic liturgy coming from past educational doctrines. On the other hand, the student has not been taught well and the doctrines are never changed. The educationally disadvantaged student needs help. Yet, assistance is withheld from the remedial student who needs help while aid is freely given to the student who can make it without help. We ask the high-risk student to pick himself up by his bootstraps, to give up more than he gets. The odds against his success are overwhelming. There are, however, a few educators who are willing to bet that he will succeed.

The foregoing allegations against higher education generally and community colleges in particular are not at all excessive. They are, in fact, true and have been presented with restraint. It seems unnecessary to say that these allegations do not apply to every single community college. If one questions or protests these generalizations, however, he has but to look at his own institution.

Chapter One

The
Dilemma

*T*he two-year comprehensive community college is enjoying unprecedented growth. More than one community college per week (seventy-four) was established during the 1967–68 academic year. In 1970 there are over 1,000 such institutions from coast to coast, enrolling more than two million students. That this institution has evolved into a very significant component of the educational system of our nation is well documented. A distinguishing feature of this college has been its open-door admissions policy. It is no exaggeration that this policy implies both a new philosophy and a new challenge for post high school education, and it defies the current selection criteria for college students. The new philosophy and challenge have been accompanied by parallel emphasis on higher education for the masses. The desire for some college training has become one of the passions of the population and has resulted in an increased enrollment of a diversified student body. This variant group is made up of thousands of able students. The most significant change in the enrollment pattern, however, has been the unparalleled increase in the entry of marginal students in the group who are able to take advantage of the open-door character of the two-year school. The community college faces a dilemma: It is confronted with maintaining standards to insure the employability of its graduates and the unequivocal guarantee of its credits to other accredited colleges and universities. At the same time, it is committed by philosophy to providing some formal education or training for all students regardless of social class, sex, race, and lack of previous academic success. In either case, the comprehensive community college has no option. It has to perform both functions.

Too often the term *open-door* [1] is hypocritical rhetoric. It is a catch phrase which implies every student can enroll in the college. Open-door means more than the idea that every student with a high school diploma can go to college. It also means that the student, regardless of his level of achievement, will receive the best education possible in the college commensurate with his needs, efforts, motivation, and abilities. In reality, however, most community colleges develop the traditional programs and curricula which prepare able students to transfer to the senior institution, or terminal students to go directly into employment. The overwhelming majority of two-year institutions neither develop the same commitment, establish the same priorities nor utilize the same precision and creativity in developing the programs and curricula for the educationally disadvantaged student as they do for the able student. This student is one of the academically overlooked— or, perhaps, ignored. Disregard for the marginal student is one of the provocative footnotes which demonstrate the inability of higher education to come to terms in dealing with the non-traditional college student. In this way, post-secondary education has made little or no attempt to manage change or to match the prevailing needs with the times.

There are several other labels used in this volume and they are herein defined. The terms *high-risk, marginal, educationally disadvantaged, academically unsuccessful,* and the like are used interchangeably to specify students whose erratic high school records, economic plight, unimpressive standardized test scores, and race/cultural/class distinctions succeed in placing

[1] The terms *open-door college, community college, junior college, two-year college* are used interchangeably.

them at a disadvantage in contention with the vast majority of students applying for entry into college. The students appear to have little prognosis for success. Yet, many of them possess those intangible qualities of creativity, personality, and tenacity which counteract the customary indicators of academic prowess.

Students seek admission to community colleges for a variety of reasons. The reasons range from the most practical considerations to the most frivolous: There are students who make application to the junior college because they have been denied admission to four-year institutions—or have been dropped from them. Some students are not interested in pursuing a baccalaureate; they prefer to go into the nation's work force after they have learned a technical skill in a two-year terminal program. Others come to the college because they recognize the economy of attending a public tax-supported institution. (There are, of course, private and parochial junior colleges.) Many enroll because their parents insist that they do. A few students exercise their only option for additional post-secondary education. "It's the thing to do," for some, and a sizable number of the male students hope to avoid the military draft. Regardless of the real or stated reasons why students come to the two-year community college, a significant number of those applying are students who have been academically unsuccessful, inept, slow, and uninterested, and are classified as being educationally disadvantaged. Many of them are Negro, or Blacks as they are now called. Most of them are not.

A considerable number of the community college registrants are older than the typical college students. They are women who deferred their education to raise a family, grandmothers "with nothing to do" who wish to learn a skill for pleasure or profit. They are also young adults of both sexes who are returning to school after discovering that the opportunities in the work world are most accessible to those with some college training. Many GIs, returning from the military services, are among the entering students. Some of these older registrants are high risk because they have a history of poor academic performance, others are high risk because they have been away from active academic pursuits for a long time and sometimes find it difficult to make the readjustment to school. But once the adjustment is made, these older groups tend to make fewer failing marks, have the patience and tenacity to stay with the job and there are fewer dropouts. They establish their educational, vocational, and personal objectives with more realism and precision than younger students.

According to a recent investigation of remedial programs, it was reported that the overwhelming majority of colleges (95 per cent) identified and assigned students to developmental or remedial programs on the basis of test scores. A third of the colleges used the School and College Ability Test (SCAT). Twenty-one per cent used the American Council on Education Test (ACE), and the American College Test (ACT) is used by 18 per cent. There also are many other tests being used by various community colleges, including the Scholastic Aptitude Test (SAT), the College Qualifications Test (CQT), and other tests administered by the various states for the purpose of placement. Florida, New York, and Washington are examples (Schenz, 1963). There are also other criteria used to identify and assign students to remedial programs. Class rank at graduation and grade point averages are used. Some colleges use a percentile ranking from one of the above-named tests alone (usually the 15 percentile or below). Other colleges use a combination of the percentile ranking and class rank at graduation as criteria for placement into a remedial program.

There is an impressive and unmistakable disparity between the aspirations and the abilities of marginal students. Among such students it is common to find those who indicate that they are interested in certain professions and careers but who have demonstrated neither the aptitude, interest, means of financing (in the case of poor students), nor the persistence required to accomplish their goals. This is not a homogeneous group by any means. The members of the group have come from suburban and inner city schools, rural and urban schools, integrated and segregated schools, and private (including religious) and public schools. Students from these diversified educational backgrounds do come to the community college with aspirations (that in many cases have been indoctrinated by their

parents) which are not commensurate with their past performances. They are pressured by their parents, friends, and others
to select programs in which they have no interest as opposed
to a career or vocational program that the student might enjoy. This is because the former programs are thought to be
more economically or socially respectable.

As a consequence of much of this disparity, marginal
students must inevitably face conflict at home, in school, and
in their respective communities. Those who have no desire for
college must, nevertheless, prepare themselves to live in a highly
sophisticated society. Others want to attend college but do not
appear to be able to handle the minimum traditional curricular
demands. In this latter case, many of these students will not face
the reality of the situation. Still, these students will be expected
to operate in a complex society.

The predicament of the high-risk or marginal student
is complicated by a growing technology, one that displaces human labor. Traditionally, the student who failed to perform
satisfactorily in high school did not attempt to enter college.
He had a place to go. There was a job he could perform that
did not require college training. Now, however, as Reynolds
(1965, p. 2) points out:

> Technological progress has caused a near revolution in
> the field of occupational opportunity. Many of the old
> occupations have become obsolete. The newer ones in
> the technical fields very often require longer periods of
> preparation. The advantage once conferred by the high
> school diploma has decreased materially.

Today some college training or other advanced training
beyond the secondary school is almost one of the prerequisites
for employment; to some extent higher education is responsible. Its representatives have vociferously articulated the need
and value of college training to fulfill the requirements of em-
ployers with quality personnel. Yet, higher education has done
little to provide for the increasing numbers of the educationally
disadvantaged who lack scholastic preparation for even the least
rigorous curricula. Only the two-year college faces this burden

of truth. It is a burden that was clearly stated in a proposal for assistance that staff members submitted for the Forest Park Community College of the St. Louis–St. Louis County Junior College District to both a national foundation and the federal government:

> The increasing numbers of [educationally] disadvantaged students may be reviewed either as an overwhelming problem or an enormous opportunity. From either point of view, the degree of challenge for the two-year college is beyond question. It should not be overlooked that the form and extent of educational opportunity provided for this group of students will shape the future of the two-year college as surely as the future of thousands of disadvantaged students will be shaped by the response of the college.
>
> There are two basic directions observable among two-year colleges as they face the opportunity and challenge of the disadvantaged students. The first parallels the university model of sharp retention policies and high attrition. The unvoiced thought behind such policies is that the college's responsibility may be fulfilled by simply providing the opportunity, without concern for whether the opportunity to the individual is real or only an illusion. The second basic direction follows the path already trod by the comprehensive secondary school with the ever-increasing number of successively lower level courses to the end that all may complete secondary school. With retention the basic objective, the product is functionally illiterate, unable to find employment, and frequently not even able to pass requirements for service in the armed forces.
>
> It should be clear that while this proposal concerns itself essentially with the disadvantaged student, it bears a vital relationship also to the future of the two-year college. A beginning must be made to find new adaptive responses that will at one time both preserve the integrity of college parallel-technical offerings and provide countless numbers of disadvantaged students with a genuine opportunity to seek out constructive roles within the context of community, state, and nation.

Enrollment of the high-risk student in the community college, therefore, challenges the stated philosophy of the col-

lege to fulfill its pronouncements with a bona fide education.
Many seriously question the quality of the education provided
for marginal students. In a large number of community junior
college catalogs, a "Developmental Program" is listed; close
inspection of these documents reveals that the term "developmental program" means in most institutions several remedial
courses in the language arts (reading, grammar, spelling, and
so on) and mathematics. It does not mean a complete, well-
conceived, and well-designed program of education for the marginal student. Gordon and Wilkerson (1966) agree that:

> It is probable . . . that most of the compensatory pro-
> grams and practices reported by institutions on this level
> (junior college) are not at all special, but are a part of
> their regular ongoing programs of public education be-
> yond the high school. Of course, many socially disad-
> vantaged young people are enrolled in these programs.

The authors further state:

> In a very important sense, the regular programs of most
> junior and community colleges are inherently compen-
> satory; but they are not special programs addressed spe-
> cifically to . . . disadvantaged youth.

The open-door college purports to provide a quality
education for the marginal student. Why does it apparently fail
to fulfill this obligation? There is a sameness about the answers
college people give: There is too little research on the slow
learner at the college level, there are no models to observe, too
few experts in the area, low priority, little commitment on the
part of faculty and administration, and no tradition. One dean
of a community college in an eastern state sums it up, "We need
precedent; we don't have anything to go on." Neither did
Adam and Eve.

It is more than a lack of precedent which prevents the
community junior college from developing effective programs
in higher education for the educationally disadvantaged student. In spite of the fact that there are no *Children of Bondage*
(Davis and Dallard, 1940), no *Handbook for Teaching in the*

Ghetto School (Trubowitz, 1968), no *Learning to Teach in Urban Schools* (McGeoch et al., 1965), and none of the thousands of other books, studies, and journals describing how to teach disadvantaged students at the college level as there are at the precollege level, there are still few valid reasons why the community college cannot develop quality programs for the high-risk student. Before 1962 most of the current printed material on understanding, interacting with, and educating the marginal student at the elementary and secondary levels had not been written. There was no research, no stated commitments, and no models.

Authors like Sexton (1961), Riessman (1963), Clark (1965), Deutsch (1962), and the Ausubels (1962) are pioneers in the education of the economically deprived since 1961. These authors have become pioneers because they were willing not only to accept and investigate change but also to effect it—and in the absence of precedent. It is true that a lack of patterns or models has served as a good excuse on the part of the community colleges for nondevelopment of complete programs for the educationally disadvantaged. It is not the whole story. There are other problems.

Let me reiterate: the community junior college faces a dilemma. The dilemma is trying to provide a quality education for both the academically able student and the high-risk student. For the able student, the college does a creditable job. The faculty understands him and is happy to be associated with him because he is thought to be "college material." The school's reputation is secure with the qualified student. His accomplishments establish and maintain a good image for the college and reinforce its stature. On the other hand, the community college has not learned how to deal with, and it cannot count on, the abilities of the marginal student. It has not developed the knowhow or the real commitment for dealing with him. His academic prowess does not have a history of reflecting on the college in a positive way—if at all. The fact that this student was accepted by the community college in the first place is considered by some persons as an inherent weakness in the college.

It is no exaggeration to say that the dilemma has many

components. Any one of them may prevent the community college's effectively planning a program for the educationally disadvantaged. Four of the components are explored here: identity, the challenge of numbers, sparse research, and the conflict of faculty.

The community junior college is still in search of an identity of its own. People inquire, are a junior college and a community college one and the same? They ask, is the two-year institution more like a high school or a vocational school than a college? Other members of the public, especially high school seniors, want to know whether the credits earned at a community junior college can be used in a "real" college. There are many other queries in the same vein. The questions seem to indicate that some people view the two-year college as something less than a higher education institution. The true concept of the community junior college has only fragmentary understanding or is completely misunderstood. Too many laymen do not know what the role and function of this institution are, and too many professionals seem unsure. Consequently, the quest for identity persists.

The lack of identity of the community college is complicated by its relationship to both the secondary school and the four-year college or university. It is closely associated with the precollege institution. Often it is part of a public school system and is under the authority and leadership of the local school superintendent; because of this, it is considered the thirteenth and fourteenth grades. In many places the local two-year college operates only at night in a public high school building. It is not unusual to find former high school teachers who have become faculty members in the junior college. There is a heterogeneity of abilities among community college students which is not tolerated at most four-year institutions. Like the high school, the community college not only appreciates but also solicits the concerns of parents. Faculty members are not required to do research or to publish in order to hold their positions or to be granted tenure where this applies because the primary function of the teacher is to teach. The junior college has no vested interest in students (in sports, for example) beyond providing a sound education. The above characteristics describe some of the tenets of the high school. Although the community college should not, could not, and dare not sever its relationship with the secondary school, it is in quest of a distinct identity of its own. There is a new vocabulary which emphasizes such an identity: "salvage institution," "second-chance college," and "open-door college."

The two-year college also has close contact with the college and university. The original junior college idea was developed by people from the four-year college who originally designed the two-year college as a "feeder institution" for the senior college. Whether the community college is state, local, private, church related, or maintained as a branch of a university, by its very nature it must have contiguous relationships with the senior college. It resembles the four-year school in various ways: It is governed by a board of trustees. The minimum credential requirements for faculty are now virtually the same as in many four-year colleges, that is, the M.A. in the subject-matter field or the equivalent. A larger portion of its faculty are beginning to come from existing liberal arts colleges and graduate schools. The administrative structure of the two-year college is similar to that of the university; and the curricula patterns for transfer students in the community college must parallel that of the university which, after all, will be the recipient of the students from the two-year school. The whole idea and reality of academic freedom is enjoyed by the junior college faculty as it is with the senior college faculty. We hear such labels as professor, dean, and provost. Those factors of admissions, scholarships, loans, counseling, placement, and so on, which are a part of the university syndrome, have had some influence on the lower college. In these ways and in many other ways the public community college often appears to mimic the four-year college to such a degree that one sometimes finds it difficult to distinguish the former from the latter. It would appear, therefore, that the community college is amorphous. It is expected to bridge the gap between the high school and the senior college without clearly establishing an identity of its own. It is accepting the challenge of bridging the gap but rejects

any attempt to obscure its own identity. There is little virtue
and no advantage in the community college being absorbed in,
or being described as, the thirteenth and fourteenth grades of
high school. Rather, the junior college must be viewed as a
bona fide educational institution in higher education with a
definite role and function. Too long, the attitude of the four-
year college to the two-year college has been one of tolerance.
Actually, the university has frequently responded to the community college as though the relationship was illicit; the latter
being assigned the role of mistress—all right to woo but not to
wed.

  The two-year comprehensive college, although it shares
several characteristics with the high school and the university,
has features that distinguish it from both. Perhaps the most
distinguishing characteristic is the policy of admitting to college
students who would otherwise be economically, socially, and
academically alienated from higher education. To begin with,
the community college is a tax-supported institution, and as
such, there is either little or no cost to the student. Because of
the public ownership, and low cost, there is no attempt on the
part of the college to recruit students from well-known "status"
preparatory schools or students who are the children of pres-
tigious people. The open-door college admits students who
exhibit the entire range of academic abilities. The community
college has the flexibility to meet the needs of both the honors
student and the student in the developmental curricula. This
flexibility permits acceptance of students whose diverse interests may span the gamut from transfer, technical, vocational,
and developmental programs to students (primarily adults) who
are concerned only with community service courses. Without
getting involved in an emotional binge about the value of an
educated citizenry to a democratic society and the guarantee to
every student of an opportunity to succeed commensurate with
his level of abilities and efforts, let it suffice to say that the
community college is the only institution in higher education
which attempts to be all things to all people. Clark (1960), writing in *The Open-Door College,* says it well:

A secure status for a junior college finally depends largely on perception of it as something different and acceptance of this difference. A recognition reasonably consonant with the character of the junior college thus seems dependent on the building and communicating of an identity. Such a college needs to spread the word locally about much of the particular combination of tasks and roles it has assumed. An identity also needs to be shown to the college world. This suggests that the building of a communicable and socially acceptable identity is the problem resulting from the character of the unselective junior college.

An effort, then, to sell a new junior college to outsiders and to achieve a secure status in the general society is likely to be successful if the organization has a sense of identity and communicates it in acceptable terms. The first requirement, the building of a somewhat distinctive image, is made difficult for the public junior college, however, by its overlap with better known types of schools. Duplication in one direction lies in its role as a lower division for senior colleges and universities. . . . In addition, there may also be a jurisdictional overlap with technical high schools and adult programs. When asked to assume programs formerly conducted by regular high schools, there is additional confusion. The gaining of a reasonably clear identity is further complicated by the interplay of conflicting needs and orientations. The need of the junior college for status in the academic world pulls orientation toward transfer work; but the need for a unique function, to be able to do something that no other organization does, pulls toward the terminal, as does the non-college nature of the majority of the student body. The uniqueness of the terminal work is of special value, at first glance, in building and projecting an identity, since a unique operation can be used to claim a distinctive place in education.

The public junior college is free of the heritage and time-worn tradition which would bind it inextricably to the past and thereby minimize its flexibility. Although there is a board of trustees to make policy for the community college, advisory committees from the public at large—who represent business, industry, and the service occupations and who know the needs, appetites, and demands of the public—are included in the planning and development of the curricula. The junior college makes use of the talents and skills of educators who work at educational levels other than the collegiate level (elementary and secondary) as well as non-degree educators—for example, an individual working in a technical field. Non-degree educators are viewed as not being academically respectable in four-year higher academic communities.

The counseling in the community college is student-centered. It is not designed to use the students as research subjects. The counselors are not involved with delinquent behavior referrals, excessive student records, and other such routines found in the secondary school, or what some describe as the detached clinical approach of the university. All of their time is given to the student. Sports are well balanced but not as highly organized and competitive as they are in both the secondary school and the college. Consequently, more students can participate.

Perhaps the outstanding community college is most unique in its attempt to develop teachers who not only are excellent educational practitioners but also are concerned about the students. This is most discernible in the accessibility of the teaching faculty to the students in the community college as compared to the lack of faculty availability to freshmen and sophomores enrolled in the senior college. This faculty inaccessibility is also noticeable in the high school. Although the secondary teacher may want to give more time to the student, he has five classes daily. His one free period each day and the study period of a given student may be scheduled at different hours. Consequently, neither is free at the same time. At the university level (particularly the large university) the freshman and sophomore student rarely sees the professor. In the absence of a professor, too often the student finds himself taught by a graduate student who is more concerned with completing the requirements for his own degree than helping the student. The professor frequently will not know the members of his class. Sometimes he is brought to a given institution solely because his name and reputation will attract huge financial grants. Consequently, he may be so involved with research that he never schedules office hours for undergraduates, especially those who are freshmen and sophomores. Some students who demand the time of such college personnel are considered impudent. Others are ignored.

The cry for academic freedom on the part of faculty members in the four-year college prevents much of the needed criticism and evaluation of their teaching, and instruction as a whole, in higher education. By contrast, in the community college there is an organized attempt to improve the quality of instruction at all levels. Instructors are frequently evaluated in the better comprehensive colleges. Whether his rank is "instructor" or "professor," no individual or classroom is taboo. If an instructor is having difficulty, it is discovered early. In most junior colleges, some corrective steps, rather than immediate dismissal, are taken to assist the instructor. Consequently, the instructor learns, grows, and improves. Finally he becomes a better teacher. This is rapidly changing. Garrison (1968) describes the new teacher in higher education.

> The junior college teacher is—or may be becoming—a new breed of instructor in higher education. Markedly different in significant ways from the usual situation of his four-year colleagues are his conditions of instruction, his aims, and his professional-philosophical attitudes toward his task. Not simply a post-high school instructor of grades thirteen and fourteen, he is, in his own desire and view, a colleague in a new kind of collegiate effort, as yet ill-defined and in furious flux. He is unsure of his status in the educational spectrum, for he fits few traditional categories. He is aware that he is being asked to function professionally in an unprecedented situation, and he is deeply concerned about this professionalism, in the best sense of that term. He is the servant of several demanding masters, and he is groping to bring such demands into a compatibility, a coherence, that will give his work a clear rationale and thrust that will command his loyalty and his long-range commitment.

One is compelled to be impressed by the surprise reaction of educators when they observe the obvious, the inevitable, and the expected. For two decades they watched the symptoms of an expanding population. The predicted baby boom of the late nineteen forties and early fifties materialized as expected. In spite of the well-documented predictions on the acute increase in births, boards of education and school people acted surprised when school enrollment doubled and tripled a few years later. The elementary schools quickly became overcrowded. The shortage of space forced school officials to operate some educational plants on double shifts and to resort to other educationally unsound practices. There was also a corresponding shortage of qualified teachers. In urban areas, many school play yards were replaced by additional buildings. The secondary school, with a longer time to prepare, had some of the same problems. Due, in part, to a thriving economy, liberal GI educational benefits, and an unparalleled emphasis on and availability of higher education, students came to the colleges in massive numbers also. All of these symptoms have been concerned with the schools and education; they were all obvious and inevitable; they should have been expected. They were a part of the excessive enrollment syndrome. There were other signs of population growth. Traffic became unmanageable; one-way streets became a way of life. Much of the mass production of materials formerly done by a human work force was preempted by electronic technology. There were, of course, many other indications of population gain and the growth has been handled in different ways. The birth rate was counteracted with "the Pill"; traffic congestion was "relieved" by building free ways; and production was made more efficient with the computer; to deal with all the problems of education, we set up committees.

Committees probably cannot solve the problem. According to the *1968 Junior College Directory*, the average annual rate of increase in junior college enrollments over the five years 1963–67 has been 15.41 per cent. In 1967 there was a 14.16 per cent increase over 1966. Harris (1964) estimated that one and a half million students would be enrolled in public junior colleges by 1970; in 1969 that number had already been surpassed. At the current enrollment rate, the community college will have to construct more colleges in the next ten years than in the previous fifty. Concomitantly, four-year colleges continue to raise the requirements for admission. As a consequence we will find thousands of able students who could not qualify for admission to senior college, but who, nonetheless, are better than average students. Similarly, there are thousands of other able students who do not apply for entry because of financial difficulties. Both groups will be eligible to attend the public community college—and will. As the number of able students seeking admission to the two-year college increases, so does the number of high-risk students. The community college philosophy and its open-door admissions policy will be challenged. Eventually the community college will find it necessary to restrict enrollment. It will be forced to turn away able students in order to make space for students who are considered to be less able. The alternative is to deny enrollment to the high-risk student. To exclude the marginal student is to forfeit both the community college philosophy and the open-door admissions policy, and (in most states) the college will be in violation of statute. Eventually a quota system or a lottery, or some other system stripped of the human dimension, will be developed to select students applying for admission to the community college. If we follow this logic, it is inevitable that the competition for admission to the two-year college will be as keen as it is for admission to the senior institution. When this happens—and it will—the selection committee of the junior college will be compelled to exercise a twofold option: "Pick the best of the eggheads and the best of the dummies," is the way one dean of student personnel services puts it.

As we have seen, the horns of the dilemma of increasing numbers are sharply honed. This problem of the increasing junior college population is already monumental for some schools. Since both the marginal and the able student are petitioning with equal vigor for a share of education's rewards, college people will not be able to postpone action. It would appear that the community college will have to substantiate and support the need for providing a quality education for the high-risk student with the same enthusiasm and priority as it

does for the capable student—more so. College representatives
will have to be able to say with conviction that a program for
the educationally disadvantaged student is as important to the
community, indeed, to the nation, as is the program for the
transfer or technical student. They must meet the current
dilemma. One way to resolve a part of this conflict is to give
the marginal student more attention because this student can
make a contribution in excess of what he is calculated to be
able to make. Already he secures employment and performs the
job efficiently beyond his level of ability as indicated by tests
administered by the college.

We are constantly told that virtually no research has
been done to assist the educationally disadvantaged in learning
at the college level. We are also told that no materials are available to teach the marginal student. Both statements are incor-
rect. There are hundreds of books and thousands of studies
which have investigated learning, low ability, and underachievement. The fact that most of these studies and materials have
not been written specifically for the two-year college is irrelevant; most of the research conducted and books written for
primary, elementary, and secondary school students are written
by college professors. In psychology we study the abnormal in
order to understand the normal. There are, however, resources
available about the junior college. There is an ERIC (Educational Resources Information Center) clearinghouse for junior
college information at the University of California at Los Angeles. A joint project of the UCLA School of Education and
the University Library, this ERIC clearinghouse began operations in summer 1966. Its overriding purpose, according to its
director, is "to process studies so that information would become available for people making important decisions in junior
colleges. Accordingly the clearinghouse set out to acquire, in-
dex, and abstract research documents and research-related materials and to disseminate them to the field in a variety of ways"
(Cohen, 1967).

The junior college is a toddler in the area of research
but there are sources available in almost every area. There is
printed material on innovation, testing, programs for the low

ability student, problems and needs, performance of transfer students, and many other subjects. The ERIC clearinghouse on the disadvantaged stores thousands of studies. Yet, one would have a less-than-sharp eye on reality if he did not admit that a great deal more research is needed on the junior college, particularly as this college relates to the educationally disadvantaged student. In like manner, it must be granted that there are very few models for the community college to emulate. Still, the lack of precedent cannot become the code phrase for apathy.

There is still another component of the dilemma: the sense of frustration of the faculty who will be responsible for devising programs for the low-achieving or nonachieving student. Teachers no longer attempt to conceal their lack of knowledge and understanding of the marginal student in college or their lack of training which would help ameliorate his learning problems. Teaching a high-risk student is a highly skilled, intellectually demanding task, requiring instructors with unique skills. Teachers who have these skills learned them. They tend to be open-minded, genuine, patient, and want to learn. They do not construe working with the educationally disadvantaged student as an illegitimate extension of their proper function. There are other faculty who feel differently. This latter group of teachers feel that their proper function and that of the college is maintaining standards. Almost no one disputes the legitimacy of the faculty's concern for educational achievement. Yet it is equally legitimate to be concerned about educational failures. To reconcile these two justifiable anxieties is an evident source of conflict.

The biggest problem of the faculty appears to be a lack of information and training. Books, even good ones, written on the community or junior college have not been specifically addressed to the identity, problems, and needs of the low-achieving student. The three most quoted books (Clark, 1960; Medsker, 1960; Thornton, 1966) in junior college literature since 1960 do not specify the distinguishing characteristics of the academically unsuccessful student. It follows that they have not suggested a curriculum for him. There is nothing found in teacher training techniques designed to teach college instructors how to teach high-risk students. The individual differences in students which are highlighted, analyzed, researched, and inculcated in the training of elementary and secondary school teachers are not tenets for consideration for teachers in higher education. The natural sympathies for students who are slow, parental opinions, concern about what the next instructor will think, and pride in their skill as teachers are pressures which do not appear particularly threatening to teachers in higher education.

There are steps that have been taken to understand the underachiever. The correlates of academic performance have been isolated. Techniques have been devised for improving the poor performance of slow students. Commitment has been voiced. And the presence of the high-risk student is a firm educational reality. Yet, the arbitrary assertions and assumptions made about the student who needs help in basic skills preempt the attempt to ameliorate the problem. This has spawned a unique pedagogical controversy which will force faculty and administration to go beyond the traditional and routine educational boundaries. The definitive and restrictive ways of past techniques which are effective in instruction of the able student are being challenged, if not by new and well-developed processes, certainly by a kind of intuitive expertise. In either case the teacher is in the middle. Either side he chooses causes him to be rejected by the other. On the other hand, he can remain where he is without direction, information, firm involvement, and skill.

College people have always known that there is a large number of able students whose scholastic performance lags far behind their intellectual ability. Disadvantaged students are represented by this same inconsistency. Even faculty members who are willing to subscribe to the idea that marginal students are lacking in learning rather than ability to learn are disappointed when these students enroll in college where they have an opportunity to learn but fail to do so. College people have also understood the conflict of culture and expectation between themselves and many high-risk students. They do not appear to understand the intra conflict of cultures between academically unsuccessful students: black and black, white and white, black and white. The common ground between these groups is their low achievement.

As we have seen, the absence of a clearly defined identity, the challenge of numbers, sparse research, and the conflict of faculty are all components of the dilemma and, as such, must give junior college educators cause for concern and an intimate sense of conflict. If the problem of devising a program for the educationally disadvantaged is ever resolved—and of course, it must be—a great deal more will have to be known about the student who is to be taught, the teacher, the curriculum, the educational setting, and the rest of what have been called the pivotal problems of education.

Chapter Two

The
Student

*T*here are many descriptions of the junior college student. All of the measures of central tendency have been applied to delineate him. These measures reduce him to little more than a statistical caricature having neither sharp distinction nor complete obscurity. He is a variant breed concealed in that vast wasteland called average. A few years ago this meant white, male, nineteen years of age, holds a part-time job, is enrolled in a business curriculum, has an aptitude for academic pursuits less than that of a university student, and has never challenged the system. This description does not characterize the "average" student today. The current student represents many diverse people, interests, and communities that cannot be readily identified or muzzled. When one considers the description of the educationally disadvantaged student, which is but one classification of junior college student, the same anonymity prevails. There are several subcategories of the high-risk student. They will be described here to emphasize their cultural and experiential differences rather than their academic compatibility. The stereotype of the low-performing student needs no documentation. Too frequently his description is synonymous with the lower-class, poor white student or any black student. The middle-class student who is marginal is considered almost an exception and is thought to have psychological problems when he is slow. This stereotype, like most, is inaccurate. The high-risk student is not confined to our slums. He is indigenous to the total class structure. Whether this student lives on the curving lanes of a suburban drive or the teeming streets of Harlem, he is spawned in our own homes, in our own schools, and in our own communities. He is among us a marginal discard. And there are more differences among marginal students than there are similarities.

Research has a way of being redundant. All of the studies on the student characteristics of community college registrants which the author has seen reveal findings which show the distribution of students according to academic aptitude, socioeconomic status,[1] age, sex, geographic distribution, and other such demographic inputs. These data deal with numerical apportionments; and statistics have a way of obscuring quality and character. Too many of the studies on the student characteristics of junior college enrollees are too old to be currently applicable to the needs, changes and ever-increasing enrollment of community college registrants as a whole, and do not get at some of the fundamental problems of understanding the high-risk student in particular. A more definitive description of this student is necessary. More specifically—who is he?

The ten brief case histories of community college students which follow are real cases. They are included here to emphasize not only the great diversity among high-risk students but also the similarity of the method used (that is, attendance at a junior college) by these students to ameliorate their common predicament, namely, their low performance and achievement. The names of the students have been changed but their stories are recorded here with permission. The names of institutions they will, or do, attend have not been changed.

Andrea's parents are divorced. She has lived with her mother since she was nine years old. She claims to recall the constant bickering and nagging of a mother who wanted every-

---

[1] This is primarily earning power rather than social class status.

thing from a husband who had nothing. Her father taught
school. Where there is tension and stress in a family, someone
always gives. The father did; he became an alcoholic. The
mother used his affliction as grounds to be awarded the divorce.
Andrea's father moved to another city while the mother—we
will call her Mrs. Wilks—set about getting the things she
wanted. Mrs. Wilks did not remarry. She was, however, per-
petually betrothed to an impressive list of suitors. With the
termination of each engagement she had acquired another mink
coat or expensive car. Yet, she never had a bank account of more
than a few hundred dollars.

In March, 1969, Andrea was a candidate for high school
graduation. At seventeen, she was envied by both her classmates and her female teachers. She was a "fashion piece" in
her high school. Everything about her emphasized one quality
—glamour. She wore false eyelashes, several changes in hair
attachments and clothes that would probably cost more than
half the salary of a beginning teacher who might have taught
her. Andrea is pretty—like her mother, who is still a glamorous
woman in spite of her forty years. Mrs. Wilks has made the
cover of several magazines, drives an expensive car, has several
changes in fur coats, is known as a party girl and a "bunny-
mother." [2] She lives in that area of Los Angeles enviously called
"mink canyon." Sometimes, behind the closed doors of her
lavish quarters and hidden from the view of others, Mrs. Wilks
batters Andrea around because both are known to compete for
attention from the same men. Andrea is really quite bright: she
is articulate, sophisticated and charming but, nonetheless, a "D"
student. She could not successfully apply herself to the routine
and monotony of study, or the restrictions and rules of going
to school. She would cut classes, claim a free period and "hire
herself out" as service-worker to a counselor or teacher, leave
school to keep appointments at the beauty salon, and play
truant in the school building by spending the entire day in the
girl's toilet primping. The counselors who worked with Andrea

[2] Girls who are pretty but are too old to be bunnies (waitresses)
and work in the Playboy Club sometimes work in the club as chaperones,
wardrobe people, and so on.

recognized her many "hangups" but had difficulty communicating with her mother, who seemed always on the defensive, who
abdicated her responsibility, and who put the burden of proof
on the school. School people really pitied Andrea because there
was little they could do to help her either academically or atti-
tudinally without more assistance from her home. Teachers
knew that she was a creative liar but so charming they could
not get exasperated with her. When confronted with her fabri-
cation, she would often break down and cry. She would then
mouth all of the expected penitence. The other students in
the school rejected Andrea. She was not only ostracized by
the girls, as might be expected, but she was also shunned by the
boys. Students did not want to stand beside her to be photo-
graphed for the yearbook. One student readily admitted
her sophistication but hastily followed this admission with the
statement: "She is a dumb broad." The students did not reject
her because their own behavior was more puritanical; in many
cases their behavior was worse. They appeared to reject her
because in spite of her poor performance in school, she was more
sophisticated and had more of the items and symbols of things
that many students want. They could not compete with her.
Andrea was sarcastic with them and would always "put them
down." It is a fact that Andrea has not done well in school and
apparently has many problems of adjustment, but she has been
convinced that a career as an airline stewardess would be one
well-suited to her interests, talents, and demeanor. Andrea will
go to college about 112 miles north of Los Angeles at Bakersfield College. She hopes to enroll in the Airline Stewardess program in that two-year school.

Pedro lives in a dismal tenement on Fiftieth Street near
Tenth Avenue on New York City's west side. He can walk to
Broadway, Rockefeller Center, the National Broadcasting Company (NBC), and other nearby centers of great wealth and
power in a matter of minutes. This young man, now nineteen
years old, came from Puerto Rico along with his parents and
five brothers and sisters. His family moved in with relatives
prior to coming to the Fiftieth Street location. The father deserted the family, leaving the mother to support the family on

a low-salaried job. There are no English-language newspapers, books, or magazines to be found at Pedro's home. The mother speaks a little English but Spanish is the language spoken both in the building where Pedro lives and in his home. A television set is the only luxury in the home. Pedro learned much of the English he knows from watching TV. Living in the tenement where Pedro lives is like living out of doors. The triumphs of a tenant as well as his adversities are exposed. People are everywhere—on the stoops, in the corridors, on the roof—everywhere. Simply by turning the volume of the television down Pedro can hear people in the apartment next door as they make love, and argue, and fight—and sometimes laugh. He passes women in the narrow hallways who smell of cheap perfume, men who smell of sweat, and babies who smell of sour milk and urine. He struggles for a space at the window to share the infrequent breeze. He lies awake at night and listens to the rats, which defy all but professional exterminators. There is not enough of anything but people. Privacy is nonexistent. Pedro lives on the threshold of poverty. In his community, the resentment, hostility, ferment, and tension are built in. In spite of Pedro's background and environment—or because of it, depending upon one's point of view—he did not get into difficulty with the police. He did not become a gang member, or fight, or get involved with dope or any of the other items, behaviors, and symbols reputed to be indicative of moral turpitude. His high school counselor talked about him. "He's a great kid, never in trouble, liked by all of the other kids—the saints and the thugs alike. I don't know how he does it but he keeps his nose clean." Although the problem with English was almost insurmountable, Pedro still managed to graduate from high school in 1969. He had made high grades in most of his courses. It is obvious to all who knew this student that the conventional tests of mental ability, which are based on a student's facility with language and knowledge of American cultural patterns, were inappropriate for him. Pedro's file gives an invalid picture of his ability. Nevertheless, he enrolled at the Bronx Community College, Fall 1969.

    Max, twenty, is redheaded, freckled, and the son of a

highly paid computer designer and his wife. In addition to his
parents, he lives with a younger brother and sister in a beautiful $40,000 four-bedroom colonial ranch home in Montgomery
County, Maryland. From all indications Max is a popular, well-
adjusted young man. He lives in a home where there appears
to be sufficient love, understanding, attention, communication,
and all of the other requisites used by educators to describe
students they can teach. His parents are involved with a few
church and other activities designed to maintain and improve
the community. The Boy Scouts, father-and-son events, and
camping and fishing trips have always been occasions shared
by the family, along with sports and photography. Money is
not a problem. The boy's family gives him most of the things
he wants. First, however, they attempt to see that he does something to earn it. They can afford to send him away to a "good"
college if he is accepted for admission to one. Max was not admitted to any of the colleges where he applied. He is a low
achiever. From the very beginning, Max had trouble in school.
Long before the subdivision where he lives replaced the virgin
acreage, he went to school in one of the rich suburbs of Chicago. There he was slow in kindergarten as well as every grade
in his entire elementary and secondary school experience.
Throughout his school years his parents have hired tutors and
purchased some of the best materials they could find. None
proved successful. Max could barely pass his courses. Max was
graduated when he was eighteen years of age (1969). He had
applied to several colleges but none would accept him. Since
he was not enrolled in a college, he was inducted into the military service. While in the service he became fascinated with
tutoring soldiers whose performance was less than his own. He
was made an instructor and was considered by his superior officers to be an excellent tutor. Max began to study on his own
and apparently has profited from his goal-directed study. After
his discharge from the army, and since he had been denied admission to several four-year colleges, he applied to the local
community college. His ultimate goal is to work with adults
who have learning difficulties. He is confident that his own
scholarship will improve. It is as if working with other persons

who demonstrate low performance will improve his own. He is
a freshman at Montgomery County Community College in
Maryland.

In the district where *Archie* attended school the dropout rate is high. When he was graduated from the eighth grade,
there were thirty-four members in the class. Two years later,
an audit of those alumni revealed that of the girls two were
unwed mothers, two were forced to marry because of preg-
nancy, five were high school dropouts, one was a suspendee, and
four were still in good standing in the high school. The activities of the boys in the class were equally unusual by normal
standards, although they were typical of Archie's community:
one of the boys was dead—killed committing a robbery; two
were in jail; one was in Lexington, Kentucky, taking the cure
for narcotics addiction; five were in the military; and six were
dropouts—working at various unskilled jobs. Only five were
graduated from high school and Archie was among the graduates. Archie can see the tallest national monument in America
(The Gateway Arch in St. Louis, Missouri) from his window
in the three-room apartment where he and seventeen other
people must eat and sleep. Archie is a black student who has
the scars from rat bites on his hands and face because he was
put to bed at night with a penny sucker (candy) to pacify him
when there wasn't any milk. He also has the memory of a baby
sister who died after being bitten by a rat. At seventeen, he still
sleeps with another sibling. The people in the house eat in
shifts. This student grew up in the inner city. He has watched
his peers—one by one—go to prison, become winos, pool sharks,
and pimps. In fact, Archie was a problem himself. The police
picked him up many times when he was truant in the elementary school and infrequently he was considered a behavior
problem in high school. Archie lived in a fatherless household.
He would go to school in winter because school was the only
place he knew where he could keep warm. As a youngster he
was always hungry. The lunchboxes of his classmates were
never secure when he was around. The castoffs of his mother's
employer constituted his wardrobe for as long as he could remember. When Archie was a sophomore in high school he got

a part-time job waiting on tables. He saw how people other than those he had always known acted. He listened to people talk and use words he had never heard. The words, he discovered, were like those he read in his schoolbooks. Guests in the hotel were polite to one another; this impressed him. He saw people argue with a passion who never resorted to force. As he saw the way others lived, he was dissatisfied with the way he lived. Archie became a mimic. He tried to do at home and in his community what he saw done where he worked. Many of his friends and even some of his teachers in the high school felt he acted snobbish and detached. His mother considered him unrealistic. Former gang members were hostile toward him because he would rather play chess than shoot craps. Although he had never been a good reader, he pretended to be. He took several boards and a few bricks and made a makeshift bookshelf. On this bookshelf near Archie's bed one found himself in the company of some time-tested titles: *Grapes of Wrath, A Tale of Two Cities, Death of a Salesman,* and many, many others. Archie could not understand and interpret much of the literature on his shelf. It took him a week to read a book that a student with more demonstrated ability could read and comprehend in two days. Archie was also slow in mathematics, that is, he never seemed interested in the subject beyond what was necessary for him to function. He could work well with motors. Archie could dismantle a motor or a transmission or any other power plant on an automobile and reassemble it with efficiency and precision. Yet, he was frequently unable to read with facility and understanding the manual which gave instructions as to how it should be done. He built a car out of spare parts from thirteen other old cars. This student has the aptitude and skill to become a first-rate mechanic. He does not demonstrate the academic competency nor the motivation. In the first case, academic competency, he hopes to improve in the General Curriculum program of the Forest Park Community College in St. Louis, Missouri. In the second case, motivation, Archie has been erroneously indoctrinated to believe that it is more important to be a professional than to be a mechanic. It will require a formidable counseling job to convince this student that if he finishes the General Curriculum program successfully, he should consider the school's Automotive Technology program.

Julie Steiner has had to spend too many of her nineteen years attempting to refute the stereotype that "all Jews are smart." She is the first to say: "All Jews are not smart. I know. I'm a Jew. It's not that I'm unmotivated, a late bloomer, and all of that other jazz that they come up with; the fact is, I am not very good in school and never have been. Why can't people be as realistic as I am? Everybody tells me I can do better than I do. First, it's my mother saying that I don't apply myself; then, it is the rest of the relatives. As far back as I can remember teachers have been writing on my report card: 'Needs more time.' Well, I am almost twenty years old and that ought to be time enough to improve. Besides, I am going to get married to Solomon Rosenthal, have babies, and be a full-time housewife. As soon as I graduate from high school, and, incidentally, I'm a year and a half behind, I am going to the local community college because it is the only college which has accepted me. I can't go to any of those fancy schools that my parents want me to attend and that's fine with me. I'm tired of all the pressures and comparisons my folks throw at me. Maybe I can get out of this college rat race in two years and forget it." Julie Steiner will attend St. Petersburg Community College.

In 1967, *Darlene* was in San Francisco's Haight-Ashbury. Her parents convinced her that if she was not satisfied with society, she should not drop out of it; she should rejoin it, then do something about improving it. She did. She went to Chicago and worked with Dr. Martin Luther King in his Operation Breadbasket until his assassination in April of 1968. She then went to work as a supporter and volunteer for the presidential campaign of U.S. Senator Robert Kennedy until his assassination in June of the same year. She was back in Chicago in August at the national Democratic Convention. This time, she was working for the presidential nomination of United States Senator Eugene McCarthy. Her candidate, of course, lost. She was also one of the people trapped in Chicago's Grant Park and beaten by the police. In the spring and summer of 1968, Darlene was a loser of causes. Darlene's disillusionment did not start in the summer of 1968. It had started three years before in her upper middle-class home in a suburb of Chicago. It was one of those uneventful days when a chance remark or a turn of events ignites the spark which changes the lives of people involved. Darlene had always been a good student in school, and had never caused her parents or teachers or anyone else any difficulty. She attributed her model behavior to her being reared by good parents. Her parents and teachers alike had taught her the ideals of fair play, honesty, and the other virtues, including work. The church too had constantly taught her the Golden Rule, the Beatitudes, and so on. Then, at age sixteen, she had her sudden confrontation with social reality when she brought a black girl home and suggested that she be a weekend guest. This gesture not only disturbed her home but also disturbed the whole community with its curved streets which, Darlene says, "lead to nowhere." Neither her parents, nor the teachers and counselors at school, nor the minister at her church were willing to turn their abstract platitudes into concrete action and statements. Their reasons need no documentation here. Darlene, nonetheless, wanted reasons. She got none which were valid. This was three years before the summer of 1968. The months and years which followed revealed all of the hidden bigotry and bias in Darlene's home and community that she never knew were there. There was an almost unbelievable naivety about her. She had always thought that the things she had heard which happened to Jews or the things she saw on television happening to black people were things which happen to other people in other communities. It never occurred to her that the suburb where she lived was really a little insular society. She knew that there were no black residents in her community and that there were no Jews she could identify in the country club to which her parents belonged. But she had never really thought about it. More and more Darlene discovered what she called "the big lie." "It's all a pack of lies: The school books lied, the teachers lied, my parents lied—I didn't know who to believe. Even my minister didn't have the guts to say something when something needed to be said." Darlene had two years left to complete high school at the time of her

confrontation. Almost immediately she was a problem at her
school. She would support everybody's cause that was anti-
Protestant, anti-provincial, and anti-puritanical. She joined
civil rights groups and went on protest marches; she picketed
with fair housing groups. She brought civil rights literature to
school and passed it out to the other students. The school
administration quickly prevented this procedure, so she distributed the brochures to students who were en route to and
from school. She was arrested several times. Her academic
record slipped to the point where she was a "D" student. In
June, 1967, Darlene was graduated from high school. At that
time the civil rights movement was obscured by the newer
emphasis on black power. Darlene felt that the idea of black
power, as she understood it, was as distasteful to her as the ideas
she was rejecting. She quit the civil rights movement. She did,
however, become interested in social work, deciding that this
might be "a better way to clean up society." Her school record
was not of sufficient quality to get her into the college of her
choice. Moreover, she scored lower on the placement test than
her level of ability would warrant. Darlene now attends Rock
Valley Community College in Illinois.

Richard is deeply religious. He had been an altar boy.
He acted as though every single act and human behavior was
a sin: If he took a girl on a date and kissed her, he would go
to confession; if he was late for school or mass or any other
function concerned with the church he would go to confession;
when he played football—or attempted to—he came back to
the huddle after each down and said a prayer. His team members did not want him on the team because he concentrated
more on his prayers than on the plays. His locker did not have
the usual array of pin-ups and other such adolescent distractions
found in the average high schooler's locker. Richard's locker
was filled with pictures of Christ and the Virgin Mary. He
collected religious medals and crucifixes the way many young
children collect charm bracelets. His family was religious, too;
but they were not obsessed with it in the same way. Moreover,
they were disturbed about Richard's myopia. Being a priest
was the one great ambition Richard expressed. In school every-

thing he did led to this end. The nuns who taught him in the elementary and secondary school were delighted with his angelic behavior and encouraged him in his vocation. Although Richard appeared to have better than average ability, he often found it difficult to concentrate. He would doodle during class time. And the doodles always revealed his preoccupation with religion. After graduation Richard went to the seminary. There he found that the requirements for the priesthood were more rigorous academically and demanded more discipline. He soon learned that wanting to be a priest and learning to be a priest called for a totally different kind of commitment and skill that Richard did not have. He did not make good grades. It was the decision of the school officials that he should not continue in the seminary. This decision was made on the basis of two criteria: Richard did not exhibit the right kind of personality for that part of religious involvement that transcends saying the mass, hearing confessions, and other such duties; and he did not maintain the required academic standards. In almost every college you will find students like Richard. Students who have come from the seminary, or flunked out of some other school because of the disparity between their aspirations and their performance. There are probably many reasons for this problem. The reasons may be centered in the home, or the college, or inside the student himself. Richard says he will attend an open-door college in North Dakota which he refused to name. He will be twenty-two years old. Perhaps he can learn to be content as a parishioner instead of a priest.

Marian came from the southside but east end of St. Louis. She is from that side of the city where the least amount of change is evident. The people, the property, and patterns of behavior do not reflect much modification. They simply survive and persist. There are several ethnic enclaves located in that part of the city; the ones most talked about are the Germans and the Dutch. Both groups carry the slang name (with pride), "Scrubby Dutch." They are famous for scrubbing their front porches and steps. Young people, artists, liberals, and others reported to be more open in their thinking are considered outsiders when they move into the southside neighborhoods.

The few blacks who live in that part of the city are those whose families have lived there for generations. Some of these families have resided in the area since Civil War days. Many teachers in the St. Louis Public Schools live in South St. Louis and consider a teaching assignment there a choice one. In fact, the best public school district (best in terms of academic performance of the pupils on the standardized tests) in the entire city is reported to be on the south side. Yet, in the 1950s–1960s this part of the city never supported school bond issues or tax levies. Obviously, this part of the city is united politically. Marian now calls where she grew up "another country." Although her childhood was pleasant enough, when she became a teenager she did not like the area where she lived. "The people always seemed to care more about what their neighbors thought of them than what they thought of themselves. Actually, the neighbors tell them what to think of themselves. You always had to scrub steps on Saturday morning whether they were dirty or not. It was a status thing. People looked down on you when you didn't scrub your steps on Saturday. It was like violating a taboo. How do you bring meaning to that absurdity?" The residents of the community always treated Marian well and her movement through the public school system was ordinary, almost uneventful. She was barely an average student, but nonetheless, safe in that obscurity. Marian enjoyed sports and was a cheerleader at her high school. She was a student who was well behaved; and she did not cause her parents much trouble until she began to date. She explains it best: "It was worse than the inquisition when I took a boy home. My parents cross-examined him from the moment he walked in until he almost ran out. They wanted to know his father's job, lodge, and politics, what baseball team he rooted for, his feeling on civil rights, and the church he attended. If the boy was of another religion *that* was like original sin to my family. If the neighbors saw the boy come to the house two or three times, they began to ask questions that weren't any of their business. I guess it's safe to say that you needed community approval to go out on a date. Sometimes I used to get so fed up on tradition and neighbors I would nearly choke. What really bugs me is that it never changes."

Marian met her husband, Bob, when they were both juniors in high school. Both were seventeen. Because Bob was of a different religion Marian did not take him to meet her parents for several months. In spite of Bob's maturity and apparent genuine affection and respect for Marian, he was not acceptable to the family. After a few dates Marian was forbidden to see Bob again. No amount of reasoning would change the decision of her parents. Finally, the young girl was forbidden to discuss the matter further. As a result, Marian began to deceive her parents by meeting Bob elsewhere. They discussed their predicament and decided they would continue to see each other. Later, they decided they would be married after high school graduation with or without the consent of Marian's parents. To summarize, Marian and Bob were married the day after commencement. They have planned not to have children until he finishes college. In the meantime, he holds a full-time job at night and attends Meramec Community College in St. Louis. He expects to transfer at the end of two years and attend the University of Missouri. Marian's placement scores were low so she enrolled in Forest Park Community College's developmental program. After she remediates her skills, she plans to enroll in the secretarial program at the college.

Alonzo's father was a principal and one of the less than 4,000 black Ph.D.'s in America. His mother was a schoolteacher who held a master's degree. All his life, Alonzo had been exposed to educated people and to an educational climate seldom duplicated in the homes of black children. Books and other printed material were always in evidence. Alonzo had traveled, been a Boy Scout, taken piano lessons and had all of those experiences normally associated with a wholesome middle-class environment. This student did not appear to have a problem of adjustment or identity. He was active in sports and showed no overt hostility toward authority. He had attended school with both white and black students and did not seem unduly impressed by either group. Alonzo was interested in the things most of the students his age are interested in. He had all of the encouragement and gentle persuasion that one might expect him to receive living in a school-oriented household. Alonzo graduated in the lower third of his high school class and on the School and College Ability Test (SCAT) ranked at the tenth percentile. This disturbed neither him nor his parents. They wanted the best for their son without putting undue pressure on him. Fortunately, Alonzo found himself after being placed in a program of basic skills and is now attending school at Miami-Dade in the "regular" college. Alonzo was about as middle-class and normal as a student could be. His background, environment, and all of the other indices which many accept as ingredients of success in school did not make for success in the beginning. Perhaps things were too normal—too much without tension.

Tina's mother wanted a scholar. Tina wanted to dance. This was the thing Tina did best. Mrs. Gorman wanted Tina to make A's and B's. Tina earned C's and D's. The situation remained moot. Finally, the mother refused to let Tina dance in the school's choreography club. The girl began to earn D's and F's. Mrs. Gorman would come to school and berate the girl in front of others. She constantly told the student that she was not going to be embarrassed by her underachievement. This mother was visibly more concerned by her own embarrassment than Tina's problem. She felt that since she had restricted Tina from the dancing club, her academic performance would improve. It did not. Mrs. Gorman blamed the school for her daughter's poor academic showing and demanded that she be transferred to another high school in the city. The school administration complied with the demand. In the new school nothing changed. Tina again resumed her dancing and her grades returned to C's and D's, but Mrs. Gorman continued to pressure her daughter to make A's and B's. Tina could not earn the grades. She was again taken from the dancing class. Her grades dropped again. Actually, Tina is working as hard as she can. Her mother cannot resolve the idea that her daughter is less than average. The author knows Mrs. Gorman well and attended the same high school and shared some of the same classes. She was less than average, too, when she was in school. When Tina graduates—if indeed she does—she claims she will attend Cuyahoga Community College in Cleveland, Ohio.

Many community college educators have a way of refusing to call a spade a spade. In the language of the ghetto, "They won't tell it like it is." A case in point is the seemingly innocuous and idealistic pronouncement of wanting to provide an educational opportunity for "inner-city youth." Translated, "inner-city youth" means black students living in the core city. Few people in the two-year college have demonstrated that they have the techniques, communication, attitude, or even the desire to tackle this problem. Moreover, when they do attempt to meet the situation the attempt is made without making any real changes in the existing structure, faculty composition, curriculum development, and established priorities.

The high-risk black student in the community college or the black student who is matriculating in one is a special concern for colleges. Until relatively recent years there were only minor concern, little persuasion, abstract commitment, and no priority for giving special attention to the black student. In fact, he was ignored. For an undergraduate to be ignored in college is not unique. However, the middle nineteen-sixties spawned two of the dramatic movements affecting higher education which also affected dealing with the black student: the phenomenal increase in community colleges established with open-door enrollment policies; and the rise of the controversial black power movement. The first movement brought with it increased enrollment of marginal students in college. This created new problems but educators were willing to meet the challenge and set about solving the problems. Although few changes were made in the planning of community college curricula which would make it relevant for the educationally and socially disadvantaged student, and few faculty members departed from tradition in their presentation of subject matter to marginal students, community college people did not attempt to obscure the fact that the low-performing student was there. In the second movement, there were—in the beginning—attempts to ignore it, ridicule it, oppress it. The phrase itself (black power) was misinterpreted, reinterpreted, polluted, pros-

tituted, and damned. Books were written about it (Carmichael
and Hamilton, 1967). The public reacted to it with ambiguity.
Some people got angry when they heard the term. Others
thought it was exactly the kind of "shot in the arm" that black
people in America had always needed. It frightened the white
liberal, obscured the conservative black, and shocked the so-
called "responsible Negro" who had traditionally been palatable
to everybody. Hundreds of articles appeared in magazines and
newspapers across the country commending or condemning it.
Black students, using Eldridge Cleaver's words, began advising
the college hierarchy that if it was not a part of the solution it
was a part of the problem. Other symptoms of the movement
were apparent. Among college students, teenagers, young adults,
and those young people reputed to be militants, the term *black*
replaced the term *Negro* to designate race. In one study *Negro*
was found to be next to the least preferred term. Other than the
label *black, Afro-American* became the term acceptable to designate black people.

"Black is beautiful" was the new motto. This slogan was
seen on bumper stickers and T-shirts. Boys wrote it on the walls
of restrooms. Preschoolers, too young to speak distinctly, learned
it by rote. Teenagers wrote the slogan on their sneakers. High
school composition classes wrote themes and essays about it.
Congregations across the nation listened to Sunday sermons
addressed to : Black is Beautiful. Black had a sudden and new
mystique. Everything connected with it was emphasized. When
one heard "soul music," "soul food," "soul sister," these were
terms (used for generations in the ghetto) which established
immediate identity between blacks. Perhaps for the first time
in the total "colored" community, it was the black female who
was in demand rather than the girls of lighter hue.

Black awareness came quick and sharp like the pains of
labor to the colleges and universities across the nation. The
black Ph.D.'s who headed the Negro colleges of the South were
shaken from their pedestals and labeled. Because they did not
understand the "black experience" that the students talked
about they were branded "Dr. Toms." From the Ivy League
colleges of the East to the great state multiversities of the Mid-

west and West, a vocal minority was being heard. This minority protested that higher education was not designed to reinforce them and their culture in any way. They insisted that white education did not address itself to the poor, to the landlord and tenant in the ghetto, and to applied humanity. Students said they were coerced with threats of poor grades to learn about the three B's in great music that the white students learn, but they did not get any B.B. King and Joe Williams with which they could identify. Their protest was sometimes violent, like the shoot-out at Texas Southern University in Houston, Texas; sometimes subtle, like the implied threats at other universities where the administrator capitulated. Their tactics were almost always effective. For these reasons and many others, the students made demands for everything black—black instructors, black studies, black homecoming, more black admissions, black dormitories, and so forth. The students were almost irrational in their demands. The symbolic motion made by Ralph Abernathy, president of the Southern Christian Leadership Conference, to continue the sit-in, nonviolent method of protest that Martin Luther King, Jr., had started, died for a lack of a second from the black students who were willing to fight back. He was joined by some white students who supported his cause. He was joined by others (some SDS groups) who exploited his cause. The black student knew this would happen. The liberal (faculty member and layman alike) began to find out that he was not as liberal as he thought he was. The black student knew this would happen also. The black student began to feel who he was and what he was. For this brief moment in history he felt the power in blackness.

Regardless of the distress of faculty and students, the demands of black students continued. At a conference, Higher Education for the Disadvantaged: Problems, Progress, Prospect, held in Washington, D.C., in March, 1968, it was made crystal clear that attention to the problems of the black student would not be ignored. This conference was but one of four held in 1968 where black educators and others caucused and forced the conference to take a new direction with emphasis on the education of the black student. Forty-four speakers, including college administrators, directors of poverty programs, research persons, and others, repeatedly, almost to the man, spoke the same indictments of higher education. More specifically, they focused on administration, faculties, curricula, institutions, and commitment. These speakers addressed themselves to: who will teach high-risk students (low-income, members of minority groups, and poor whites) and how; what will be taught and why; and when do we really expect to start moving beyond the tokenism that is practiced over the whole country. The conference directed itself to some basic assumptions and can be summarized as follows:

Black youth are being denied college entrance because of a white standardization measure (entrance exams and high school rank) of what part of the culture a college student should have assimilated by the age of eighteen. This criterion measure is irrelevant and completely inadequate to a youth rich and knowledgeable in a culture for which standardization instruments have not been developed. They are too often being screened and educated by people who see only their lack of competence and familiarity with the educator's own acculturation system. This results in the educator's generalization that the student is inadequate, not cultured and perhaps not amenable to being educated. Such a reaction is a gross misunderstanding of the fact. The really educated black who comes up out of the ghetto is beginning to define a more reliable standardization instrument of intelligence for the black: survival —and with it, creative use of available ghetto power—gang leadership, hustling, pimping, and so on. White values label this as offensive bad behavior when, out of moral context, it does in fact indicate an objective measure of potential.

Since present educational leadership by institutions is inadequate in terms of the problem and often selfish in really sharing its power with others, education should be turned over to those who are experienced pupils of the culture to which education is being directed. Credentialing for the new educators should also consist of number of years in the ghetto, leadership activities while there, understanding of its language, customs, and daily experiences. This would result in the replacement of a largely incompetent "degreed" staff by an experienced, thus educated, competent staff. This new staff could redirect the recognized, potential ability of students to societally useful behavior. Redirection of students might take two years rather than one—in some cases three—but wise use of time is not measured by GPA but by a teacher's evaluation of a student's progress and responsibility in change.

Inbreeding, or almost segregation, for the time being is often considered to be essential until experiences can be accumulated which can be generalized, thus allowing for transmission of these experienced educational methods and techniques to those who do not have experience with both systems but want to be involved.

Students from minority groups and other low income groups have been systematically denied opportunities for higher education based on assumptions that these students cannot or will not learn anything anyway; and institutions use research to back up these assumptions. The disadvantaged student can learn and benefit from education; moreover, the institution can benefit from the students thereby making education more relevant for both. Educators must face the facts that there must be curriculum change and if it requires changing administrations, faculties, and policies, make the changes.

The blacks insist on being involved, in a meaningful way, in what affects their lives: what they are taught, how, why, and to what ends. This includes both the black who has adapted to the system (Ivy League suit and the rest) and the one who is trying to adapt. In short, "The house nigger and the field nigger has to make it," states James Goodman of the University of Washington.

There is still no commitment to working with the disadvantaged student. Even where there are programs, administrators and faculties are the first to plan their demise and these programs amount to "a pimple" in the total setup of the institution. Most programs represent "a backyard effort." Yet, no program is too expensive since thousands of students are being short-changed, particularly blacks, other minorities, and poor whites. The fact is, professors, institutions, graduate students, and others have been subsidized (through government grants and so on) and derived more benefit from the plight of the poor student than the poor students themselves.

Programs for the black and other disadvantaged students and staff who are a part of the programs on campuses all over the country are like satellites or appendages to the institutions. Both the programs and the people are tolerated—not integrated. Educators do not know what is going on because they confer with each other only at a gilded level. It was made perfectly clear at the conference that these things could not continue and the persons saying it were articulate, determined, and were not to be turned off. The conference participants involved themselves with criticism of institutions, administration and faculties:

Institutions: Junior (and senior) colleges have remained traditional in terms of priorities and the faculties which served these institutions; the curricula taught in them and the men who administer them do not change. The methodology, selection of students and staff, and policies remain the same. It is also clear that institutions refuse to do anything significant about admission policies and placement of these (educationally disadvantaged) students. It was further emphasized that institutions practice institutional racism, and when institutions cut back on programs, they start with the programs for the high-risk or disadvantaged student if such programs exist.

Administration: It has been charged that administrators attend conferences to recruit staff, to look for new positions, to search for methods to counteract pressure being brought to bear in their respective communities, and to get on committees to bring status to themselves and their institutions. They should attend conferences in order to exchange information about current educational problems and to explore innovative solutions to the problems raised. It is also rather clear that administrators demonstrate that they are more concerned with control, channels, and reports than they are with what happens to students, specifically black and other minority students of low income. They are more concerned with credentials of the people they hire than they are with quality teaching. Administrators are not concerned with and may not be aware of the kind of education which is relevant for a large percentage of young people (black and white) today. They are charged with practicing institutional racism and with being aloof. This creates barriers to communication and develops in them a lack of sensitivity to the problems in their own institutions. This lack of sensitivity translates them from the leadership role in education to managers of buildings, budgets, and so on, and if this statement is valid then the educational leadership should be given to someone else in the college. Finally it is no exaggeration to say that administrators disregard the logic of events while they call for innovation which must always fit the system.

Faculty: In many ways faculty members are the worst culprits of all. In higher education there is little or no involvement of teachers in teaching. Teachers are concerned with class loads, salaries, fringe benefits, and academic freedom. They seldom seem to have the dedication to students that they have to salary and working conditions. Teachers want to influence conditions, curricula, administration, and every other facet of the college; however, they are like morticians. They want to go into their classrooms and close their doors and let no one see what they are doing. They call this academic freedom.

Most college instructors can lecture but not teach and students have a right to good teachers. Instructors in the college parallel program in junior colleges are not significantly different from instructors in the universities, although they claim to be. Teachers are unable to handle students whose cultural, economic, and educational handicaps are different from those of the regular student body. It appears that teachers do not pay any attention to their own research. It is an irony that the most important and best work in learning and education is now being done outside of the field of education. As a result, faculty members are following rather than becoming the leaders in the field of education.

The conference adopted the following resolutions:

I. A. Whereas the majority of white faculty of predominantly white institutions of higher education still appear to be unaware and insensitive to the humanity of minority and low-income students: Be it resolved that institutions of higher education initiate aggressive and compulsory in-service training programs for developing sensitivity to minority and low-income students' problems.

B. Moreover, the traditional credential requirements for administrators, teachers and staff must be abandoned. Also greater scrutiny should be made of attitudes of staff and faculty to the end that the racist structure that prevails in institutions of higher education is abolished. Persons applying for positions at institutions of higher education manifesting racist attitudes are not to be hired.

C. Moreover, educational programs serving nonwhite students must be administered, taught, and counseled by staff representing the racial or cultural backgrounds of the students. Also, there must be an increase in nonwhite representation in administrative and educational capacities within all educational programs conducted by the institutions at large. Inasmuch as the particular educational needs of black youth can be best served by resources from the black community, a central consultant team should be established to assist the universities in their attempts to educate black youngsters.

II. It is resolved that all college curricula be reexamined to the end that minority and low-income students see a relationship between higher education and life.

III. Recruitment and Admissions: Be it resolved that the present admission codes and practices be abolished and replaced by new practices which meet the needs of minority and low-income students.

IV. Financial Aids: Be it resolved that massive grant-in-aid programs be established. All grant programs should be sensitively administered to meet the total needs. This conference goes on record advising the Congress to immediately enact legislation substantially increasing federal funds in support of grant programs specifically for minority students.

V. Federal Programs: Whereas, institutions of higher education are receiving federal funds, be it resolved that those institutions not complying with the philosophy outlined by these resolutions be cut off from all federal funds (including research contracts and grants) until clearly demonstrated changes have been instituted.

This attention to the education of the black student is what community college administration really means when it proclaims to be looking for ways to "help inner-city youth." "Inner-city youth" is the code phrase meaning black youth. Obviously, community colleges must be concerned and for good reasons:

There will be more black students in community colleges than in four-year institutions because of the lower cost; of the large number of black students who cannot meet admission standards in four-year colleges; many of these students are employed while they attend college at home; community college students expect to learn a skill or vocation they can use in two years; and many male students are attempting to avoid the draft.

Black students in large four-year colleges are primarily middle-class youth who have not encountered the poverty cycle, cultural deprivation and academic failure that the student from the black ghettoes knows. As a consequence, he is more amenable to negotiation, discussion, and "proper" channels before he acts. He is likely to be concerned about the consequences. On the other hand, he knows what is due him and has the intelligence and sensitivity to create confrontations with far-reaching effects, especially since he can demonstrate and document the condition which perpetrates his actions. The educationally disadvantaged black tends to respond to frustration with aggression instead of discussion.

High school counselors in inner-city schools are counseling more black students into the community colleges.

The black taxpayer is demanding more from his dollar. He is beginning to compare the cost of equipment, facilities, and personnel to turn out the small number of nurses, dental hygienists, and other such persons which require large capital but turn out few products with the number of people who could be going to school on a smaller budget.

The community college cannot shirk its responsibility to educate certain segments because that segment is more difficult to educate.

Black organizations are turning up in many communities

and are looking at the so-called democratic institution (community college) that has few if any minority group members among its faculty, counseling, and administrative staff. They are looking at the recruiters from these colleges who seldom if ever recruit from Negro colleges; many recruiters do not even know the names of Negro colleges. This is truly a paradox since Negro colleges have been dealing with high-risk students for decades. They are watching the administrators who never come to their communities to speak. They see displays from the college in other parts of the city and never in their own.

Community colleges, because they are designed to be a part of the urban complex, cannot avoid ever-increasing contact with the black community.

Black students who have subjected themselves to no teaching, poor teaching, many failures, and personal debasement in ghetto high schools will not subject themselves to such abuse in college because they are older, free of parental control, and some are financially independent. There is also a movement toward the development of the use of arrogance by black students as a technique for handling educators.

There will be an increase of inner-city ghetto youth taking advantage of much of the federal legislation to pursue education at the post-secondary level.

As the community colleges meet the increasing and varied body of black students (as well as white) who are educationally disadvantaged, they must make the content of programs essential, relevant, and realistic.

Marsee (1968) points out that increasing attention will have to be paid to the education of the underprivileged, particularly the Negro, whose population will increase from twenty-one million to thirty million—or from 10.8 per cent to 12 per cent of the population—by 1980. Repeatedly, men like Marsee make educators aware of change and the need for preparing for it, specifically as it relates to the black student.

It appears, therefore, that the black student who is marginal in the community college will be either a threat or an opportunity. From either point of view the two-year college must come to terms with the facts of life. It must give special attention to the way the black student differs from the traditional college student for whom the present system of higher education is planned. At the same time, it must provide for the learning difficulties of this student as it does for the student who may be an honor student.

If college people are to be effective in dealing with the black student, they should know his habits, behaviors, and attitudes. Many of these characteristics are never documented.

The black student who is educationally, socially, and economically disadvantaged is likely to be quite different when compared to the white student of the same class. To begin with, the black student is more cynical. He does not believe in God, Mother, and Country with the same fervor as his white counterpart or his own parents. He is candid, not given to the little charades of guile. If he does not like the teacher he does not pretend to like him. The black student has few heroes. He knows that society destroys its heroes even while it creates them; so he looks for the feet of clay earlier. He can probably take disappointments better because in his world disappointment is a way of life. The black student will tend to be more worldly though less sophisticated academically. He shows much more ingenuity outside of the classroom. Inside the classroom he has always been more of a spectator than a participant because he does not have a great deal of confidence in his ability. He considers the bits and pieces of knowledge middle-class students verbalize as trivia used to show off.

The black student is probably more tolerant of injustice, stupidity, sarcasm, dirt, profanity, and illegitimacy. He chooses his leaders from among those who can best represent him. He is willing to listen and associate with students that school officials do not consider good citizens because he does not feel that association produces contamination. The black student does not confide in his parents. He will rarely let a teacher or referee or some other arbiter handle the problem or confrontation between himself and another. He has been independent too long for that and he has had to solve his own problems and often bear his own misfortune without assistance, sympathy, or compromise. Many of these students, especially those from the lower socioeconomic environments, have been completely on their own since their early teens and have had to function as adults—in all of the dimensions of adulthood—while playing the role of children in school. This continues in the community college; some of the students playing the role of Joe College leave the campus and sleep with their lovers; later they go home and are forced by economic imperatives to retire with a little brother because there is so little space in their homes. They have neither their own rooms nor their own beds.

About the above discussion, nearly everyone can say, "but I know white students who are exactly like that; and I know Negroes who are not like that at all." Both observations are true and need no documentation. One does find, however, that this situation appears to apply more to the black student than the white student.

The literature which describes the blacks is voluminous; but these are not the books likely to be found on the shelves of college educators, although they can be found in the personal libraries of elementary and secondary school people. They are more likely to have a volume such as *The Testing of Negro Intelligence* (Shuey, 1966). Whereas this is an excellent and scholarly book, it explores only one facet of the Negro and then, as most books of its kind do, compares the Negro students with white students.

HIGH-RISK STUDENTS

Many people are surprised to discover that there are more differences between the middle-class white student and the lower-class white student than there are between the middle-class white student and the middle-class black. In the first case, it is a research fact that students, black or white, coming from educationally privileged environments have higher aptitudes, more persistence, and greater motivation for intellectual exercises than those from lower socioeconomic backgrounds. Middle-class whites often reject lower-class whites. The same is true of middle-class blacks. They, too, look down on lower-class blacks—and whites, too, for that matter. One has but to observe the behavior of students on the college campus to see that there is more fraternization between the races among middle-class students than there is among lower-class students. There is also less hostility.

Attention to the black student in higher education is not new. The paradox is that business, industry, and large foundations such as Danforth, Ford, and Carnegie are making more direct contributions toward dealing with the black students than are the colleges and universities themselves—although institutions of higher learning are sometimes the agents for government, industry, and foundations. More and more the public community colleges are becoming agents also. Project Ahead, funded by the Ford Foundation, and the General Curriculum, funded by the Danforth Foundation, are examples. The importance of the public junior college in this sphere was singled out for comment in a statement by the Commission on Higher Educational Opportunity in the South:

> If there is a single great problem involved in providing equal educational opportunity for Negroes . . . it is to find ways of extending post-high school educational opportunity to the masses. The public, community-centered, multi-purpose two-year institutions are the primary hope for doing so. They cannot do so, however, unless they confront the needs of disadvantaged Negro and white students and devise methods of meeting them.
> Their tuition and fees are relatively low. Their proximity allows most students to live at home. Their mixture of pre-baccalaureate, vocational and technical programs equips them to serve a wide range of needs and abilities. Their free-wheeling curricula permit also limitless experimentation with remedial and compensatory programs. Above all, their open-door admission policies make them accessible to anyone with a high school diploma and an interest in furthering his education.

The high-risk black student, however, is a special case requiring the community college to develop special measures. He is but one of a wide variety of students who will not meet the predesigned mold that the educators often attempt to force him into, and he will reject being treated like data. In an article, "Students Are a Lot Like People," McInnis (1968) discusses this Procrustean approach:

> We educators are the modern version of Procrustes. Some students come to us with knowledge which does not conform to our data, and we promptly cut them down to size. Others come with insufficient background to manipulate our data, so we shove it in all the harder. All who pass through our classes are thus standardized to the specifications of our data. Just as Procrustes could not bear to allow people to make their own accommodation to his bed, so we educators are reluctant to allow students to make their own accommodation to our data. *Our* choice, arrangement, and interpretation of the data is the only one we care to allow. The assembly line model of education is inefficient, dehumanizing, dishonest, and just plain stupid.
> Community college students at the extremes are representative of two worlds. One of those worlds is full of blight, despair, unrest, and ferment. This world is replete with violence, blood in the streets, black and white confrontation, crime, riots in the city, poverty and frustration. It is also characterized by dissent, change, and the demand for relevance. The second world is affluent, comfortable, and apathetic. It is a world that is uninvolved. There is a whole range between the extremes which have introduced an entirely new kind of student to higher education and the two-year college.

CULTURALLY DISADVANTAGED STUDENTS

No discussion of the high-risk student would be complete without reference to the "culturally disadvantaged" student who is socially, economically, and educationally out of the mainstream of urban society. This student is of no single race or color. He has come from a region of the country or a section of the inner city which is very rich in its own traditions but which fails to prepare its members to operate successfully in society. Moreover, the student who comes from this background brings to college with him a culture and mores which are either misunderstood, rejected, or ignored. Consequently,

the student and the educational agents and agencies quickly
become adversaries rather than complements and the logic of
their associations is weakened.

Until fairly recently college was out of the question for
the vast majority of students who were economically and educationally deprived. Neither the school nor the student held
reciprocal and positive expectancies about the other. The things
that the student expected college to be were often different
from what college really is. In like manner, many of the traditional assumptions that the college has been able to make about
the student are totally inapplicable to many of the students
from the central city and the rural communities of the country.
Yet, students from these regions are going to the two-year college by the thousands. The prospect is that many more will go.

Although the number of community college students
continues to increase and a substantial group of them will be
classifiable as poor academic risks in the strictest interpretation
of this term, few people describe a portion of these students
as being culturally disadvantaged. In fact, the term *culturally
disadvantaged* is usually associated with elementary and high
school students. Only a few, a very few people have called attention to this situation: Knoell (1968) is one who not only
alerts college people to this phenomenon but also points out
that the community college itself is made inaccessible to many
disadvantaged students. In an article "Are Our Colleges Really
Accessible to the Poor?" Knoell indicates that the deadlines,
fees, forms, and lack of information may close the "open door"
for disadvantaged students. She further suggests that the community colleges run the risk of subtly violating the obligation
to serve the disadvantaged educationally:

> In principle, community junior colleges are accessible
> to all, without respect to race, color, social class, degree
> of affluence, parentage, or prior educational experience.
> Community colleges are by nature open-door institu-
> tions—free to those who cannot afford the low tuition
> and fees, comprehensive in curricular offerings, located
> close to population centers, and responsive to local needs
> for education beyond high school. Yet, in the name of

administrative expediency, procedural barriers are often
erected—subtly discriminatory barriers which may have
the effect of rendering the colleges inaccessible to the
poor, the educationally handicapped, and others lacking
the necessary "savvy" to cope with a bureaucratic system.

At a counseling roundtable, Rosetta T. Moore, a counselor in an inner-city high school in St. Louis, recognized this
problem and commented on a realistic approach to the solution:

The culturally disadvantaged may need institutional social work. Why not? That is a part of our responsibility.
Too many of us in education seem to forget that it is
our job to support students who need support and to
guide those who need direction. Sometimes we have to
spoon-feed deprived students. In many cases this is what
is necessary. We would not ask a sick man to cure himself. In a way, I suppose many of these students are sick.
What I am really saying is that many of the things we
can expect educationally competent, motivated, and affluent students to do on their own, the disadvantaged
student will not do unless you stay right on him. This
may mean filling out forms for him, asking admission
officers to send to you copies of all correspondence sent
to the student so that you can be certain that there is
the appropriate followup. It may mean checking to see
if the student is getting his money together because he
will probably be paying his own tab. It means the whole
bag. And if you do not want to get involved to this extent, perhaps you would be better off working with the
advantaged student who will not procrastinate. Curi-
ously enough the advantaged student often needs even
more spoon-feeding than the disadvantaged student. We
just feed him different stuff.

Knoell and Moore know their students. These are the
students from the black and white ghettos of the central city.
Many of them are the offspring of the uneducated and unskilled
rural in-migrants—who exchanged the drudgery of life in the
mills, mines, and fields of another America for the unemploy-

ment, confusion, and frustration of the city.[3] In the early 1960s
the children of these in-migrants attended the elementary and
secondary schools in inner cities and rural communities. They
were then labeled the economically restricted, culturally deprived, low socioeconomic group, and so on. Now, although the
problems and conditions of these same students have persisted,
the labels have become obscure, at least at the college level.
Many of the students still live where every conceivable human
degradation exists. They live in the black ghettos and poor
white enclaves, which are filled with the whole cadre of problems found among the disadvantaged. The students live in
crowded conditions, in filth, in poverty, in ignorance and re-
jection. Although they have been spawned from many of the
same conditions, they are different from the disadvantaged
described by Riessman (1962), Clark (1965), Deutsch (1968),
and others, primarily because of age and experience. Nevertheless, they still belong to "the other America" described in the
book of the same name by Harrington (1962). They are the
largest portion of that 70 per cent of junior college students
who hold full-time and part-time employment. They come to
school after an eight-hour work day ends or before one begins.

A considerable number of the disadvantaged are young
girls. Many are older women. A portion of both have been
school dropouts. Some have quit school to help out at home.
Most still do so. Others have quit because they did not like
school. Some have GED's. Some are trying to earn the GED.
They represent the unwed mothers, deserted wives, barmaids,
nurse's aides, waitresses, and many others. A surprising number
of these women have the sole responsibility for maintaining a
household. There are others who attempt to avoid accepting
responsibility, and a few do not know why they are in school.

The males who come to the community college from disadvantaged homes, backgrounds, and environments are not significantly different from the females; still, there are differences.
The disadvantaged males enrolled in the junior college out-

[3] For a more complete discussion of this in-migrant, see my book,
The Vertical Ghetto: Everyday Life in a Housing Project (Moore, 1969).

number the females at a ratio of almost three to one. This ratio is not true when applied to the black males. The reverse is probably more accurate. There are other differences. The male student as a whole dresses better. He is probably not as responsible as his female counterpart. He procrastinates more than his female counterpart and dissipates more. Infrequently he has had minor scrapes with the police. Sometimes he is trying to dodge the draft. This student is self-sufficient and worldly. He is often obsessed with owning cars. On the other hand, the majority of the disadvantaged males are in many ways like the females. Some are right out of high school. Others are returning to school after many years absence. Some are returning from military service. Still others simply hold jobs, have families, and are responsible citizens. Unlike the girls, however, the disadvantaged male student has probably enjoyed most of the privileges of adulthood since his beginning teens without the same amount of parental control.

Disadvantaged students—regardless of sex, race, region, or religion—have usually come to the community college from rural areas, inner-city ghettos, and other decaying communities. Almost all have come from crippling schools. Many deprived students hate the schools they attended. They have been often taught by teachers who could not excite them, using content they consider irrelevant. They have neither achieved, nor been challenged, nor had offered to them many of the educational resources that should be available in today's schools (Gleazer, 1968).

Almost without exception, disadvantaged students are students with a staggering number of problems. In this way they are not unique among college students. There is, however, one significant difference: The problems of disadvantaged students never seem to get solved. There is constant uncertainty related to family stability and harmony. There is persistent worry about being able to provide the basic needs even when they are employed. The place where many disadvantaged students are forced to live is a frame of reference for regular embarrassment and irritation. Such things as a quiet place to work free of distraction is a problem for the disadvantaged as he pursues the routine required for effective study. The casual observer would not see the full range of problems that many of these students must handle daily along with the business of attending college. The problems are as common as breathing. And the students are forced to devote a disproportionate part of their time coping. Most of them have always had to solve their own problems. This type of self-dependency is, of course, laudable. There are situations and times, however, when the knowledge and resources of others, if brought to bear on the predicaments of disadvantaged students, would evolve more efficient solutions than the sole reliance of the students upon themselves. Realistically, however, such students do not readily go to a counselor. The counselor must go to them. This is the way it is done in the General Curriculum, a program for high-risk students at Forest Park Community College in St. Louis, Missouri. One of the General Curriculum counselors relates:

> If I waited for these students to come to my office, I wouldn't see a dozen a semester. I take each class list and contact the students on that list. Sometimes this means setting up an appointment for him and writing him a letter to come in and see me. If he doesn't respond to my note, it may require calling him at home or elsewhere and inviting him to visit with me. I have even gone down to the baseball diamond and the gym to get students. I don't mean to imply all of these students have problems. Many of them are extremely well adjusted. I just have to make sure that when a kid needs me I'm there. Often they talk about their grades and their futures. I need to hear that. Once and a while they talk about themselves and their homes and families. I like to know about these things. Sometimes, they just want to bitch. I need to hear that too. When these kids do open up, the quantity and magnitude of their problems are staggering to the imagination. Actually, when they talk about their hangups, I'm embarrassed when I appraise the little inconveniences I label as problems.

For decades disadvantaged students have been rebelling against the same system and authorities that privileged students began to react to and fight against within the last few years.

The contrast and results of the way these two groups handled the situation has been readily observable: The affluent students have been organized and have been able not only to attract the public but also to make demands on college administrations that the administration agreed to. In almost every case these students have had at least some faculty support. By contrast the disadvantaged students were mavericks without organization, could not—until fairly recently—attract public attention, did not have faculty support, and were expelled or seriously reprimanded for their activity. Yet, disadvantaged students have a history of rejecting the prescriptions of authority and the older generation. They have refused to acquiesce to the proposed conformity of their parents and other authority figures in order to avoid the criticism that appears to threaten the privileged student's sense of security. Disadvantaged students have their own vocabulary, develop their own customs, choose their own diets, clothes, friends, and heroes. They reject much of the social order dictated by adults. They are super-sensitive to the hypocrisy of adults and the various social institutions adults represent, including the church. To the disadvantaged student, authority is that inquisitorial and inflexible tyranny that one sanctions only in order to subvert it or to use it for one's own gain. Paradoxically, while such students refuse and reject the imposed rules, regulations, and restrictions which make up the guidelines authority figures use to insure conformity, they are rigid exemplars of the conformity of their peers. Actually, the disadvantaged student hates authority most when it is imposed with sarcasm, arrogance and oppression and when it is impervious to change. The student rejects authority when it is bigoted and refuses to listen, and when it is unavailable to answer questions or arbitrarily refuses to answer questions. On the other hand, the disadvantaged student will work with authority when the approach of the latter is acceptable or when there is no other alternative.

Many hasten to point out that the vast majority of disadvantaged students are slow learners. This may very well be true. Learning slowly, however, is no vice, just as learning rapidly is no virtue. It must be readily admitted that the rapid

learner fits the education system best. In fact, much of what
the system does, the curriculum it uses, the techniques used by
its teachers, and the goals established for it are selected to meet
the learning rate of the average or better-than-average learner.
The ability to learn rapidly is an advantage for the learner and
a convenience for the education system. In like manner, there is
much to be said for the student who is careful because he
checks and rechecks his work, who is scrupulous and finical
about details, and who is cautious about making generalizations. Many disadvantaged students cannot shift readily from
one method of learning to another. They do not raise their
hands to respond in class and do not take an active part in class
discussion primarily because of the unpleasant experiences they
have either had or observed with teachers and the education
systems during their elementary and secondary school tenure.
And their lack of verbal response is little evidence to justify
an appraisal of their abilities as being dull.

One of the things which must be understood about the
slow learner is that he does learn. It may mean that four-year
colleges will find it necessary to reduce his load and to extend
the undergraduate curriculum to five or six years. For the community college enrollee, the tenure in the two-year college may
have to be extended to three, four, or even five years, if it takes
the student that long a time to accomplish his goals. Although
slow learners may take longer to deal with a concept or a given
body of knowledge, they can usually stick to a task with great
tenacity, particularly when they can use their bodies as well as
their minds in the learning process. All of the available evidence indicates that the disadvantaged student and the slow
learner like education and see its value. The evidence also indicates that these students often hate school.

Above all other things, disadvantaged students know
that there is little dialogue between themselves and higher education as a whole. Most of them are convinced that when they
talk to college personnel, the college people are not listening.
They are convinced that people in higher education neither
really know about their problems specifically nor understand
them generally. They believe that it is only a matter of time

before the selection process of the community college becomes, as it it is in the university level, a process to eliminate the vast majority of the poor. In short, disadvantaged students do not feel that the community college really gives a damn. When one takes a look at the total attempts made by community colleges nationally to reach the high-risk student who may also be culturally disadvantaged, he too is convinced that the feelings of the students are probably right.

Yet, the average high-risk community college student does have some distinctive characteristics above and beyond those usually documented. They can be described: Young, white, poor (not destitute), and conforming, this student comes from a neighborhood feeder high school. He comes from one of the clean little side streets in the city, although there is an increase in the number of students coming from suburbs. The student often lives in a tight little ethnic or religious enclave that is not being pushed by racial mobility. The students from these little enclaves come to the community college with their groups intact, unless they are from a large urban community like New York or Los Angeles—and even then a group from the same high school will tend to remain intact. In cities where there are multiple campuses, any one of the campuses may be located where there is a housing pattern which would, by its very location, tend to exclude certain students of certain religious groups, races, and social classes. The parents of this student did not go to college; some of them did not complete high school. This registrant has watched his father bring in the weekly paychecks from the breweries, factories, shoe stores, transportation companies, and the thousands of other routine and bread-and-butter jobs that have traditionally kept the poor honest. These persons are characterized in Clark's *The Open Door College* (1960) as the lower white-collar and lower blue-collar workers.

Not infrequently, this student comes from a home where the father is a craftsman and belongs to a closed labor union. A few of these craftsman earn more than many professional workers. They belong to the American Legion, a bowling league, and often like hunting and fishing as sports activities.

They still go to the neighborhood tavern but do not take their wives. Most studies will show that this group votes the Democratic ticket but they are not usually democratic in their attitudes.

The sons of these fathers are not dissenters like the hippies or yippies. They have not torn up the community college campus,[4] gotten involved in civil rights activities or any of the other activities many deplore in college students. For the most part, except for their numbers, there appears to be very little outstanding about these particular junior college students.

> In other words, America's newest college student has spent the first seventeen years of his life in a different cultural environment from that of the students we're accustomed to teaching in college. He is less likely to have seen good books and magazines around the home, less likely to have been able to retreat to a room of his own, and less likely to have been exposed to discussions of world affairs at the dinner table. Research to date indicates that students reflect rather faithfully the interests and concerns of their parents (Cross, 1968).

On the other hand, there is a new group of community college students (the marginal as well as the academically talented) who are demanding their "own thing"—their "own bag." They are seeking their own roles and—possibly—themselves. They are asking, "What is the whole higher education absurdity all about in the first place?" It was inevitable that the community college student would mimic the four-year student. "Why not? Junior college instructors mock university professors," chides one articulate student. "We just want the right to ask a question and have somebody to listen to the question, even if they can't answer it. We are neither sitting in administrative offices, nor burning papers, nor closing campuses down—yet. We are, however, learning all of the techniques for doing it. We have got to know why those who write the rules which prevent each of us from doing 'our own thing' never ask us to help make the rules."

---

[4] There are less than a dozen exceptions which I feel would be inappropriate to reveal here since I do not know all of the facts.

The students are the first to point out the rigidity and lack of amenability to change. Obviously, marginal students in the community college come from varying geographic areas and attend schools in areas just as varied. They are of different races, religions, abilities, economic levels, and social classes. Some are foreign-born. Many are war veterans and housewives. Some appear to have psychological problems; others appear to be free of such afflictions. There is but one characteristic common to all these students: They have not performed well academically. Marginal students come from high schools in urban and rural areas, religious parishes, neat suburbs and dirty ghettos. They come as full-time and part-time students, day students and night students, old and young students. A small number of them turn out to be good students, some rise as far as they can go when they become average performers. Others remain as they were before they came—marginal. It would appear, therefore, that except for the quality of their academic performance, community college students who are academic risks are not significantly different from college students as a whole.

Chapter Three

The
Teacher

*T*oo many teachers consider the task of teaching the high-risk student in the junior college to be academic social work; and making special remedial curricula available to this student is often thought to be academic welfare. Yet this student must be taught—and well. And he must be exposed to a relevant curriculum. It is well-documented that the two-year college has not generally succeeded in providing quality instruction or educational programs sufficiently potent to counteract the academic deprivations of the marginal student or to build on the talents this student brings to the college with him. A way now must be found to do just that. The rapid emergence and growth of the community college introduced high-risk students to higher education in the first place.[1] In many ways the college which introduced him will have to help develop the prescriptions used to teach not only him but also his teachers.

There was a time when missionary zeal rather than teaching skill motivated many teachers to give instruction to the educationally disadvantaged. That day has passed. The teacher in junior college today is faced by an inquiring, ambitious stu-

---

[1] Negro institutions have been performing the function of compensatory education since the Civil War.

dent—even when he is marginal. Helping this student to compensate for previous social and educational deprivation, while preparing him to compete in a highly complex society, demands teaching skill of a high order. The teacher who faces these problems can hardly remain unprepared or futile or complacent or depend upon his zeal and intuition. He must, on the contrary, be interested, inventive, and hard-working; but most of all he should be well-trained and sensitive.

With regard to instructors in the community college, Thornton (1966) observes that "teachers are largely recruited from other positions into the junior college, with comparatively little opportunity to study in advance its distinctive purposes and problems." Men and women have been recruited from the high schools. They have come from the graduate schools of education and arts and sciences. They are ex-schoolteachers, graduate students, policemen, housewives, technicians with on-the-job training, lawyers, and retired military personnel. It is obvious, therefore, that the teachers in the community college, as a whole, represent a potpourri of skills and expertise.

A small number of junior college teachers are also Ph.D.'s who prefer teaching to research and who reject the publish-or-perish syndrome implicit in an assignment to a four-year college or university. Thornton also points out "that the smaller proportion of doctorates held by junior college faculty members is appropriate, because their instruction is limited to lower division." On the other hand, there is great need for well-schooled personnel at the junior college level with an orientation toward teaching instead of research. Pyle (1968) has emphasized, "it is time for our graduate schools to come to grips with the fact that not everyone needs to be driven through the same research forge. Sure, research needs to be done, but 80 per cent of the people who go into higher education have teaching as their major interest. Why should there not be some actual experience in teaching as part of a graduate student's program? Why should there not be inter-institutional internship programs between the graduate schools and nearby junior colleges?"

Traditionally, the majority of college-trained junior college teachers have come from the ranks of the liberal arts colleges and universities and hold master's degrees. This is still true. Cohen and Brawer (1968) put it this way:

> Historically, the preparation of junior college instructors has been the function of liberal arts colleges and universities. Normal schools for teacher training arrived upon and left the American scene before the junior college movement got under way. Even teachers' colleges, successors to normal schools, lapsed into a minor role in the preparation of teachers prior to the full flowering of the junior college as an institution. Twentieth-century phenomenon that it is, the community college has been able to select its instructors almost exclusively from the ranks of the university and liberal arts college-trained applicant.

Yet, there are many teachers on the junior college staff who teach the applied subjects and would have no need for advanced degrees. Some instructors in the technical areas do not need degrees at all. A part of the foregoing teaching personnel are nonprofessionals who can, nevertheless, teach slow-performing students. Others are professionals who cannot teach them. There is no guarantee that either the professional or the nonprofessional will be effective in teaching developmental students for any sustained period of time. Any current appraisal of the situation indicates that neither is doing an adequate job.

It is a disturbing but nonetheless generally confirmed fact that few teachers come to the junior college today well prepared for the job of teaching the great diversity of students, especially the educationally disadvantaged student. It is no secret that the very sharpest, best schooled, and most pedagogically promising students have been systematically redirected from teaching assignments in community colleges to graduate study and therefore to college and university teaching and research or to business and industry. A few competent and talented ones do take junior college positions regularly. But they have not always had the skill and the vital commitment to persistence in the creative instruction necessary in the two-year school. Customarily, though certainly with some exceptions, community colleges have been faced with a restricted choice—"seconds" from the M.A. rosters, veteran teachers retired from, and definitely influenced by, university and college experience, persons with college training (for example, housewives) who seldom or never expected to teach at all, and high school teachers, many of them excellent at their former roles but not necessarily properly oriented to the new one. Some of them are years behind in professional orientation to teaching. And almost all of them are innocent of the many functions and multiple needs of the junior college. The majority of them are uniformly unprepared, substantively and psychologically, for this responsibility, particularly as it relates to the underachieving students. Moreover, they leave vacancies as they move from one sensitive area of education to another. The high school is an example. "The junior college which continually fills its positions by employing local high school instructors soon may find creativity and receptiveness to new ideas lacking in its faculty. In-breeding not infrequently breeds stultification" (Cohen and Brawer, 1968).

TEACHER TRAINING

No one area of undergraduate or graduate training appears to receive the adverse criticism that teacher training does. The most vociferous critics are from the world of academe.

Roger H. Garrison, chairman of the literature and language department at Westbrock Junior College in Maine, a former vice-president of a junior college and a former staff member of the American Association of Junior Colleges, wrote a paper for the Council of Graduate Schools in the United States in December of 1967. Excerpts from that paper (Garrison, 1968) pose some pertinent questions and issues and some significant statements applicable to the preparation of teachers for the junior college. Implicit in the statements from the paper were references to the marginal student. First, he predicted that in the next ten years three or four million students who will not go on for additional undergraduate work for the bacca-

laureate degree will be enrolled in junior colleges. He asked
these questions:

> Are we making teachers who are both willing and pro-
> fessionally equipped to teach effectively these freshmen
> and sophomores? Are we preparing them, both intellectu-
> ally and temperamentally, to do this job at a reputable
> professional level? Are we preparing them, for instance,
> to teach—and teach well—general courses, with four or
> five sections of 25 or 30 students each? Are we equipping
> them to diagnose, prescribe, and effectively instruct stu-
> dents whose abilities range from the brilliantly competent
> to the unaroused illiterate?
> Are we preparing teachers for students who are not—who
> never will be—interested at all, or ever arrested by, schol-
> arly interests, yet who are, in their own ways, magnifi-
> cently challenging students who press always for the utility
> of knowledge? Permit me to doubt that we are. And permit
> me further to doubt—not cynically—that we do not yet
> care enough to do so.

Garrison's paper further revealed that he thought the typical
graduate school product (in English) is about as well equipped
to teach English composition "as a rabbit is to bite a lion to
death." Continuing, these were other suggestions:

> It would be the rare graduate program that would have
> prepared him for the realities of his first job; for students
> who hate to read; for students who wouldn't know a run-on
> sentence from a three-gaited horse; for students whose
> language habits have long since been distorted by the
> verbal barbarities of the rock-'n'-roll disc jockey, the TV
> commercial, the peer group jargon; yet for students who,
> if they realistically saw the need to write clearly, would
> eagerly learn to do so. Or try to learn.

Garrison said the same situation exists in other disciplines. He
called for a rethinking and recasting of graduate material "with
new goals in mind." He reiterated what has been suggested by
others: that the last ten years have been the "decade of the researcher," and the next ten would be the "decade of the
teacher."

Other educators are equally critical:

Graduate schools have not been particularly concerned
with preparation of any kind of college teacher, junior or
senior (Cohen and Brawer, 1968).
It is evident that research into teaching is non-existent in
most universities and is only an incidental activity in
others. The infinitesimal percentage of the higher educational budget devoted to research into educational results
and the improvement of teaching is shameful (O'Dowd,
1967).
We should *not* count on the four-year colleges and universities to train teachers for two-year colleges, especially
when experiences show that the universities tend to do
this in isolation from the realities of two-year college needs
and circumstances (Kiernan, 1967).
Traditionally, many graduate schools and univei ity faculty members have been unaware of or uninter sted in
the special problems of junior college faculty evelop-
ment. Many university educators have been frankly skepti-
cal of or hostile to the junior college (Mallan, 1968).
Large sums have been spent to better prepare elementary
and secondary teachers, and although impressive steps
have been taken to attract and qualify college teachers, the
effect of the latter program was to move candidates along
to the doctorate as well as to a university career. The university undoubtedly benefited, but few if any of the people
trained by this route joined community college teacher
ranks (Gleazer, 1968).

The biting rhetoric of the statements above is voiced
not by the adversaries of graduate education, but by men who
are vitally concerned—intellectually, educationally, and practi-
cally—with the preparation of teachers in higher education.
Half of the critics above are men directly involved with the
junior college movement. They would be less than responsible
if they refused to take a realistic appraisal of how teachers are
trained for the newest and fastest-growing segment of American
education. The cold facts are that teacher training institutions
as a whole, with all of the inadequacies associated with them,
do make at least some attempt to prepare teachers for every
definable educational level below the junior college level—

only. This is a condition of long standing. Gleazer (1968) notes that, "Some two hundred colleges and universities have reported that they do something toward preparation of community college teachers." Singer (1969) claims a lesser number. "Exactly how many is still to be determined, but data now being compiled indicate that between 75 and 100 United States colleges and universities now provide an organized program of graduate studies at the masters or post-masters level for junior and community college teachers." New standards are being called for and developed. Phair (1969) writes:

> [T]he tenured faculty, department chairmen, and administrators involved in the selection process are constantly seeking standards to judge the adequacy of preparation of those who want to teach. In an attempt to provide criteria for these selectors, the California Junior College Association, with the cooperation of the University of California faculty members at Berkeley associated with the Junior College Leadership Program, is trying to evolve a set of preemployment standards.

Cohen and Brawer (1968) have said, "Where university and college programs for preparing junior college instructors have existed, they have typically been organized on patterns similar to those used to prepare elementary and secondary school teachers."

Further lamenting, deploring, criticizing can serve little purpose here. And it would seem that additional documentation of the poor preparation of community college teachers can provide only an exercise in academic distraction. It is obvious that junior college teachers, as a whole, are not well trained to fulfill the function of the community college, although most of them are well trained in their subject-matter disciplines or their applied technologies. If we follow this latter statement to its logical conclusion, it can be inferred that if instructors in the two-year college are generally not prepared by their training to teach the normal achieving freshmen and sophomores as a group, then there must be a total lack of competencies among faculties to teach high-risk students, who make up a special category in higher education. This is a category that does not exist for most four-year colleges and universities and too many two-year institutions do not bring their resources to bear on this problem.

Some steps are being taken to rectify the problem of teacher training. Gleazer (1968) indicates some of these measures. He points out that several national organizations have joined forces with the American Association of Junior Colleges to encourage universities to devote more thought to this problem of teacher training. The American Association of Junior Colleges (AAJC) has been funded by various private foundations and is involved in many projects (such as the Faculty Development Project funded by the Carnegie Foundation) designed to improve the preparation of junior college teaching personnel. Proposals requesting millions of dollars have been submitted to the federal government for funds to provide better teacher-training and are a part of the idiom and literature related to the community college. Yet, I am unaware of a single source reporting the preparation of teachers for the educationally disadvantaged student at the college level. Similarly, I am not aware of any institution being specifically funded to carry on this task.

Teachers of remedial students at the college level are, for the most part, self-trained. They have operated on a "learn-as-you-go" or "on-the-job-training" basis. Their jobs have been without description, structure, theory, or methodology. Bossone (1966) would corroborate this point of view. Many of these teachers who have been assigned to remedial classes have neither the desire nor the temperament to work with such students. One teacher, resigning his position, wrote in his letter of resignation:

> Dear Dr. _____:
> I am sorry, but after a year working in this program, I find that I have neither the dedication, motivation, nor patience to work with these students. The thing that really bothers me is that I don't have the training to teach remedial students.
> I tried to locate a course that would give some instruction on how low-achieving college students

should be taught. I could not find a single school that offered such a course.

If there is no place in the college where I can better use my graduate training, this letter, then, will serve as my notification of resignation.

Sincerely,

Implicit in the above letter are the common frustrations of a remedial teacher in the community college: attitude toward the students to be taught, lack of training to deal with them, no place to get the needed training, and not even books or other literature that is appropriate for college-age students. There do not appear to be any existing prescriptions or programs to train teachers of high-risk students. Some guidelines for such training are badly needed.

Even before he is properly trained, the teacher who is to work with marginal students should approach the task with certain basic [2] knowledge about the student and the working situation. His job is greatly facilitated when he knows the following facts:

High-risk students who enroll in the community college are (at the time of their admission) operating in the society at a level higher than their achievement scores on subject-matter testing instruments indicate they are able. Marginal students have mastered most of the necessary skills, knowledges, behaviors, laws, and other confrontations with the culture with satisfactory results or, at least, acceptable results, except the academic dimensions, which they can still learn.

Teachers of remedial students must be both sensitive and objective. They must be aware of many of the needs, appetites, problems, life and learning style, and other dimensions of the student. In short, they must have the ability to empathize. From an objective point of view, they must be objective enough to deal with the student's limitations without becoming emotionally bound to him. If the commitment to a program for the marginal student is not a firm one at all levels (that is, board of trustees, administration, and faculty), the program will prob-

[2] The basic knowledge and assumptions listed here can also be found in Moore, 1968c.

ably be unsuccessful. If remedial students are taught well, they learn, assuming they have some ability. The reverse is also true. High-risk students are almost never told what they need to know, what they need to do, or why, or how. Students need this information.

The institution and its staff is rarely willing to make changes in curriculum, teaching techniques, and, if necessary, philosophy and personnel. The institution and staff who will attempt to assist the student in helping himself will abandon all of the academic charades and labels such as "late bloomer," and so on, and set about developing specific activities designed to teach the student what he has been exposed to for more than half of his life, but has not learned. The teachers who instruct the high-risk student must believe that the student can learn and wants to learn.

High-risk students who belong to minority groups have unique problems which are not completely academic in nature; therefore, the program must be designed to meet some of the special needs of these students. The teaching methods for marginal students have probably been wrong for years. The remedial student is supersensitive to the "phony teacher." He is as aware of this insincerity as the "phony" himself. He can frequently tolerate his failure more than his teacher. He has a definite contribution to make and must have a way to make it in a positive way. Many marginal students would rather not try than to fail. On the other hand, they are likely to be more patient than their teachers. This type of student cannot readily switch from one learning style to another until the first one is well internalized.

Experience has validated most of these premises. They are not the only considerations which can be suggested; and some of them vary according to the individual student, the school, the community, and other variables.

Instructors of remedial students must know the nature of the student to be served. The marginal enrollees in the same institution, as we have said, may come from diverse urban, suburban, and rural backgrounds with all of the classes, subclasses, income levels, races, and other distinguishing features of the special groups peculiar to those backgrounds. It is obvious that instructors need some course, perhaps under one title, which deals with the sociology of these different geographic, social, and cultural frames of reference of community college students. Such a course is necessary to help junior college teachers to recognize and understand the life styles, language patterns, and other unique characteristics of this variant student body. There is a specific need for the teacher to be thoroughly familiar with the psychology of dealing with the young adult as a whole. On the other hand, there is a definite psychology of the remedial student which should be known and understood by the instructor in order for him to cope successfully with the unique attitudes and behaviors of marginal students. Such courses do not now exist.

Prospective teachers for the community college should study the philosophy of the two-year college. The course in philosophy would not be the typical, broad, amorphous, and irrelevant education course normally found in teacher-training curricula. Rather, it would be a course which would clearly inform the prospective teacher of the distinct role and function of the open-door college in relation to the student, community, and other educational institutions. It would also emphasize the role of the teacher in the role and function of the institution. Perhaps in this way instructors would not find themselves in the conflict of having a senior college attitude in a junior college setting.

There are, of course, many other courses needed in the curricula for training community college teachers. Courses in guidance, test construction, audio-visual aids, and curriculum construction must be developed and oriented to the high-risk student at the post-secondary level. Method courses in the language arts (reading-writing, English, and so on) and mathematics for college-age developmental students must be a part of the course pattern of teachers of the academically low achiever. In like manner, the faculty member needs several courses in the management and organization of learning activities. More specifically, he needs to know how remedial students learn and how to teach them. It is a rare occasion to find a

faculty member in higher education who has had learning
theory unless he is in education or psychology. The techniques
of diagnosing, remediating, and evaluating learning disabilities
are the dimensions of teacher training that must be included
in the educative process if the teacher is to be effective in
dealing with the educationally disadvantaged student.

Pure teaching can be learned. Although it helps to have
some natural ability, sympathy, keen intuition, a wholesome
personality, and the other helpful intangibles, the skill of how
to provide purposeful and effective instruction can be taught
to teachers, if deliberate systematic and determined efforts are
used. If the prospective teacher has the appropriate training
(courses, apprenticeship, and so on), a part of the job is complete. On the other hand, complete dependence on formal
courses, textbooks, and the official curriculum alone decidedly
limits the faculty member in his attempt to provide for the low
achiever. These tools only give him knowledge about the students he is to teach and a frame of reference. There is no
shortcut to experience. He must hoe that row alone.

Blocker and Richardson (1968) have said:

> [T]he teacher and learner are engaged in a cooperative
> process in which there is an active interchange of intel-
> lectual stimulation, knowledge, and affective relation-
> ships. Tutelage of the students inside and outside the
> classroom is an active psychological relationship in
> which both parties participate in the learning process:
> the teacher as a stimulator, leader, and evaluator; the
> student as a reactor, formulator, and evaluator. Within
> this context the teacher is simultaneously aiding the
> student to identify and solve problems and also helping
> him reassess himself in the light of his new understand-
> ings.

Is the above definition any less true for the marginal
student? Obviously the answer to this question is no. The reality of the definition for high-risk students is less apparent.
Teachers neither stimulate nor do a very effective job of leading
and evaluating remedial students. They do not know how. The
teaching strategies necessary to work with low achievers at the

college level have not been organized. Objectives have not been developed in behavioral terms. The mundane dos and don'ts have neither been catalogued and made available to students learning to become teachers nor are they accessible to those who are already faculty members. The following strategies can be employed as the student-teacher or the in-service teacher prepares to work with the remedial student. Thus the effective teacher is well organized. This may mean preparing an outline and distributing it as a handout to the student so that he can follow in sequential order the format of the lesson. He makes sure that the material is written below the student's reading level. This does not mean that the ideas and concepts must be unsophisticated. He requires students to respond. He does not permit them to give one-syllable answers, although he encourages them to answer in their own words (idiom or slang), at least in the beginning. He is careful to make his explanations succinct. He uses concrete examples and he makes sure that the examples are always appropriate, relevant, and as interesting as possible. He makes sure that the guidelines (test schedule, method, attendance, and so on) are established early and are observed in a consistent way and that the student is reminded often about the guidelines. He listens to the student most of the time.

The effective teacher with the low achiever does not use subtle corrections when the student is wrong; he uses concrete ones that the student can see, take with him, and question. It is necessary that the instructor of the low-achiever be flexible. He cannot hesitate to depart from tradition. He must demonstrate often in contemporary terms even if what is to be taught is historical in nature. Most remedial students do not appear to have a well-developed historical frame of reference. The instructor must understand that the female members of his class will have more concern with what is to be learned than the male students. He cannot use the textbook as an all-purpose medium for the high-risk student. For many of these students it is not an effective medium at all and it tends to limit the teacher who is not resourceful.

The remedial student is always in need of more educa-

tional experience than basic skills and the effective teacher sees
that he gets it. Most remedial students are "ear-bound." However, they must have an opportunity to talk some and to listen
some. High-risk students must have an opportunity to produce
knowledge. They cannot accept a random selection of obsolete
facts as inputs but have little or no opportunity for outputs.
Lecturing is not an outstanding teaching technique and is almost disastrous with remedial students unless the lecturer is
unique.

PROBLEMS OF DIAGNOSIS

The learning problems of remedial students in college
are much more difficult to diagnose than they are among elementary and high school students. One reason is because the
symptoms of the students' learning deficiencies are frequently
obscured and teachers do not always know where to look. Typically one would examine the physical disabilities (loss of hearing, visual anomalies, and the like) as a first step to determining
whether or not a student's deficiencies were due to some physical
malfunction. However, these disabilities have usually been corrected by the time a student reaches college. Frequently, an impoverished experiential background has been blamed for low
achievement in students. Whereas a considerable number of community college students come from poor communities, a large
majority of the students come from homes where all of the experiences, possessions, attitudes, and traditions considered to be important for learning are present; these students, even the poor
ones, have been exposed to books, newspapers, field trips, muse-
ums, concerts, plays, and libraries during their twelve years of
schooling. Still, they have not achieved well academically. Consequently, an impoverished educational background is frequently
more an excuse for than a reason why they have not learned.
The college student brings with him the experience he has used
to solve his problems for most of his life. He also brings with
him the ability to hide from others things about himself and
what he really thinks and feels. He has already experienced
many of the routines of study but he cannot study effectively.
The records of the poor learning habits and methods

used by the remedial student are not normally available to the college teacher. For example, poor reading habits (eye span, eye fixations, mouthing words, and so on) are not immediately, if ever, known to the teachers of high-risk students in general education courses or mathematics. These poor reading habits may be known only to the teacher who teaches reading. The extreme behavior (negativism, antagonism, and resistance) that is frequently observable in elementary and secondary marginal students is not always readily apparent in college-age students.

There are other glaring contradictions that characterize the intellectually different student which make his learning problems difficult to diagnose. A case in point: The same low-achieving student who cannot read *Ivanhoe*, *The Iliad*, or *War and Peace* can frequently read and understand *Sports Illustrated*, *Valley of the Dolls*, and the *Autobiography of Malcom X* without a great deal of difficulty. The ability of a remedial student to grasp a complex and sophisticated idea goes beyond his ability to express it orally or in writing; this is another contradiction.

There is little doubt that some of these students are intellectually deficient; and it is to be expected that some have emotional and personal problems. There are also some of them who may be described as unmotivated. Since most teachers are not psychologists, these latter problems are only speculations and require professional attention before a conclusive determination can be reached and made available to the teacher. There is, however, some information already known. In the area of emotional problems, it is well documented that students who are anxious cannot concentrate, and this inhibits performance. Many educationally disadvantaged students appear anxious. There is evidence which shows that depression decreases the memory span. It is also rather well documented that the student who continues to experience failure stops trying. The student who feels humiliated, frustrated, and embarrassed because he has not been able to succeed can develop many emotional problems which are not readily identifiable to the teacher in the college.

The problems involved in finding out why high-risk

students have difficulty learning are too holistic and there is too little research for us to be capable of treating in discrete, encapsulated categories. Teachers have neither the training nor the opportunity to analyze the problematical situations in which they find themselves as they attempt to diagnose the marginal student's learning habits and behavior.

It is fairly obvious that a rather comprehensive roster of situations faces the teacher as he plans to teach the marginal student. Diagnosis of learning difficulties is usually associated with testing students. The complement to evaluating students by using tests implies that the teacher will have the skill and ability to interpret the data from the measuring instruments. Teachers who have not had training in education, psychology, or guidance do not have such skills. Most diagnostic evaluative instruments are administered to students by some person in the college other than the teacher (usually the counselor) if they are administered at all. Because teachers cannot always handle the data from these tests, their diagnosis of a student's learning difficulties is incomplete and their remediation process is, therefore, either incomplete, inaccurate, or both. Most instructors do not have to make a determination at all since they have no teaching responsibilities for remedial students. Those who do find it difficult.

STATUS AND ATTITUDE

The status an instructor enjoys when he teaches elementary and high school students is not the same when he teaches high-risk students at the college level. The favorable circumstances that the teacher has in greater experience and maturity, which are supported both legally and by custom as he teaches precollege students, are not normally advantages he can enjoy when he teaches marginal students. For one thing, the experience in adult involvement of the high-risk student in college is frequently equal to, and sometimes greater than, that of the instructor. The high-risk student is less likely to ask the teacher for help or advice. The student's capacity for independence makes unique demands on the teacher. Roueche (1968) notes:

Instructors are concerned about "status" and being properly identified with higher education. To teach a remedial or developmental course does not identify them with higher education, whereas teaching specialized and advanced courses affords instructors personal and professional prestige.

Later in the same publication he writes:

The questions of status and prestige must be resolved if instructors are to become interested in the teaching of remedial students. Jargon is clouding the issues. If junior colleges are identified as institutions of higher education, then those who teach in two-year colleges are automatically associated with higher education. If the lives of the students are important, all teaching assignments have value and worth. The pecking order of preferred teaching assignments is worthy of serious question and challenge.

Although there are many exceptions, the reaction of the academically slow student to the teacher is frequently uncomplimentary. "By the time we reach college, we have had a belly full of teachers," one student states bluntly. "It's hard to believe that all of the kids we see now are as stupid as their teachers say they are. It's about time somebody makes them responsible for the job they get paid for doing. They are the only experts left who can continue to get paid and not do the job. You've never heard a doctor say I can't cure you because you're too near dead, or an architect say I can't build a house over a swamp; but the first thing you get around here is that they can't teach you because your SCAT scores are too low. If a teacher is supposed to be an expert, he ought to do his thing. If he's not an expert he ought to quit—or get fired." More and more we are beginning to see this type of criticism of teachers creep into the literature. Sobel (1968) writes:

If there is anything revolutionary on the American educational scene, it is not experiments with talking typewriters. . . . It is simply that we are beginning to hold

teachers responsible for much that is rotten in schools.
If truth is the beginning of wisdom, then we may at long
last be on the road to educational enlightenment.

Not even from his colleagues can the instructor in the
remedial program expect recognition for his work. It appears
that the ability of the teacher is often compared to and associated with the abilities of his students. He is frequently responded to at the extremes by his colleagues, that is, he endures
either their detachment, their sympathy, or their hostility.
Sociological research shows that what Roueche calls "something
of a 'pecking order' " exists in most institutions and in divisions
within those institutions. This order is based on seniority and
tenure. Tenured faculty get first choice at their teaching loads.
Bossone (1966) points out that research has shown that the
inexperienced faculty member is the one most often found in
a remedial classroom. Roueche (1968) corroborates Bossone.
He writes: "It is ironic the inexperienced teachers are sometimes considered to be unprepared to serve on major committees
but yet are given one of the most difficult teaching assignments."
It is indeed rare to find a permanent faculty member assigned
to the remedial program. When an exception is found, the
person is not considered to be among the outstanding teachers
on the faculty. Often the teacher in the remedial program is
untenured, young, and inexperienced. Some instructors who
work with marginal students are hypocritical. The lip service
they pay to the students and the programs in public is refuted
in private. Repeatedly, one gets off-the-record information from
teachers in developmental programs which indicates that they
do not like the job or support the program in which they work.
Teacher status, then, becomes an elusive dimension when
working in projects designed to serve high-risk students. The
reasons are clearly apparent. The faculty members who have
a real choice will not usually accept the job. Those who are
"forced" to work in the developmental program are found to
be bitter about the assignment. This is tragic. The teachers in
the remedial program not only should be especially trained but
also should be volunteers. Esbensen (1968) emphasized that

there is no faster way to kill a program than to staff it
with reluctant dragons. The unwilling teacher is the
deadliest critic there is. To place the fate of an educational venture in their hands is to court disaster.

The truth of the matter is that more criticism and hostility
toward the developmental program come from the faculty than
from any other source. Many teachers believe the program
should be designed according to their own specifications, even
though they wanted nothing to do with it in the formative
stages. Too many suggest that it has no place in college curricula
—"open door" institution notwithstanding. Every faculty member who has a research ax to grind will want to use the developmental program. This should never be permitted. The program
should never be the scapegoat or whipping boy for other programs, departments, or divisions in the college.

It is probably true that a majority of teachers in the
community college, as elsewhere, would prefer to instruct students who represent the academic elite. In the "working man's
college," however, as the two-year institution is often called,
they find themselves in competition for more academically
talented students and in search of academic competence. This
is an attitude commonly found in colleges and universities.
Medsker (1960) points out: "The attitudes of junior college
teachers may reflect the educational values or attitudes of teachers in four-year colleges and universities." His observation certainly seems valid with relation to teacher attitude toward the
remedial student. Many teachers assert that low-achieving students and the developmental programs and projects necessitated
by their presence are of little or no concern to them. Roueche
(1968) also points out:

> Teacher attitudes are probably related to student
> achievement; accordingly, no teacher should be arbi-
> trarily assigned to teach a remedial class who prefers
> not to do it or who is only mildly interested. It is un-
> realistic to expect uninterested teachers to motivate
> students who are characterized by their lack of motiva-
> tion. Teachers must motivate students toward a desire

to learn, and this may not be possible if teachers themselves are not enthusiastic.

Medsker further reports the results of a study which shows the attitude of the faculty toward the function of the college in relation to the remedial student:

> Twenty-eight per cent indicated that it was "not important" for the junior college to offer remedial high school level courses for students whose academic record makes them ineligible to enter directly into conventional college courses. Nineteen per cent said it was not important that the junior college offer certain programs for adults. A fifth of the respondents thought it not important for the junior college to offer vocational or in-service classes for adults.

Schenz (1964) reported that in a national survey 91 per cent of the community colleges surveyed agreed with the open-door concept but only 55 per cent provided special remedial courses for their high-risk students.

Since the teacher is a key person in any developmental or remedial program, it is imperative that various dimensions of the teaching function be explored. No one area needs examination more than the attitude of teachers. From Maine to Oregon, one hears some interesting and revealing questions and comments that appear to reflect the attitude of many junior college people:

"If a student didn't learn how to make subject and verb agree in the twelve years of elementary and secondary schooling within his eighteen and nineteen years of living, how can I teach him this in college?"

"It's hard enough to try to teach *these people* in the first place, but I have been waiting three weeks for the bookstore to get the texts in. How am I supposed to teach them without books?"

"I didn't know it was the job of the college to do missionary work with weak students. There are too many qualified students who need help to waste our time with those who can't cut the mustard."

"How can I teach a student science who can't even read the textbook?"

The first question was asked by an instructor teaching remedial English. The odds are that the students in that class will not know how to make subject and verb agree when they have completed the course. There is an implicit question here: Will the student fail to learn because of his inability to learn or because of the expectancy of the teacher? Rosenthal and Jacobson (1968), authors of *Pygmalion in the Classroom,* would suggest that it is the latter. For a qualified and creative teacher, the student's previous lack of academic success and lack of available resources are, at worst, only inconveniences—not barriers. For the good teacher they are challenges.

One assistant professor who claims he is in pursuit of relevance suggests, "We're teaching the wrong thing. We ask students whose cup of tea is not writing at all to sit down in an hour or overnight and write a theme. I am a teacher and I have trouble doing that—and I know all the rules. How many times can an instructor sit down and turn out a new and creative piece of work? Most college professors cannot identify all of the rules, techniques, and intricacies of the expository writing which they themselves use. Were it not for the editors, many who get published would not—if the language properly written was the criterion."

It would appear that we do get frustrated and penalize students when they cannot produce on cue like a symphony orchestra that runs through Beethoven's Ninth when the conductor steps up and raps on the podium a couple of times. Even then, the orchestra can perform with perfection only after many rehearsals. In educational jargon we call this "practice" or "drill," or when we are really snobbish we call it repetitive experience designed to solidify a learned response. When we ask a student to begin writing a theme at 2:00 P.M. and complete it by 2:50 P.M., we are frequently asking him to do what the instructor cannot do. The difference is many marginal students have sense enough not to try. Actually we are asking the students to be creative on cue. Few possess such creativity. The writing format offered by Roth and Altshuler (1969) for assist-

ing remedial students is one of the most effective techniques.
The method suggested by these writers gets rid of the lack of
precision on the part of English teachers and provides for a
realistic approach to teaching high-risk students to write. They
point out that:

> Teachers can be mysterious creatures to remedial stu-
> dents in a junior college writing class. They stand in
> the position of authority, in front of the room. They are
> arbiters of rules, dispensers of grades. The student knows
> that his future depends in part on the way a teacher
> views him; yet he often finds it hard to break through
> the mystery of what he is expected to do. At the begin-
> ning of each course, "The Great Guessing Game" is
> played. "What does he want?" wonders the student. This
> worry reaches its high point the day a theme assignment
> is made. Already worried about the ability to write any-
> thing which can elicit enthusiasm from his instructor,
> the student's concern is deepened by the assignment to
> "Discuss . . ." What? How? . . . Instructors who care
> about good teaching in the junior college do not want
> students to play the guessing game. The solution is to
> take the mystery out of what is expected on a writing
> assignment.

The high-risk student is an educational reality. Like a
latent disease, he will not go away. Unfortunately, few teachers
can, or want to, teach him at the college level, even fewer understand him; many reject him academically and socially and a
large percentage of people in higher education consider his
presence in college as a prostitution of higher education.

Chapter Four

The Counselor

T he counselor is a specialist. Not only must he bring to the developmental program the special preparation required of his profession and a knowledge of his function, but also he is asked to take an active part in the learning process. In short, he is an educator. There is little doubt that he is one of the emerging giants in remedial education in the community college. As he deals with the high-risk student he must be concerned as much with what the student is as with what he does. Interacting with marginal students requires that he understand the immutable values, persistent reticence, and the recognizably distinct habits of this student compared to those of the traditional college student he has always known and served.

With regard to counseling the high-risk student, Thelen (1968) makes several generalizations: First, the high-risk community college student has accumulated a number of deficiencies by the time he enrolls. Second, research on counselor effectiveness with the high-risk student from four-year institutions is scant. That which is available predominantly shows a null or negative effect. Authors suggest that primary use of grade point average as a criterion of effectiveness may be too limited. Third, research from community colleges is almost nonexistent. Although the author made additional generalizations in her study, the above three are quoted most in the literature. Thelen's generalizations further reinforce statements which have been made earlier; and these statements imply what the counselor's task must be in working with the high-risk student.

There is mounting evidence that in the community college the counselor is the pivotal staff member in the remedial program. Around him revolve the functions of teaching, learning, scheduling, and program planning. He acts as the liaison person between the remedial division or department and the other divisions within the institution, and he is often a contact between business, industry, and much of the community as a whole. He represents the core of any program designed to assist the academically unsuccessful student. Sometimes his assistance is more effective in helping students improve than academic courses. DeWeese (1959) found group counseling more help to high-risk students in academic achievement than a remedial reading course. If the counselor in the program is to be successful, he must be student and community centered. Witherspoon (1966), a counselor in one of the more successful remedial programs, emphasizes, "It is the counselor's task, through the use of a variety of informational materials accumulated through varied techniques, to assist the student in making use of available data concerning his psychological, educational, and occupational situation."

The counselor's job is sometimes more difficult in the basic or developmental program in a community college setting than it is in the four-year institution. Several reasons account for this difficulty: First, he is expected to work with students who have not succeeded and who are normally not expected to succeed. Second, the counselor does not have the support of the entire faculty that the counselor could expect to get from a university faculty because of the nature of the students being served. Third, there is usually a lack of financial support for the remedial program. Fourth, as a rule, the developmental program and the personnel who serve it are "squatters." They are always housed in temporary space. They are allotted only the space some dean or department chairman is willing to "let" them use. Fifth, the community college is a commuter college and the students work on either full-time or part-time jobs and do not develop the school spirit that is usually found in a four-year institution; in fact, those students who do attend a two-year institution and later complete their work for the baccalaureate at a four-year institution do not consider the two-year college as their alma mater in terms of either compliments or endowments. Sixth, a sizable number of the marginal students (about 70 per cent) do not plan to continue their education beyond two years even if they are able. Further, because of the open-door policy, there is, of course, a growing black student population. Their presence with regard to the current emphasis on black awareness and black activity is a new influence in the community college. This influence can cause tension between racial groups. This is a definite problem for the counselor from one racial group who counsels a client from another racial group. Smith (1967) postulates that Caucasian counselors may have more difficulty establishing rapport with black students than would black counselors. This is obviously a clue to hiring personnel. Finally, students view the community college experience as a transitional period in their lives.

The counselor's task is also made difficult because of the several functions he performs. He must provide major services to the students, teachers, and administrators, and to the general college program. In a few community colleges, the counselor teaches courses in group guidance to the same students he counsels on an individual basis. Fields (1962) reports that in some colleges the counselor is asked to teach remedial courses. Counseling in a remedial program can often involve a conflict of values between the counselor and his client. Because counselees come from such broad and diverse educational, economic, and social backgrounds, the counselor finds himself at times working with those whose values, attitudes, and commitments are the same as his own. The counselor is expected to serve other clients whose beliefs are not only different from his own, but antagonistic. His function is further complicated when he

works with the educationally handicapped student because of
the social stigma directed toward such students from other
people. Maurice, a second semester freshman enrolled in a
remedial program, explains: "When you're in this program,
you are the ass in the crowd. Teachers give you a kind of 'well
I really don't expect you to know' look when they ask a question.
Some are hostile to you without reason—and they call us stupid.
Every time you pass a group of students in the hall you're being
auditioned; they sort of get quiet until you pass. Sometimes you
would rather hear them laugh at you. I have even borrowed
other guys' books to carry around all day because I'm ashamed
to let everybody see the books I use and let them know I don't
learn too fast. Even my folks at home are always comparing me
with my little brother who does well in school. When you don't
learn too fast the word gets around. Last year, when the men
from colleges came to my high school, my English teacher told
me I shouldn't bother to go talk to them. I knew it was because
I didn't do too well in her composition class. But she always had
us writing themes—and about the damnedest subjects. I just
couldn't get a charge out of writing about 'How a Chipmunk
Got His Stripes.' I tried though. The only thing I really know
anything about is cars but my high school counselor kept saying
I shouldn't want grease under my fingernails for the rest of my
life. I don't see anything wrong with grease. He certainly didn't
have anything better to offer. The counselor in this college is
different. He tells me if this is my thing to go ahead and do it.
I guess I could take being in this program for slow students
better, if others didn't treat you so different."

There is also consistent contradiction found among high-
risk students: Many of them grow up too fast; and many others
refuse to grow up. One observes extreme, almost psychotic,
shifts in mood from optimism to pessimism. There are students
from poor families who look forward to the future and there are
other students who come from the same types of families and
environments who fear the future. Williams and Cole (1968)
imply this latter group has a poor concept of self. Many remedial students, especially those from low-income areas and

broken homes, are adept at solving their own problems but
have never seen how a family cooperates to solve problems.
While middle-class marginal students are willing to defer many
of their gratifications, disadvantaged students want their rewards immediately. Bard, Lerner, and Morris (1967) explain
this accent on the immediate as it applies to the disadvantaged:

> [S]tudents typically emphasize the immediacies, the
> present reward, the at-hand realities. Involvement with
> the distant and beyond, in terms of educational and
> occupational goals, of achieving potentials, is not easily
> visualized. Present involvement of the students focuses
> attention on today—on the getting for today and letting
> tomorrow go. In many instances, the immediate concern
> is with battling poverty, and with getting the basic
> physical necessities. Under these circumstances, plan-
> ning for college by students, or parents, becomes almost
> forbidden.

Remedial students overestimate their abilities to others while
at the same time they show lack of confidence in their ability.
Their stated goals require abilities beyond their demonstrated
capacities. These incongruities have been documented by Kagan
(1966) and Berger (1967). High-risk students attempt to cope
with all of their dilemmas except academic ones. There is little
doubt that some of these students are of low ability. A considerable number of them are misdirected and uncertain of their
goals. Most do not know the areas of their strengths. Few either
see or accept their weaknesses. They do not know their resources, and the majority have never learned proper study
habits and skills. The frequency of these predicaments is well
known to counselors. In every college counseling situation, the
counselor meets a few students who have the characteristics
described above. It is most striking that in the comprehensive
community college, only a few marginal students are without
them. There is disagreement as to whether or not counseling
can help the high-risk student. Richardson (1960), Bloom (1964),
and Bowlin (1965) indicate with some evidence that little can
be done to help such students with their academic problems.

Conversely, Burck (1965), Nelson (1967), and Thoreson (1967) have data to support their contention that counseling does help the remedial student to improve academically.

The majority of a counselor's time in a remedial program is spent in assisting students in individual counseling. Tennyson (1958) calls this one-to-one counseling "the heart of the guidance program." There are, in addition to individual counseling, other supportive services necessary to assist students in making adjustments and in developing and carrying out their plans. Remedial students who are also culturally disadvantaged need a disproportionately larger amount of the counselor's time. Ryan and Gaier (1968) reached this same conclusion. Still other facets of the counselor's job are apparent. The number of high-risk students increases each year. Munroe (1964) believes that in certain large urban areas as much as 50 per cent of the students will be considered remedial. These students present unique problems for counseling in the community college because they have multiple problems instead of one or two. Most of the problems affecting the students are not school related. The origins of the student conflicts are primarily in the home, on their jobs, and in their communities. Not infrequently, the counselor has difficulty in helping these students with their problems because of the "tuning-out syndrome" many of them manifest. Crow and Crow (1951) suggest that individual problems of adjustment center around one or more areas of a person's life pattern. The authors continue by saying that the attitude or demonstrated behavior of an individual is influenced by: his physical constitution and health status; his habitual habits and behavior traits; his ethical or moral standards or ideals; and his religious experience or affiliation. Crow and Crow failed, however, to point out that in many, many cases, specifically among students representing various ethnic groups, the poor, the disadvantaged, and the blacks (as well as whites), the problem of the student's own adjustment may be due to the health, attitude and behavior traits, moral standards, and religious experiences and affiliations of others. A chronically ill parent, child, or some other relative, the atypical behavior of a loved one, and the prevailing moral standard of a home or a community which may be in conflict with the mainstream are examples; with certain persons and in some groups, all of these factors operate simultaneously.

The characteristics of high-risk students were listed by Merson at the American Personnel and Guidance Association in 1961. Roueche (1968) summarized that listing. High-risk students: graduated from high school with a low C average or below; are severely deficient in basic skills, that is, in language and mathematics; have poor habits of study (and probably a poor place to study at home); are weakly motivated, lacking some encouragement to continue in school; have unrealistic and ill-defined goals; represent homes with minimal cultural advantages and minimum standards of living; are the first of their family to attend college, hence have a minimum understanding of what college requires or what opportunities it offers.

This listing leaves a lot to be desired. Still it is worth consideration. A disproportionate number of ghetto residents and many others from culturally and economically deprived areas will possess six of the seven characteristics listed. It must be pointed out, however, that many middle-class and other affluent students have some of the same characteristics, possibly all but the sixth and seventh. And parental pressures may cause a student to manifest the characteristic listed fifth. The counselor, then, who must work with those students who have some of the identical academic deficiencies and poor learning habits also finds he is working with students who represent a wide range in economic and social backgrounds. Quite apparently, this is a compelling counseling problem.

Another problem of major magnitude confronting the counselor is helping to isolate the "can learn" from the "cannot learn enough for college." Many students feel because they are interested and motivated that they will learn, their abilities will improve, and they can be helped to do adequate and appropriate planning. Willis and Kerr (1966) found small correlation between interest and ability. The findings from this study reinforce counselor knowledge that interest is not an adequate criterion for realistic planning. Bard, Lerner, and Morris (1967) agree: "A mere desire to attend college is not enough, one needs

to be prepared to succeed once he gets in." The counselor must
ask himself questions: What serves as positive predictive evidence that a student can or cannot succeed? Do predictive
criteria for male Negroes differ from criteria for white males?
Is the instrument used to measure ability a valid one for students
from a rural community as well as for those from an urban and
suburban community? These are the age-old problems of education and counseling.

Counselors find common problems of dealing with ra-
tionalization and anxiety related to academic deficits: High-risk
students are quick to attribute their problems to their parents,
teachers, racism, "nobody else uses good study habits," and
similar causes. Many of these individuals and situations deserve
the indictments. Many others do not.

There is, of course, always the problem of communication. The counselor in the remedial program must be an effective communicant. He has to convince parents that the
developmental curriculum their children are assigned to is the
most appropriate for them at that time.[1] He does this by inter-
preting the program to the parents. Parents want to know what
the program is; why their son (or daughter) was placed in a
remedial curriculum; how long the student will be required to
remain in the program; whether the student receives credit;
and so on. Perhaps the most essential question they ask is, "Is
the program any good?" Parents must be convinced that assignment of their youth to a developmental curriculum is no reflec-
tion upon themselves, and they must be made to understand
that they need not give up their dreams of an education for
their children because of their academic placement but to postpone their dreams. In a remedial program the counselor must
make special effort to keep parents apprised of the student's
progress or lack of progress at regular intervals in addition to
the normal reports of the institution, if the particular situation
warrants it. Since in the past, a sizable number of high-risk students either dropped out or eventually failed, it is absolutely

---

[1] Some developmental programs are voluntary on the part of the
student. Others are mandatory when the student's entrance examination
is low and he has a pattern of poor achievement.

necessary that parents have been kept informed. They should also know whether any new adjustments have been made in the curriculum which will affect their sons or daughters. The counselor must be able to reassure parents that their child can be successful in some program while he emphasizes that their current vocational or career choices may have to be reassessed. Yet, he must listen while parents repeat their children's excuses: The student did not learn because it was the teacher's fault, racism, he could have done better on the entrance test but he wasn't feeling well, and so on. Thus, the ability to establish and maintain a good rapport with the parents is without question a necessary function of the counselor's ability to communicate effectively.

The counselor must also be able to communicate with his peers. He must be able to interpret the remedial program to division chairmen, department heads and faculty with such clarity that they will know exactly what adjustments will have to be made in their programs and in their teaching techniques to accommodate the high-risk student. He must attempt to change the attitude of the teachers who are prejudiced toward remedial students, and attempt to get from them suggestions which will help the high-risk student move with the least amount of difficulty from the remedial program into their academic or career areas. The counselor communicates the success stories of the marginal student to faculty and others in the institution with the hope that faculty members in the technical and transfer program will be as proud of—and as sensitive to—the efforts of the college to reach marginal students as are those persons who work directly in the developmental curriculum. He learns as much as he can about all of the divisions so that he is knowledgeable when he talks to faculty about their areas of specialization. In short, the counselor is a diplomat, troubleshooter, placator, negotiator, interpreter, and facilitator as he communicates with his colleagues in relation to the curriculum, acceptance, needs, and goals of underachievers.

With regard to the counselor's communicating with and responding to his peers, in connection with the remedial program, it is recommended that the counselors, teachers, and administrators conduct ongoing seminars on the high-risk student aimed at determining how the institution, its teaching staff and administrator can respond effectively to this student. The teaching staff, even though they have not been trained to work with low-achieving students, can nonetheless make a contribution as they attempt to determine how their disciplines can be adjusted for the marginal student.

The community college counselor working in the remedial curriculum is also the main communicant between the high school counselor and the college. He must make sure that the secondary school people know that there is a program in the community college designed to help the student who will not graduate in the upper fourth or upper half of his class. The college counselor must make available to this potential student all of the printed materials, scholarship information, registration requirements, and other such data. Most essential, he must make the opportunity known to high school personnel and high-risk students. This can be a problem because students who are not normally college bound do not seek information concerning their opportunities for education beyond high school. O'Connell (1968) makes a point of this characteristic in his new book, *Community Colleges*. Secondary counselors are usually responding to students who are academically talented, and to the college and university representatives who are in search of talented students. Some secondary counselors seem shocked when they are asked, by counselors in the remedial program of the community college, to recommend students (who are academically slow) for further training in college who would not normally be accepted in higher education. This has not been a typical role for high school counselors. It is unfortunate; but in the real order of things, the high school student who makes good grades, who can probably get his own information, and who is already motivated, gets more assistance than the high-risk student who has none of these characteristics. The "good-student-centeredness" of much of the education in America is so obvious as to need no elaboration at this point. So much is done for "good students" that they have had little opportunity to do much for themselves. Counselors are as guilty of having this

"qualified-student" myopia as other educators. They, too, motivate the motivated. The community college counselor may do
well to consider Knoell's (1968) suggestions and questions. Although Knoell was referring specifically to the disadvantaged,
her considerations apply. She wrote, in effect, that each college
should ask itself the following questions, with an eye to changing
or relaxing its procedures if the answers are negative: Do admissions procedures make it easy to admit and offer financial
aid to the disadvantaged applicant who "discovers" the college
too late to meet the admission date? Does the college have
unconventional means of seeking, informing, and assisting the
disadvantaged who might otherwise be passed by? Are funds
easily available for testing, physical exams, evaluation of financial need, transportation, formal application for admission, and
other fees? Is some financial aid—educational opportunity
grants, work-study jobs—available for very poor high-risk students, or is it given only to the "safe" students? What is the
reading level of the financial aid and admission forms? Have
they been—or can they be— simplified? Does the admissions or
counseling office use students to recruit and assist the traditional
non-college-goers? Are special recruitment materials and techniques employed to reach disadvantaged students in high school
and in the community? These eight questions may serve to
stimulate local faculties, admissions officers, and student personnel workers in general to examine the practices they follow
as open-door colleges.

Therefore, one of the many tasks of the counselor in
the community college remedial program will be to work with
high school counselors to encourage and motivate marginal
students to go to the junior college. Motivation, of course, is a
paramount problem.

MOTIVATION

Many people, when they refer to the remedial student,
agree: "You can lead a horse to water, but you can't make him
drink." True. But that is not the task of education. Our job
is to make him thirsty. The problems involved in motivating
(making thirsty) high-risk students are overwhelming. And the

counselor must act as mediator, social worker, matchmaker and confidant in order to help the student accomplish what Hamrin (1947) has stated in this way: "Helping John to see through himself in order that he may see himself through."

Because the high-risk student has very great needs in the academic and personal areas of his college experience, the counselor who establishes the rapport and gains the trust of this student will be called upon to perform many varieties of counseling and guidance. The marginal student actually seeks trust, and is not easily fooled by a false facade. Once the counselor earns the trust of the student, the client-counselor relationship is very intimate on both the academic and personal levels and there are many unique problems that a counselor might expect as he attempts to counsel and motivate the educationally disadvantaged student. The following are a few actual cases which provide some insight into the typical cadre of conflicts brought to the attention of the counselor in the remedial program daily:

Miss Q., in her early twenties, is having an affair with an older man who she knows is a philanderer. She is also a student of low academic performance and is greatly concerned about her future. Her announced goal is unrealistic. After intensive counseling, Miss Q. now feels that she is secure enough to break off her love affair and seek relations with her peers. With the counselor's support she is completing her remedial work in basic skills and is presently investigating jobs which are realistic and in keeping with her abilities.

The counselor must provide an atmosphere for students to vent hostility toward their teachers, parents, and the remedial program. Mr. L. came into such an atmosphere and had many disparaging things to say about teachers, administrators, and the developmental program. After three weeks of being allowed to speak his mind in counseling sessions, the counselor then moved the sessions toward a realistic solution of the problem. This was in contrast to the profusion of defense mechanisms being used by Mr. L.

The counselor must be willing to provide detailed and repeated explanations of information and instructions, especially on how one gets out of the program. Interpretation of the program must be given in a detailed manner to Mrs. B. repeatedly. She hears what she wishes to hear. And she asks questions to which she already knows the answers. Nonetheless, the counselor responds to her questions each time she poses them.

Sometimes in a remedial program a counselor must produce in a tangible way in order to gain the trust of the student. Mr. W. needed a part-time job. He insisted that the job must be playing his guitar. The counselor located this type of position with the aid of the college placement office. This resulted in greater rapport with the student. This latter technique was a crash method that happened to work. It was quite obvious that Mr. W. needed a great deal of counseling. He was very immature and had to discover and rectify his childish behavior.

Mrs. C. has been out of school for twenty years and has not had the opportunity to do academic work since. She's approaching mid-forties with a family of six. Academic skills will benefit her. She needs a counselor's support and reassurance that coming back to school is worthwhile, and that what she has lost in concentration and energy, she has gained in experience and depth.

Mr. P. has had father-son problems. His father feels that he should work full-time to help support the family. Though his scores and high school rank were low, after his private parental feud took second place to the necessity of assuming responsibility for self and providing for self (not father), Mr. P. is now doing well in a transfer program.

In this latter case, O'Connell (1968) calls this type of parent an adversary. He writes, "We are counseling the student to work fewer hours outside the college for remuneration; the parents are directly or indirectly pressing for more. We have enough such students to make it desirable as a general rule to deal directly with the student and not with the parent. Why send a failing grade home addressed to the parent if a failing grade is going to result in a parent's saying, not 'You must study harder' but, 'See, I told you it was a waste of time?' " This latter procedure might have worked well for Berkshire College where the above statement was penned; it is to be hoped, however, that no counselor, registrar, dean of admissions, or other staff would be willing to deal directly with a student until at least some attempt had been made to deal with the parents and that attempt had failed. Only then would a counselor recommend to a student that he might analyze his predicament in the absence of parental involvement and make the necessary adjustment to his particular situation.

Miss A. has been tracked in C track since coming from a foreign country during the elementary years. She feels she has always been classified dumb, but does not feel she really is. Psychiatric evaluation indicates she should be able to perform adequately, but is disturbed by many environmental situations: What do American girls act like in boy-girl relationships, parents from the old country, the relative weight of independence-dependence in the role of women, and so on.

Mr. H. has come from a vocational school where he learned to be a cabinetmaker—and received good grades. He does not want to go to college; he does not have the ability. He tried to get a job all over the city, but could not be hired. He has attributed this to his being Negro. He is right, in part at least. The carpenter's union will not permit him to become a member. He needs a counselor to assure him that learning an alternate occupational skill is not a waste of time and that he should continue to press for admission to the union.

Mr. S. is in school to stay out of the draft. His life pattern consists of finding angles to circumvent what he does not want to do. He is bright enough to have manipulated people in all kinds of ways to avoid what he does not like. He needs a counselor who will help him see himself as he really is, and to help him see that he must redirect his behavior in some ways.

Mr. R. is an alcoholic. He has learned to use people's sympathies to get what he wants. He has good peer relationships with eighteen- and nineteen-year-olds although he is forty. He takes an adolescent view toward responsibility. The counselor's task is to avoid sympathy—insist on behavioral standards. Psychiatric evaluation in a group or individually cannot help him unless his personal orientation changes.

Miss D. comes from an uneducated family and from a community where very few of the people have attended college. Her peers, too, see her as "trying to be more than she is." Actually she loves her parents, peers, and her community residents. She also likes the world of academe and can envision how college training could help her help her community. Miss D. is ambivalent. She has on various occasions been tempted to quit college. At other times she has considered not attempting to communicate with her elders and peers. This student needs a counselor to help her analyze her dilemma.

Because of the rapport gained via group guidance and individual sessions, the counselor must be available to the students to "just talk."

As I have mentioned before, the varieties of counseling situations are very numerous. Many students need their counselor's support on many different areas of endeavor. Sometimes no support is required but friendly conversation to smooth anxieties is. At other times students are placed in remedial programs and feel that they are discriminated against according to the instrument used. The student feels that he is being cheated since he wants transfer credit and is not getting it in remedial courses. The counselor explains that learning is a process that builds from a base and that the basic skills gained in the program should provide that base while the general education courses provide for cognitive stimulation in academic areas.

Student predicaments take the above manifestations in addition to many others. Many students have feelings of resentment because they have been placed in a remedial program. This antagonism is expressed in a variety of ways. Some students challenge the material being used in the course as being too much like high school; some vent anger against teachers by complaining about the instructor's lack of skill in teaching (lectures too fast, tone and manner are condescending, and attitude implies that the student is stupid); other students boycott classes or refuse to participate in classes even if they are present. Remedial students will often talk to counselors about these things; rarely will they talk to others.

Educationally disadvantaged students often feel inadequate, inferior and uncertain in various courses. Mathematics, for example, seems to frighten them. It is common for many marginal students to drop science courses at the first indication that mathematics is needed in the course. Research shows that mathematics (Blanton, 1964) and English (Bossone, 1966) are the two subject-matter areas where marginal students seem most uncertain. Consequently, students who can hold their own in courses which allow them to participate verbally frequently ridicule the mathematics they must take as being too elementary and irrelevant. The English they are often required to take is considered equally irrelevant. Convincing the student of the worth of the courses is another knotty problem for the counselor.

Traumatic past school experiences produce varied reactions in marginal students to present school experiences. They have learned to survive by never questioning a teacher. They will verbalize their feelings to the counselor but not to the instructor, whom they often do not trust. They feel that the counselor is concerned about what is happening to them, and that the teacher is not. Remedial students find that the counselor advises them of their resources. They soon learn that he is one person on their side.

One of the most essential factors in the counselor's effectiveness in motivating the remedial student is his belief in the student. He must have confidence in the student he is serving and must believe that the student will improve in spite of his previous academic and behavior record. Since high-risk students have been subjected to "reformers" for much of their lives in a school context, the counselor who acts, reacts, and interacts with them must refrain from the natural inclination to dominate, control, and preach to the student. At the same time, he has to believe that the student will make the right choice most of the time. This is difficult sometimes because many counselors are former teachers; and teachers have a way of over-verbalizing, moralizing, and directing. Moreover, many of them have been rigid in their attitudes toward some students and their behavior. It is not easy for them to change attitudes which have become concretized through many years of habituation. Such rigidity and attitudinal persuasions are not only poor from a counseling point of view; they are also deadly in terms of motivational methods for low-achieving students.

High-risk students must never feel that the counselor is overtly or covertly attempting to protect his own personal status against all attacks and criticism. In fact, it frequently creates a better counseling atmosphere for a student to realize that the person who interviews him does not "walk on water." Remedial students immediately reject the counselor who attempts to convert them to his value system or life style. These students frequently make many demands and the counselor cannot resent them.

If the counselors, teachers, and others who nearly destroyed many of these students in the first place and are still destroying them with the cry, "They're not college level," and are doing nothing to teach them or counsel them—if these people were as interested in the students as they are in salary increases and being called professor, they would recognize that they not only are not doing their jobs but they are also doing nothing to improve. Counselors are supposed to give students support—regardless of how they look, smell, or the grades they make. The demands of students are a part of the game. Remedial students must feel that the counselor is secure, sensitive, objective, socially mature, and emotionally healthy. In order to motivate low-achieving students the therapist must be conscious of certain characteristics often found in these students:

Remedial students repeatedly ask for the same information—such things as test results, how he is achieving in class (although he already knows), and what resources are at his disposal. Conversely, the high-risk student may not request information at all.

Marginal students with a ghetto or lower-class background frequently consider the counselor-counselee relationship a game—at least in the beginning. The student behaves as though the counselor is one to be outwitted. He will not only deliberately withhold information, withdraw, attempt to erect verbal barriers, project contemptuous attitudes, and other psychological barriers to communication between himself and the counselor, he will also consciously match wits with him. Sometimes a young and inexperienced counselor is not an adequate opponent for this type of student. Even if he is capable of handling the student it takes a great deal of time to resolve the battle of wits and get to the problem. This behavior is observed more in male students than female students. This applies to all racial groups. Black students, however, often feel that they are masters at giving white counselors a "snow job." Often they are right in this belief. White counselors do not typically have a black frame of reference. By contrast, black counselors have both a white and a black frame of reference: They live in a black world and know intimately the triumphs, adversities, mores, customs, habits, taboos, and life style of that world. The training of black counselors has been at white institutions which reinforced certain values and required certain specific skills designed to touch, by and large, a certain group of people. Black counselors have learned to "play the game." Historically, black people had to study Caucasians simply to survive. Everywhere they went they were in a white world or one controlled by whites. They worked in white homes, on the job, had to deal with the police, and so on. On the other hand, there was no real advantage in a Caucasian possessing the same knowledge of the black world. Even now whites do not indicate a strong persuasion to go into the black world. Unfortunately this is the way things are—not the way they should be. This is just one of the social truths and, therefore, one of the counseling facts of life.

The academically slow student looks for relevance in what he is expected to learn. He will not attack with all of the energy, enthusiasm, and resources at his disposal a subject or a problem simply because an instructor has assigned it. Although many students do this and others eventually learn to, today's remedial student is aware that he has been getting the short end of the stick. He now asks whether or not what he is required to learn is important. If teachers and others cannot demonstrate this relevance to the student, then the output of the student will be commensurate with what the student perceives as the significance of what is to be learned. In like manner, the motivation of the student appears to be directly proportional to the student's perception of the importance of the task to be performed. This assumes, of course, that he has the ability to learn the material. This has not always been true. It must be said, however, that there is a difference in this quest for relevance from different students. In the past, only the good student and the rebel student would question what they were asked to study. Lower-class (not culturally disadvantaged) black and white students were not, by and large, brought up in a democratic educational atmosphere where they felt free to question much of the trivia given them by their teachers. Affluent students still question what they are taught; and the so-called militant blacks question what is taught. The disadvantaged white student appears to be more concerned about whether or not he gets credit for what is taught regardless of its relevance. Disadvantaged blacks are often apathetic. This is rapidly changing in black communities. This also appears to vary in different parts of the country. In many southern communities, in private institutions, and in many conservative communities, students are not permitted to tamper with curriculum or the prevailing social order.

Many lower-class marginal students feel that they must look good from the outside in. This is evidenced in the clothes they wear, the automobiles they drive, and the conspicuous behavior they demonstrate to be seen and heard. A considerable number of these students have not had enough personal successes or the inner security to look good from the inside out. This has been pointed out repeatedly with reference to the disadvantaged and the disproportionate number of failures they experience. *Ebony Magazine* (1966) quoted me once on this score: "You see, you and I, in our day-to-day life, have pretty much a mixture of successes and failures. Here you're dealing with people with no successes at all. Success for them becomes, 'How can I *look* like a success?' So, like the peacock, the plumage may be beautiful but the ugly feet still show." The counselor must be able to appreciate what the student is doing and why; at the same time, he must be careful not to reinforce or criticize the student's current value system but to assist the student in reappraising it.

Remedial students, like other students, are motivated when they like what they are doing.

High-risk students develop security and confidence when they know specifically what to do and how to do it; more specifically, when a student knows what is expected of him and he has been taught how to perform, he feels that he can succeed. He becomes more secure because he does not have to guess what is wanted and he is more confident if he has been provided with the right prescription for success.

High-risk students learn best when they are involved with the learning process. This means, for example, that the teaching technique used to teach the student cannot always be a monologue (lecture); most of the time the teaching method should be a dialogue (seminars, discussions, and so on), or a climate where the learner can act, react, and interact with the material to be learned. The remedial student who cannot read with comprehension the instructions for tuning a car, can, nonetheless, learn to become an expert at tuning an automobile. In this latter case, he is interested; but most significant, he is involved. Remedial students are usually motoric in behavior (Sexton, 1961). Involvement motivates the academically slow student.

High-risk students like to see immediate success. The success might be small but immediate gratification is the hallmark of the disadvantaged. They also want to experience many accomplishments. Each achievement, however small, reinforces the desire for and approach to the next task. In fact, these students prefer many continuous small successes to a few large ones. Remedial students increase their goal-seeking behavior in a positive way when they achieve and their level of motivation increases.

High-risk students respond in a positive way to the individual attention from instructors or counselors. Powell (1966) reports that individual instruction is indeed a critical factor in the achievement of provisional students.

High-risk students are enthusiastic, encouraged, and

motivated when they have an opportunity to compete where they have an equal chance for success with the other participants.

Every educationally disadvantaged student is knowledgeable about something. When he is asked about his interests and has an opportunity to demonstrate some area of competency in which he is personally involved, he is later amenable to learning because he has been able to make a contribution.

In short, high-risk students are more similar to than different from other students, as can be discerned from some of their characteristics above. Therefore, the counselor who understands this student not only is able to do a more effective counseling job but also is in a position to provide instructors with certain kinds of information and insights about the student which in turn may help him to motivate the student as he instructs him.

RECRUITMENT

The recruitment of marginal students into the community college appears to be one of the least imaginative functions performed by the college counseling staff. In the past, school officials have sat back and waited for these students to come and hoped that they would not. As a result, there is little evidence that the majority of comprehensive community colleges do much preplanning for the admission of remedial students.

It is atypical for either college representatives seeking high school applicants for their institutions, or secondary school counselors who help select, recommend, actively counsel, and attempt to motivate students to attend college, to seek students who have a history of low performance. Yet, surprisingly, the mere act of recruiting a high-risk student appears to have a positive motivating effect on him. Counselors ask, "How do I go about recruiting high-risk students?"

Counselors from the community colleges, like admissions officers from many four-year institutions, attempt to make one or two visits to the local high schools each year. On these occasions, the college counselor goes in and replenishes the supply

of brochures from his college or he may brush the dust from
his college's display, which seems inevitably to have been placed
in the rack behind the door in the counseling office, where the
materials are not being seen or used by the students. The community college counselor makes a presentation at least once
a year to the seniors in the local high schools. This presentation
is made in the school's auditorium and will usually take about
one hour. It consists of a thirty- to forty-five-minute monologue
with approximately fifteen minutes set aside for questions. Not
only is the time set aside for questions insufficient; it is also
painfully obvious that only the academically talented, motivated, and well-informed student will make inquiries. The
academically slow student does not know what questions to ask
or he asks the wrong questions. Too often his questions go unasked because he is not about to expose himself in a public
assembly filled with his peers. Since the community college is
normally located in the same community, city, or district as
the local high school, the above procedures are neither creative,
innovative, nor productive for the recruitment of high-risk students. Other techniques, which show more imagination, may
be used to recruit these students.

To begin, most community college counselors and other
representatives limit their advertising and recruitment efforts
to working with high school counselors. This is a good source.
It has had the test of time. It is not, however, the only source
for the recruitment of marginal students, nor is it necessarily
the best. Take the use of brochures for example; they are rarely
found in places where students meet and the design of them
does not reflect the variant groups that the college is trying to
reach, especially the marginal student. The dropout, the disadvantaged, and the poor are not likely to come to the counselor's office to get advertisement from the college. It would
seem to make sense to place the college's printed materials in
hamburger establishments, record shops, drive-in theatres, hot-
rod clubs, Yamaha and Honda rental agencies, pool-rooms,
teen-towns, and pizza parlors. These are the places where students hang out. Since every student, sooner or later, goes to the
barber shop, beauty shop, doctor's office, and so on, it would

also seem that these are obvious locations to place the college's printed materials. Bars and cocktail lounges are not off limits either; at least The March of Dimes, American Heart Association, Muscular Distrophy Association, and other such organizations do not find that their goals are so puritanical that the placement of their displays in such places as bars would unduly prostitute them. High school newspapers are constantly looking for patrons and advertisement, as are fraternities, sororities, businessmen's clubs, church groups. These are just a few of the places where the college can say with the printed word, both to in-school youth and out-of-school youth and adults, "We're here!" There are other ways: The community college can place special boxes, similar to the suggestion boxes in industry, in the corridors of high schools. In such a box a student can place his questions, his suggestions, and his gripes in the absence of the counselor. These can be picked up later by the counselor and answered by letter, telephone, or in person. There are still other techniques that can be used to acquaint the general public with the facilities and opportunities of the local community college. For example, permanent benches can be placed at bus stops with copy advertising the college. "Mini-boards" (these are billboards about one-fourth of the size of a normal billboard) can be placed in the various communities.

In the design of brochures, the various ethnic, religious, and racial groups may be reflected. It would certainly mean more to a Mexican-American student to pick up a brochure which read *preguntan par Vd.* (you are wanted), or a member of the black ghetto to pick up a piece of written material where he saw black faces. It would also be refreshing to see community college brochures which show that although people who work on automobiles get greasy and dirty, they earn good livings and they appear to be as happy as other people.

It would also be more fruitful to assign the community college counselor to a cooperating high school for a day each week or for a few hours each week, than to have that counselor make his presentation in the school assembly described earlier. The advantages of assigning college counselors to a specific school or schools are readily observable: The counselor would get to know his high school counterpart, the teachers, the administrators, who coaches football, and who conducts the choir. Most important, he would get to know the student. He would also get to know what happens in the faculty lounge, the hideaways where students go to smoke, and where "the john" is. He would have an opportunity to see the curriculum in action. He would have his own desk, preferably in a corridor, which would be readily accessible. The same student who would not expose himself in the auditorium we discussed earlier would stop by the counselor's desk and enjoy confidence and privacy in asking his question. The advantages of the arrangement demonstrated here are limited only by the initiative and creativity of the high school and college people involved.

For recruitment, the community college counselor can look beyond the high school to the junior high school. In the spring of 1968, Forest Park Community College in St. Louis showed how this can be done. This institution, cooperating with the Pupil Personnel Services of the St. Louis Public Schools, brought 1,500 seventh graders from different schools and different districts within the inner city to the college campus as a motivational project. Each junior high school emphasized its own individuality. One school called the excursion Operation Motivation and another excursion was called The Banneker District Goes to College, and so on. The students were brought to the college campus, where they watched a fifteen-minute slide presentation. They were then taken on tours through the college. Typically in such a tour, the student who is fiftieth in line never hears what is being said. To avoid this, the students were escorted through the college facility in groups of ten, and they were asked to be participating observers. Not only did they see the language laboratories but also they were encouraged to put the earphones on and to manipulate the equipment. When the students passed through the art department, they were given brush, paint, and easel so that they could paint if they had the desire to do so. In order to avoid being completely directive, some facilities were excluded from the tour while at the same time the location of things to be seen were such that a student had to pass the facility not listed in order to get to the ones listed. The natural curiosity of the students took over and they stopped to look at laboratories, and the animals, and the skeletons, the way the planner knew they would. The college choir conducted a sing-along with the youngsters. After refreshments and after the students boarded the bus, each one was presented with a T-shirt with the slogan, *Forest Park Community College—Class of 1974* inscribed across the front.

Such a project cannot be carried out successfully unless the administration, faculty, and students are willing to assist in the activity as well as in the special services provided in the institution. This type of project is of little worth unless there is follow-up. Therefore, each student was sent a letter (not a form or mimeographed letter) thanking him for his visit to the college. The letter carried the actual signature of persons involved in the project and was mailed directly to the home of the student. In the communique, the student was asked to invite his parents to the college for a visit. Another letter was sent to the principals asking them to encourage their parent groups (PTA, Mothers' Club, and so on) to hold at least one of their meetings each year on the college premises. Thereby they could get to know their community college. Many accepted the invitation, and these meetings, too, were scheduled in locations in the building where it was necessary for them to pass one facility in order to reach their meeting place. While they met inside, students outside placed bumper stickers on the bumpers of their automobiles carrying the slogan, *No Place to Go? Try College!* This latter prerogative was one of the creative immoral acts that is probably a part of legitimate innovation.

Because the two-year college is an educational institution with a community focus, it should make greater use of the community's human resources to motivate and recruit high-risk students. Poverty agencies and other community organizers have developed a mastery in finding and developing the skills and talents of indigenous persons. The junior college can also train local residents to help them work with the areas of a com-

munity where college-age students are found and where a regular recruiter would not normally go—or even know about.
These people already know the high school graduates and where
to find them. They know the kids who will probably stay in
school and the ones who will drop out; they know the students
to avoid, and the members of the Mothers' Club (unwed
mothers) who would return to school if they knew the opportunity was available. They speak Spanish on the west side of
New York, the slang of the ghetto, the drawl of the South. They
are experts. With a minimum of training they can be taught
to carry the word to the marginal student.

There are already enrolled in the community college
students who would be ideal recruiters in their own neighborhoods. These students know both the college and the neighborhood. They are examples whose very presence in the
community can provide the unique extrinsic motivation that
the college could neither purchase nor duplicate.

The director of one developmental program secures the
list of the graduates from all of the local high schools. He sends
a letter and a fact book about the college to each alumnus of
these schools who ranked in the lowest one-third of his graduating class. The letter is an invitation. The fact book has been
designed to answer almost any question that a student, his
parents, an interested citizen, other educators, or members of
the legislature could pose. If the student decides to visit the
college, he also receives a souvenir pocket notebook which
carries on the first two pages the "mini-facts." The "mini-facts"
provide a capsule of some basic information in ten short sentences. At a glance the student is able to determine the cost of
tuition, registrar's name and office location, registration deadlines, list of official papers needed (copy of diploma, health
certificate, and so on), testing date, and other pertinent information. There is also a page showing a trial class schedule
and an accompanying billfold-size card which lists the courses
required for the program in which the prospective student says
he is interested. The visitor also receives a folder containing
the first ten forms he will be required to complete if he should
matriculate in the college and such practical things as the way

to obtain a parking sticker and how to enter and leave the parking lot.

Recruitment, then, can be creative and can be used as a motivational scheme to touch a type of college student that higher education has failed to reach for in the past. The techniques for reaching these students are limited only by the lack of imagination of the recruiters. Many foolproof plans can be worked out by the college personnel to inform the people the institution is trying to serve. In order to do this, college people make use of a little "think time." This is most important. It is worth an administrative salary to provide time to a group of people (three or four), some of whom may come from the neighborhoods and not be educators at all, to do nothing but sit around and come up with some wild ideas and do a practice run on these ideas. These persons may be given the constraint of a very low budget. In fact, it is recommended. Community people in particular will not think as educators do; they will instead think as they—the people the educators are trying to serve—normally do. Many of them will think the way they have always had to—how to survive. The typical advisory committees are made up of businessmen and technicians who function in terms of their own profit-making and vocational interest. Consequently, they know only how to reach their clients. On the other hand, the group that is described above will not be involved with profit; they will not be concerned with theories of counseling and the principles and practices of guidance; they will not be attempting to impress their colleagues; they will not write 80,000 words complete with charts, graphs, statistics, and the other academic distractions which could be written in twenty-five words or less; and they will not be seeking scholarly recognition. They will be able to devote most of their time to the task. They will be free to work with the professional educators without the inherent competition normally found among educators. In short, these are people who would be free to be creative. Some staff people in the college, with a little orientation from this type of group, could do this kind of thing in the summer as release time projects.

Wendy. "I know many people think we should not be here (in the community college). But honestly, all of us are not 'goof-offs.' I've only been here in this city two years. I have a lot of catching up to do but I can't do it unless I have the chance. In the little town where I came from they called my family white trash and the only thing we were guilty of was being poor. People hated us not because we were bad but because we were poor. There was kind of an unwritten law that we couldn't sit in certain pews in the church because they belonged to the 'respectable people' in the town. The minister once asked my family to move out of a seat because it was the pew where 'Mr. Nutlow customarily sits.' It wasn't any better at school. Teachers did not permit us, by *us* I mean the students who were considered white trash, to participate in anything. If the class had a play, the only part we could have was the one that the 'nice' children didn't want. Whenever you raised your hand to recite and were wrong the teacher would put you down. All of the people in the school, from the principal on down, would start grinning when the important people came to the school but when my folks came they weren't very polite. It was always the same. I started to work when I was thirteen. I know I am behind. I know I will have to work hard and I know all of the tests might say that I can't do too well but I know I can. I have even taken this remedial program and worked hard in it. Now they're talking about raising the standards in the dental hygiene program so that kids coming out of the remedial program can't get in. The same thing is happening in most of the other technical and career programs. Pretty soon it will be just like it was in the little town I came from. I don't see any point in

---

[2] This collection of student monologues was taken from tapes. The tapes have been edited in the following ways: (1) The counselors' questions and responses have been removed in order to maintain an unbroken continuity. (2) Some of the monologues are composites, that is, they are made up from the dialogue of two or more counseling sessions. (3) In two cases, the subjects had a distinct dialect and there was no attempt to record that dialect on the written page. (4) Sometimes a random sentence or phrase was shifted for continuity and clarity.

taking this program if we're going to get out of it and face a closed shop. The junior college was supposed to be different. Now it looks like they want students who can teach themselves like the other colleges want. You give me a suggestion of what I can do! When I came here you told me I should go into these courses for the dummies and if I did well I could take dental hygiene. Now you tell me that they have raised the standards. Seems like these new standards should be for students that you didn't tell they could get in."

Sylvia. "I don't have any problem that I know about except that I want to get out of this remedial bag as soon as I can. I'm really in here to see you because everybody is supposed to come to see the counselor in this program. I accept the fact that I am not too smart but that's not the most important thing in the world to me. You're always talking about self-concept— but nothing seems wrong with mine. I'm making good grades in this program. I'm not culturally disadvantaged; my parents love me; I don't have any hangup on teachers; I don't smoke pot; my sex life is my business; and people over thirty don't bug me. Gee, this sounds kind of defensive but everybody thinks every young person has problems and that something must be wrong between him and his parents or teachers or some other adults. That's just not true. I live in a nice middle-class community and I have come to this school because I couldn't get in the one or two or three my parents wanted me to attend. They didn't bust a gut because I couldn't get in the college of their choice. The neighbors on the right of us gamble, on the left fight, behind us lives a minister and across the street a bigot. I guess you can call us a melting pot—or maybe a salad bowl. At least in a salad bowl everything can be different and still be a part of the same thing. My boy friend is a Jew, my best girl friend is black, and my favorite teacher is an Irish Catholic. My crowd certainly upsets the neighborhood when they come out in force, especially when there are four or five blacks driving around out here looking for my house. It's like I was saying, I don't seem to have a problem. I'm not mad at anybody and most of the people I know don't seem to be mad at me. I'm healthy and I certainly don't feel left out of anything. My dad's psychologist friend says that I am completely uncomplicated. My folks are nice too. Although they don't buy some of my ideas, they never tell me I can't have them. That's certainly important, and it makes me respect them all the more. Leslie, that's the daughter of the minister that lives in the house behind us that I told you about, can't respect her parents. Her mother is an alcoholic and instead of her father accepting it and trying to get help for her, he acts like the situation doesn't exist. Any fool knows you can't cure alcoholism on your knees. He doesn't even follow the advice that he gives other people. And our bigoted friends across the street would die if they knew what their kids were doing. Especially their daughter who loves a black who doesn't give a damn about her. Their kids talk about them with contempt. All I have been saying is not what I came for. If I need some kind of help that I don't know about, please tell me and I will try to get it—either from you or whoever the person is you're supposed to get help from when you can't help yourself. Anyway, it's been nice talking with you, and I would like to invite you to meet my parents. They would like you very much."

Steve. "I have been classified 1-A and frankly I'm scared. When I was placed in this program I thought it was a joke. When you and them teachers were telling me about spending two hours studying for every hour I spent in class, well I didn't spend forty-five minutes for all of the subjects put together. Now I have been academically dismissed. It looks like I will have to go to Nam. The people down at #110 [3] said I probably wouldn't have to go if I had been making passing grades in my courses. I know my record ain't much to look at, it's been that way a long time. Up until the seventh grade I did real good; I made good grades and everything seemed like it would be okay. Then when I got in the eighth grade I started to make poor grades. Since the eighth grade is nothing much but a review of the fifth, sixth, and seventh, I should have been doing better. I started running around with these guys and that didn't help. Then I went to high school and took all of the Mickey-Mouse

[3] The number of his selective service board.

courses I could take so I would make C's. Until I came here, I didn't know how bad off I really was. My dad, he didn't get much education, has been talking to me about going to school and trying to be more than he is; well, now I know what he means. Do you think that maybe I could have another chance to get back in school? I won't even take a full load. My sister goes here and she has agreed to work with me. Will you say a good word for me to the powers that be?"

Brad. "I just got changed from that nigger counselor. That's part of my problem. I could probably do better if I didn't have to attend classes with niggers. I get sick every time I see one. I can't concentrate for thinking about them. They want everything; they want it free; and they want white people to pay for it. Pretty soon they will get all of the good jobs and have all of the best houses and everything. My dad lost his job to some nigger. He had been on that job for a pretty good while; then along comes this nigger from some school and schemed his job from under him. They're always trying to get what white people have. We had to move from Delta Acres because the niggers started moving in. Everybody knows they don't take care of their property. Soon as they move in, they started to act better than the people who already lived there. Every time you looked up they were parading down to the swimming pool; it got so the good white people stopped going. Everybody knows most of them got social diseases. They all try to ride around in big cars and wear fancy clothes. When they do get a little something, they ought to try to help each other. Maybe that would get some of them off welfare. Everybody knows that all those women do is get babies so that they can get ADC. They take them relief checks and go straight to the liquor store and drink it up, or give it to some good-for-nothing nigger to keep up the payment on a big Cadillac. Everybody knows you can't learn if you don't have peace of mind. I don't belong in this program simply because some test says so. I'm not stupid. I honestly believe that I could do better if I didn't have to sit next to the niggers, and that ain't prejudice. Everybody knows that when niggers are in the classes, you've got to lower the standards. I'd sure like to thank you for talking to me. It helps when something is bothering you to have somebody that will listen. I know you say you are against what I've been saying but that don't matter. In your heart you know I'm right. Listening to me is your job, but I bet you don't live around niggers either. I bet your children don't go to school with them; I bet you wouldn't want your sister to marry one. Deep down— you really think you're better than a nigger—just like most white folks. Everybody knows we're more intelligent than they are. In spite of what you say, deep down, real deep down— think about it now—you're just like me."

Harold. "My kid is better at this stuff than I am. How do you live with the knowledge that your ten-year-old can do his fractions better than his father? He wants to help me with mine. I guess this would be a chance for us to really have togetherness in the family but I really resent my ten-year-old offering to help me with arithmetic. It's not that I can't learn the stuff, it's just that it takes me longer than it takes my son. I guess you think its kind of odd that a man my age (thirty-five) would come right out and tell you his business and his feelings, but I just have to talk to somebody. In the army I could go to the head shrinker if I felt the need to talk, but I never did. I stayed in the army thirteen years. I got to be a NCO and I would put myself up against almost any other guy. It wasn't strange for a man with just a high school education, even a poor high school education, to lead men that had been to college. There all they wanted to know was could you produce. I was in Vietnam for fourteen months with a lot of other guys who didn't have a high school education, and I don't ever remember my squad leader asking me my SCAT score before we went out on patrol. The moment I came back stateside and started looking for a job people began asking me about my schooling. In the Army they didn't ask me if I was an automotive engineer, they wanted to know if I knew anything about cars. You have just told me I can't get into the Automotive Technology Program because my test scores are too low. I know you're doing everything you can to help, but do you realize that at one time I ran the motor pool and kept the vehicles for a whole company of men in top condition? I bet the man who wrote that test can't do that. He probably got deferred and learned to make up tests. I got a job as a mechanic but I'm chained to the machine. There is almost no chance for me to get from under the grease racks and oil pans and, mind you, there is nothing wrong with it except you ought to be able to get something better after you prove yourself. My foreman told me the only way I could get something better is to go back to school and learn to become what I have already been for more than ten years. He's just twenty-three years old. If I was a man with a six or seven thousand dollar car I would not even let a twenty-three year old kid put his head under the hood. Hey! I never thought about it, but maybe that's why he's the foreman. Anyway here I am doing fractions; and that English book we use is unbelievable. Do you know what the first lesson in that book says? *Birds fly.* Can you imagine that? *Birds fly.* When I first read that I said to the instructor 'they got to be kidding.' Right away I wanted to know what did that have to do with becoming an automotive technologist? I guess I must be fair though, at least the junior college is willing to give people like me and others a chance. And the day they decided to put counselors on the job was the best move they ever made."

Mike. "I'm not a kid running around here big on allowance and small on work. I'll be twenty-six my next birthday. I came to this school four years ago and I was more interested in hanging around in the lounge where they played cards, smoked pot—oh yes, they have smoked the stuff right in the lounge—and making the girls. Now that I've done all of that, I can see how stupid some of that stuff was. When I first came here I was on probation; then the second semester I was academically dismissed. I think some kids need more routine. You know when you come here right out of high school to college and nobody takes the roll, nobody rings a bell, you can go and come when you want to, a lot of students just don't know what to do with all of that freedom. I bet half of them end up like I did. They either drop out or they're pushed out like I was. I'm here now trying to get another chance. I'm older, I've been out in the world where you soon discover that it's not what you know but where did you go to college and do you expect to get

further schooling? Since I've got all that kid stuff and imma-
turity behind me I would like to come back and try it again.
I was reading in the paper that you had a program where if
one wanted to brush up on his math and reading and English
he could and if he did all right he could take some courses that
count. I think I am ready to do what's necessary. If not, my
wife and two babies are helping to make sure I do what is
necessary."

        Roy. "I can't study in that man's class cause he is a bigot.
I ask him something about the black man in history and he
doesn't know anything about it. They've been reading the
black man out for three hundred years. When I asked him
could I do my project about black people in the revolutionary
war, he up and tells me that 'colored people' didn't have a lot
to do with the revolutionary war. And he's supposed to be a
historian. You can tell what he thinks right away, he uses the
word *colored.* And here is something else, he asked me: 'Why
I would rather be called black instead of Negro since I'm not
really black?' I told him he wasn't really white. The idiot said,
'I never thought of that.' You're the counselor. You're supposed
to be like Mr. Wizard. You tell me how we can school this stud.
This whole school needs help. How can you expect the black
student to feel like he is a part of anything? The white and
black students hardly do anything together. I do okay in most
of my classes in this program for the dummies. But I can't
stomach this history that stud is trying to force down our
throats. I could probably do better in my class but I keep re-
senting what he wants to teach. And I resent the attitude of
whitey and them 'black Toms' we've got running around here
trying to act like whitey. In that history class they were talking
about the Boston Tea Party and they said that those criminals
were patriots. I asked the teacher, Weren't those patriots break-
ing the law? He said, 'Yes, but that was different.' He couldn't
tell me what was different about it. Yet, when I brought up
the black movement, all of the whites started talking about
law and order. I reminded them that the more than 4,000
known lynchings of black people over the last eighty-odd years
weren't exactly schoolboy pranks. I told them that raping black

women, poll taxes, and the Revolutionary War itself didn't exactly prove that whitey believed in law and order. I pointed out all of the so-called civil rights murders, especially the one where they killed those four little girls in Sunday school. Those little girls weren't exactly protesting in church. The instructor said that he didn't see how that related to the Revolutionary War. Even I can see how it relates and I am in this program for the dummies. All right, Mr. Wizard, you tell me what I can do. I know I'm going to get an F in that class. What can I do in good conscience? I like this program; it's the first time I've had a little chance to succeed in school. I need your advice. Gramma—what great big shoulder you got to cry on. What should I do?"

Marilyn. "Miss, my house is furnished in 'Early Goodwill.' Nothing in it was bought new. I have to work because I help to support the family. I don't mind working and I work hard at St. Luke's. I came to this school because I'm tired of a hundred bosses, I'm tired of soul food, and I'm tired of everything second-hand. Most of all, I'm tired of emptying bedpans. I don't guess I have to explain about what a nurse's aide has to do in some of these hospitals. I can smell a bedpan a block away and tell how old the patient was that filled it. When I get off from work and come out of that painful palace, even the smog smells good. I'm tired of beans, greens, and pigtails, and pot-liquor,[4] and all of that other soul food that is supposed to be so chic now-a-days. If it is supposed to be so chic, we've been that way in my family all my born days. I wish we made enough money to quit being chic. Miss, I'm twenty-nine years old. I got a husband, four children, two parents, and I hope I have too much sense to keep doing what I am doing. My husband is working two jobs and doesn't earn enough money to bring home what most men bring home on one. I have enrolled in this nursing program here but I do have to make up some deficiencies. The instructors tell me I can do all right. I really need some scholarship assistance if some is available. I would

---

[4] *Pot-liquor* is the slang, ghetto, and rural southern expression for the natural juice of greens. The term has been used primarily by blacks, though not exclusively.

just like to say that having to spend some of my time in this remedial program doesn't bother me. It's part of my reprieve from the bedpans, and lifting people, and listening to all of the hell that sick people raise. I know I will still get some of this as a nurse. I don't mind helping mankind but I would like to do it at a higher level with an increase in wages."

The need for drastic and extreme flexibility in the counselor in dealing with the academically slow student is painfully obvious from the statements above. This is immediately apparent among culturally disadvantaged students.

In the high-risk category of students the counselor must deal with and attempt to motivate students who are, or have been, culturally disadvantaged. This collection of students is so defined because they are poor, not socially preferred (because of minority group membership and status), and they are educationally destitute. They are different from the educationally disadvantaged because the latter group may be neither culturally, economically, nor socially deprived; and, they may only be marginal because of their lack of academic prowess.

The counselor in the remedial program must serve several age groups among the disadvantaged: (1) high school graduates (2) unemployed adults and (3) underemployed adults. The counselor must work with students from the secondary school who come to the college and are only able to perform in a college technical program after a certain amount of remedial work is done. From these same enrollees there are the students who will be able to achieve in a college program after a certain amount of remedial or preparatory work is done. There are also high school graduates who cannot achieve in college per se but who can be assisted in accepting their limitations, can perform jobs at the subtechnical and professional levels, can execute jobs in the service area, and can be upgraded on their jobs at the level just above the one at which they are currently working.

The counselor must also be prepared to assist unemployed adults who require basic literarcy, need to learn a different job or skill, wish to improve their skill as a prerequisite to moving into vocational training, need to know the resources available which may help them change their conditions, and who can become employable as indigenous personnel in poverty programs, as teacher aides, as hospital aides, and the like. Finally, the counselor must be able to help the underemployed adults who need additional opportunities to learn more sophisticated and highly technical skills, may wish to acquire some college training, and find the cost of attending a four-year institution prohibitive.

Each of these service groups has unique characteristics. There is a high probability that the secondary student will not continue in college, will marry early and, since he may have many responsibilities, he may attempt to work full-time and go to school. Not infrequently, his ability is not commensurate with his aspiration. We know that this student is motoric in learning, and is non-competitive in school and subject discipline, but highly competitive in sports. He may require basic skills. It is common to find no educational tradition in his home. Still, the student knows the value of education. Although he has sustained mental alertness and attention span in certain activities such as playing cards and dice, he does not demonstrate his alertness in school and other academic pursuits. This student accepts the depreciation of himself assigned by the mainstream of society (this is changing). He knows he is not much better off than the dropout who did not finish high school. Consequently, he feels the need to look good from the outside in. For example, he is sometimes overdressed. He is oriented to here-and-now gratification; consequently, he is often indifferent to verbal awards and is very sensitive to the inconsistency between democratic tenets and discrimination practices.

The unemployed adult also has some interesting characteristics. In terms of work, he has no marketable skills, sees work only as a job and not as a career, knows he is at the bottom of the job market, and, because he may be a rural immigrant, is often fired or laid off after short work duration. The unemployed adult frequently has a police record. Too often he is not treated with respect and as a consequence does not trust authority. This adult does not believe things will get better and he sympathizes with protest movements (Students for a Democratic Society, Black Power, and so on), though he is rarely a participant. Because of the way he is treated, he is not personally committed to civic responsibility, for example, is not a registered voter, rarely attends church; he may even consider teachers and other educators as snobs.

Finally, the underemployed adult is not working up to his potential, needs to update his skills, is more realistic in his goals and aspirations, has low rate of job attrition, hopes to escape his present level, does not always know what resources and opportunities are available, is often locked in because of discrimination in its varying forms, and is often duty-bound to family and other responsibilities and cannot take the time off to attend school.

It can be seen, therefore, why the task of the counselor in the development program must be flexible in dealing with the culturally disadvantaged student. It is also discernible why we have called him an educator. He might also be called a protector.

In the final analysis, it is what happens to the student after he completes, drops out, withdraws or is academically dismissed from the remedial program that must be a concern of the counselor. For the student who successfully completes the program, the counselor should assist this student in choosing the right teacher, the appropriate courses, and the best possible vocational plan. With regard to the right teacher, every effort should be made to avoid placing a remedial student in classes with professors who have a reputation for failing large numbers of students (remedial or non-remedial) under the stated pretext of maintaining standards. In like manner, the marginal student should not be placed in the classes of instructors who question the right of this student to attend the two-year school or in any other class where the instructor has shown hostility toward the developmental program. Frequently, this hostility comes with unconvincing politeness. Since the student assigned to any good developmental program has been carefully watched, guided, tutored, counseled, and helped through his problems, it would be less than candid and it would border on lunacy not to attempt to place this student with instructors who have a favorable and unprejudiced attitude toward the student, at least for the first semester. And it is recommended that the student who has completed the remedial program retain the same counselor for the first semester until the student is assigned to another department or curriculum in the college. The student must be given every chance for success. This does not mean that he should not work as hard as other students or receive other special considerations; it means that at least he will be given an equal chance in the classroom. Any counselor with even cursory tenure in an institution will know what instructors' classes to encourage their former remedial students to avoid because of the teacher's attitude and practices. In fact, all students should be encouraged to avoid these instructors. The counselor in the developmental program must be a realist. One has asked, "Why subject these students to some frustrated goon who wanted to be a university professor and couldn't be—so now he takes it out on every kid? I try to place him in the best possible position for success. I do what is necessary."

The counselor must be concerned with two other students. Both of them leave the developmental program before completing it. The first student can be described as a dropout. He gets fed up with the whole process. Often, he is impatient because he has not seen the improvement that he expected; and he sees himself on the road to failure again. Instructors are the first to observe his behavior. They note that he is showing a lack of interest and attention in class, not doing assignments, loitering around the campus while never going to class and exhibiting all of the other symptoms found among students who have learning problems. Finally, the student simply stops coming. In the developmental program the articulation between the counselor, instructor, and the program director must be so precise and the lines of communication so open that a student should never become lost because of the staff's failure to recognize the symptoms. There is the student, of course, who never reveals the above symptoms but encounters some problem which forces him not to continue in school. He, too, will drop out unless the instructors and the counselors, in a cooperative effort, make it a point to watch the attendance of each student who has missed a number of consecutive days from classes.

Withdrawing from most colleges requires an official procedure. Failure of the student to follow this procedure results in his punishment by the institution with the grade of F. Since the counselor is aware of the developmental student's lack of conformity and adherence to the behavior patterns normally found among college students, he must make sure that when a student withdraws from the remedial program that the student follows the procedure. This is done because the student frequently withdraws, remains out of school for awhile—and then decides he wishes to return to school. If he has received an F in one or more of his courses (depending upon the policy of the individual institution) his chances of readmission are seriously curtailed. As does every student who comes to the college, the high-risk receives a copy of the college handbook. As does every other student who comes to the college and receives his copy of the handbook, the marginal student neglects to read it. This is not particularly damaging to middle-class students because they have an educational tradition in their homes; and they have resource persons (parents, siblings), away from the school who will remind them and help them to meet deadlines and note procedures. Knoell (1968) points out that the disadvantaged student is without the same resources. She notes, "The hopeless disadvantaged youngster with no brothers or sisters in college, no parent who made it through high school, no friend in college to give counsel and information, may have nowhere to go."

The second student to leave the developmental program prior to completing is the student who must interrupt his education temporarily. He has no intentions of withdrawing permanently. He likes school, knows the value of education, is eager to return to the college, and does return. Repeatedly, this student is found to be one who finds himself with a problem where withdrawal from the educative process is necessary in order for him to solve the dilemma. Typically, he goes to his counselor, explains his decision and the reasons for it, then is officially withdrawn.

Finally, there is the student who is academically dismissed. He is a student who in the judgment of his instructors and the counselor is not making satisfactory progress. The remediation process has failed him. Neither the teachers, the methods, the materials, nor the motivation were of the right choice, intensity, or of the appropriate combination to help the student. On the other hand, perhaps it was the student's lack of ability. In either case the student is academically dismissed, or as one educator has put it, "pushed out." The counselor has a responsibility to this student whose education is being terminated by the institution. If the student is without employment, the counselor must make sure that the student is apprised of the vocational, employment, and other agencies which may be of assistance to him.

The students described above are the ones Moore (1969) has called "drip outs" and "drain outs." These are the students who drop out by choice, who withdraw because it is the only choice, and who leave because they have no choice. It is worth repeating that the counselor is the pivotal person around which the decisions and action of high-risk students must revolve.

Chapter Five

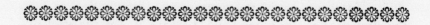

The
Administrator

*T*he administrator is a key figure in the success or failure of any developmental program. He is the liaison person between the program leader and the board of trustees, the community, the faculty, and others. He presents the budget requests and other proposals to the policy-making body. Since every member of the board will not necessarily share his enthusiasm for compensatory education or the salvaging function of the community college, the favorable response of that body to the proposals submitted to it may well depend upon the administrator's support of the program, knowledge of the remedial department, ability to interpret the program, sensitivity to remedial education, knowledge of the trends in the community college movement with regard to high-risk students and their needs, and support and knowledge of the experimentation that has taken place in remedial education. At times, in order to sell the program of the low achiever, the administrator will have to play the role of persuader, mesmerist, maverick, and patriarch. He will find it necessary to plead with a few people, demand from a few, submit to some and coerce others in order to justify and retain the remedial program. To put it more succinctly, he will be required to do what he normally does best. His influence can provide for the sustained attempts at success in a developmental effort or guarantee the immediate failure of it.

It is obvious, therefore, that the administrator must play an active role with regard to the program for the academically less able student. He can never be defensive, apologetic, or embarrassed when he assumes this role and interprets the compensatory program to others. He cannot be so bound to the tyranny of past statistics that he supports remedial education with less vigor than the transfer or the career program. As a planner, he must be sure that when new buildings are proposed, the developmental program will have space and equipment especially designed to serve the needs of high-risk students in the same way that space and equipment are planned for the technical program. If he is willing to provide an entire wing of a building for one division and only a room for the developmental division or department, he is discriminatory and he is not informed about the space and equipment needs of marginal students. It follows, therefore, that he is not providing adequate facilities for them. The quality of the staff he hires for the developmental program must be as competent as that hired for the science division. If the chief officer of the college is not recruiting the remedial-education faculty with the same vigor, imagination, and, indeed, "inducements" as he is with transfer faculty, this implies that the pursuit of excellence is more important for the able student than for the less able student. The administrator who is not as concerned about the image of his teachers in the compensatory program as he is about the image of the instructors in the honors program is setting a poor example that his faculty will surely follow.

Just as it is logical and reasonable that the transfer and career program will normally be expected to have a special budget, personnel, equipment, supplies, and other resources specifically determined to meet the objectives of the program, it is equally logical and reasonable to expect that the same type of resources will be available to the developmental program. And it is the responsibility of the administrator to see that those resources are available. If the administrator fails to establish equal priority for the developmental student as he does for the transfer or the career student, he is in effect saying to that developmental student, "You are less important than the transfer student or the career student in this college."

If the administrator is not as involved with the curriculum development, offerings, and quality of the content designed for the high-risk student as he is with the program for the academically talented, he demonstrates by his behavior that the content for the able student is more relevant than the content for the remedial student. If he is not intensely interested in the methodology used with the remedial student as he is with the techniques used with the liberal arts student, he is not committed to quality instruction for the total institution. If the administrator is willing to accept less than the best for the high-risk student, too often this is adequate indication that he is committed to, or intimidated by, the traditional sacred cows and outdated taboos. It may also indicate that he is easily distracted by such pronouncements as, "This is not college level," "This type of education certainly cannot be among our priorities," "Are we supposed to be everything to everybody?" There are many other irresponsible and irrelevant subsidiary statements and questions which break the bond that precedes reason. It also means that he is refuting the open-door philosophy of the community college and he is dishonest. He is lying to his community. In an overwhelming majority of community colleges, this is the case. There are, of course, exceptions. The educationally disadvantaged student receives much less than he is due. He gets what is left, what no one else wants, and only enough of that to keep him pacified. It is no exaggeration that he is an object of academic and administrative tokenism. And this is prima facie evidence of administrative incompetence in all cases.

Attend any conference of community college administrators, take part in any workshop, listen to any symposium, and you will hear an anthology of monologues concerning the marginal student. There is always a collective prologue of abstract commitment to educating the high-risk students followed by an analytic concession of conscience and admission that little is being done in a concrete way to serve these students.

Many administrators will admit: Just enough is done to keep the "natives" quiet. The "natives" are the accrediting agencies, the citizen who demands that his son be served, the so-called black militants and other dissident student groups who might decide to raise hell. The token efforts have been used as pacifiers for these groups. There is little doubt that remedial students and their parents will not be content to continue with the pacifier. They want milk. And they have a right to it. From nowhere have they a more legitimate right to expect leadership than from the administrator.

It is an irony that never before had so many individual parents of marginal students devoting so much of their time, attention, support, and the power of their votes to the community college and, by implication, to its leadership, only to find that after their moral, civic, and financial support, their children suffer the pervasive disease of academic neglect. It is neglect that the student readily senses. Little by little, almost imperceptibly, parents of these students have sensed also the indifference to their children. With the current population explosion of marginal students in the community college, what was an imperceptible awareness is now a tense sensibility. This recognition of educational neglect is dramatized in the excessive number of low grades awarded marginal students, the number of academic dismissals among them, the lack of meaningful and effective programs designed for them, the dropout rate, the failure rate, and the that's-the-way-the-ball-bounces attitude of teachers and especially administrators. Obviously, such conditions show irresponsibility and lack of leadership with regard to the education of the educationally disadvantaged. Since many in this deprived group have the last opportunity for an education when they come to the two-year college, and their subsequent employment may be dependent upon some school success, community college people may be courting disaster not to provide an adequate educational program and effective administrative leadership, if the activities of students on college campuses across the country are any criterion. We already know that the number of unskilled jobs is decreasing while the number of unskilled people, high school dropouts, pushouts, and poorly

prepared graduates is increasing. When these people get sufficiently frustrated they can strike out at any moment and in any
direction. A hurled brick has no conscience and a fire bomb
does not discriminate (Moore, 1968a).

Whether or not the community college administrators
construe the above statements as a threat or an opportunity is
subject to speculation. In either case, universal higher education
is already a reality. The day of the marginal student is at hand
and he is seeking his fair share of educational spoils. He is a
part of what can only be described as an abrupt change—or
even a revolution—in education, for there is an academic and
social revolution going on today in higher education. This
revolution is dramatized by new techniques for educating marginal students, the unprecedented growth of community colleges, the increased emphasis upon higher education for the
masses, the great demand for trained persons in supportive
services who are not professional but who need post-high school
training, and the emerging demands of racial and minority
groups who deserve equal access to more education and an
equitable share of its rewards. These and other changes emphasize the growing numbers of disadvantaged students who may
be regarded as either a monumental problem or an immense
opportunity for two-year institutions (Moore, 1968a).

The administrator can become either a facilitator, director, and leader of this dynamic change or a victim of it. What
are the responsibilities of the administrator related to the developmental program? He has many jobs: He must set the tone,
understand the program, know the remedial student, be aware
of the trends in remedial education, be sensitive to individual
differences, avoid aloofness, and be conscious of the total community.

The chief administrator must set the tone for the rest of
the college. Since the negative attitude of faculty toward high-
risk students is well documented (Medsker, 1960), the administrator, by his positive words and activities, not only supports
the existence of the remedial program but also does everything he can to see that the program is improved. He takes every
opportunity to praise the staff of the program to other members

of the faculty and administration. The chief officer must see that the members of the remedial faculty serve on all committees, and enjoy all of the same fringe benefits and promotions which accrue to other members of the faculty. When the administrator meets the community at large, he must give equal attention to the remedial division. The improvement of the image of the college can be achieved as effectively through the remedial program as the transfer program if the administrative leader exerts the same influence in the development of the remedial program. He has to say to business and industry that just as there are students in his institution who qualify for highly skilled jobs, there are students in his institution who qualify for jobs requiring lesser skill that he supports just as fervently. He will recommend the developmental program with the same enthusiasm that he emotes when he recommends the liberal arts program. In short, he conveys in every way that he is as proud of his compensatory curriculum as he is of his honors curriculum. He must show his interest to the entire community and collegiate sphere of influence.

Setting the tone is but one job assigned to the administrator. Yet, he cannot set the climate for the rest of the institution unless he completely understands the developmental program himself. A thorough knowledge of aims and objectives of the project is absolutely necessary for him as well as the means used to accomplish those objectives. He should know the history, strengths, and weaknesses of the program operating in his institution. If he does not have a program in his school, he should be working with the few qualified consultants and others he can find in "brain-picking" sessions to understand what remedial and compensatory education is all about before he attempts to institute such an educational program on his campus. The administrator should be able to explain why a specific group of techniques is being used in lieu of other methods; or why one group of techniques was changed and a different set was substituted. He is expected to be well aware of the problem areas and what experimentation is currently in progress. The findings from all studies on developmental students should be well known to him. It follows that he would be expected to be able to interpret those results upon request. The administrator should be able to outline the organizational structure and the educational and academic function of the remedial program in his institution in terms of some sound educational principles. He should be completely familiar with the selection, diagnostic, and remediation function of the program for the low achiever. He should know the success and failure statistics and what is the prognosis of his program. Some idea about the kinds of materials needed, used, and why those materials were chosen to instruct high-risk students in his college must be a part of the administrator's information. Knowledge of faculty attrition and why adds to his understanding of some of the problems that might be anticipated. He should know who in his organization has the answers about the remedial project if there are questions that he is unable to answer.

In addition to setting the tone and understanding the program, the administrator should also know his remedial student body. The characteristics of the high-risk student were described in Chapter Two. When the suggestion is made here that the administrator should know his remedial student body, an eyeball-to-eyeball relationship is envisioned. Low-achieving students should be as well known to the administrative staff as honor students, as those in the student government. If, however, the student chooses not to meet and know the administrator, this is a student option. The burden of proof is on the administrator. The key is *accessibility*. We frequently hear that administrators are too busy to spend much time with students in their own schools, yet we find them criss-crossing the country as consultants with, and guest speakers to, other students in other institutions administered by educational leaders who are away being consultants. The irony is that the second administrator is on some occasions actually visiting the campus of the first.

It is almost imperative that the college head or his designates understand both the rhetoric and the imagery identified with the low-achieving student. At times, this rhetoric and imagery will be violent, disquieting, uncomfortable, and well directed. At other times the students seem incoherent, dismayed, non-threatening, and without direction. There can be no denying the reality of discomfort and uneasiness for many administrators and high-risk students when they encounter each other in the day-by-day situations. The reality is vivid and replete with suspicion. Nevertheless, the administrator must "keep his cool." The disparity between the student's desire to know authority figures and the skill to get to know them needs to be understood by the administrator. Although the positive attributes (and there are many) of remedial students are rarely known, delineated, or described, the administrator must be able to readily identify these attributes.

The administrator who really knows the high-risk student listens to him. He listens as the student recounts his experiences, notes his concerns, shares his curiosities, indicates his needs, explains his wants, protests his dislikes, ridicules his fears, and describes his technique for making sense out of the world at large and the college in particular. He continues to listen to the student when he is wrong, uncertain and confused; and he listens while the student points out that the school bribes, bullies, tricks, and punishes students in order to make them accept without question what is taught. In other words, the administrator must make a pact with himself that he is going to listen to 100 per cent of what the student says before he reacts. This is a formidable goal. Few people, and probably no administrators, will listen to everything another person says without interruption or thinking about his own response. Yet, only if he listens to the student can he exercise his responsibility in informing the student when he feels the student is wrong and tells him so. It is only if the administrator is there to listen to the student that he can point out to him that his uncertainties are among the legacies of youth. In like manner, it is only after listening that the administrator can say to the student that "Your confusion may be the result of not having the facts. Here is where you can find them." Most significant, however, if one listens intently, he finds he has much less to say.

The administrator has to be able to get genuine pleasure from contact with low-performing students (as well as other students) because he will find that some of these students can be as intellectually stimulating as any other students and they are certainly honest. Consequently, the college leader should remove as many of the barriers to communication as possible so he can remain accessible to the student. Good judgment should lead him to make every attempt not to spend all of his time acting out his role as an authority figure. He must act as a man meeting friends; exhibiting a genial but never a condescending manner. These qualities are good for any man meeting any other man; they are especially significant for the administrator who wants to know and understand students who are academically slow.

It has been pointed out that the administrator should set the tone, know the student, and understand the program. In order to fulfill this last goal, the administrator has to be familiar with what is going on in the area of developmental education, not only on his own campus but also in the nation as a whole. There are several ways he can get this information: He can travel to other colleges and look at their programs. He can write and ask colleges to send information about their developmental programs. Sometimes, he can secure information when he is at conferences or when the members of his staff attend meetings. He can spend some of his time reading the literature. The first alternative is expensive, the second unreliable, and the third and fourth are fragmentary. Actually, he should employ all of the techniques mentioned for gathering information about high-risk students. Although there is not a lot of definitive research of programs for the marginal student, the literature abounds with information concerning this student. The administrator should make sure that the articles, professional journals, and books that he seeks and reads are routed through the college so that other members of the staff will have an opportunity to read about the educational activity that is taking place in remedial education. Many companies, foundations, and government programs are being reported in business, management, and government publications. When the administrator has an opportunity to view these publications and read the information on the high-risk student contained in them, he should make provisions to order reprints of the publication and have them issued to the faculty as items of information. The administrator can use a section of the library to circulate materials on the high-risk student. In this way, the educational leader is not just learning things for himself, he is acting as an enabler. He is not simply telling people to do things; he is providing the resource. There is no better source for keeping community college people alerted to what is going on in remedial education throughout the country than the *Junior College Journal*. But the reader has to make sure that he reads everything in the Journal.

The administrator must be committed to the whole community. Only a few are. Although the average community college president in a large urban setting or even in a rural community will make many speeches each year, he rarely speaks to many of the people who have a right and a need to hear him and share an equitable amount of his time. The college leader may join many organizations; it is rare, however, to find one who has joined a small neighborhood organization or one based in the ghetto. The Rotary Club, the Kiwanis, the League of Women Voters, and other such organizations enjoy the president's membership and hear his speeches. The residents of some areas of the city from which a large number of poor students and blacks come never see the college president. He never joins a club in their community. It is quite easy to find the local community college president with his institution located in the city while his home is located in the suburbs. For six consecutive years, one college president in a multi-campus district turned down an invitation to speak to an inner-city organization. The fifth year of the annual invitation, the president was requested as the speaker for the following year and turned the invitation down a year in advance. His reason each time was that he had a prior commitment. This phenomenon is not peculiar to college presidents. It appears to be true of deans and other administrative personnel also. The very nature of the community college is contradictory to this type of isolationism. This type of behavior on the part of school leaders carries with it the implication that there are two levels of taxpayers—one to be nurtured and one to be ignored. The reality is that at the ballot box each taxpayer is equal—one man, one vote. Not only should the administrator make sure he touches the entire community, but he should make sure that he remains a professional when he is among his fellow school leaders. The following example shows not only the lack of professional responsibility on the part of an administrator, but also a lack of individual integrity:

In an off-the-record statement among his colleagues at the 1969 AAJC Conference in Atlanta, one administrator quipped: "I am a practical man and whatever works in these 'idiot programs' (remedial programs) we use it at my place if it doesn't disturb things too much. Nothing is going to work very long." The thing that was most distressing among this academic and administrative quorum was that the majority of those assembled nodded their heads in agreement. No person there seemed willing to challenge the speaker. Finally, I suggested that Nazism worked in Germany. The response to my suggestion from my fellow administrators was as if I had been the offender rather than the offended. Nonetheless, I pursued the point by asking the speaker directly and the group by implication why it was necessary to make the developmental program, which after all was an educational venture, an object and instrument of derision, and why he was willing to disregard (even off-the-record) the most consistently proclaimed and explicit philosophical tenet of the open-door college. While the original speaker groped for an answer the delegates were summoned back to the meeting room.

The administrator, regardless of his level in the hierarchy, needs to know something about how the student who is academically slow learns. More specifically, marginal students have a distinct learning style and the instruction must be tailored to his mode of learning. Many low achievers are not receptive to learning in the conventional classroom, they do not readily respond to lectures, or to exhaustive written and reading assignments. They are more stimulated by seminars and other group learning situations where their responses can be made orally and in reaction to people. Marginal students do not like ideas hidden in a sophisticated verbal vocabulary, couched in compound complex sentences, obscured in complicated paragraphs, and written by professional educators to impress their colleagues, rather than written to help the student. These students will not always put *isn't* and *aren't* in the right place but they can handle sophisticated ideas. Remedial students want their complex ideas in simple language. At the same time, they do not learn efficiently when the material chosen to instruct them is an insult to their intelligence. As we have said earlier, the interest level of the material must be commensurate with the age of the student, the times, the mood, and be relevant to what is taught. There is little doubt that traditional methods are ineffective. Certain media can be used with developmental students with positive results, but it appears that the person-to-person contacts are the most effective means by which a remedial student learns. The teaching method should buttress, not contradict, what is to be taught. One of the greatest contradictions I have witnessed in instruction is seeing a course in audio-visual aids taught by the lecture method.

In the past, the administrator in higher education as a whole has not concerned himself with the individual differences in student abilities. Except for the efforts made by school leaders to provide for these differences at the elementary and high school levels, only the community college leadership has made any claim to serving the wide range of abilities among the student body. There is more claim than practice in providing for these differences. This is particularly true as the assertions apply to high-risk students. One student in a California two-year institution blurted out in a meeting (really a confrontation) of administrators and students, "You deans are no different than other people your age; you talk that talk [1] but you won't 'walk that walk.' [2] Everytime we look up, another one of you is claiming that he is going to do so much for everybody. Baby, you got something for the 'sharp tops' (eggheads, scholars, and so on) and you got something for those near top, but you ain't got

[1] "Talk that talk" is an old slang expression used in the inner-city to respond to a speaker who has just made an important point.

[2] "Walk that walk" is an expression from the same origin, and it means: to do what you say you will do.

nothing for people like me. Still you try to give all of us the same thing. What you ain't got sense enough to know is, 'There are different strokes for different folks.' " [3]

The above student was remedial. He was not at all awkward and inarticulate. He was poised and completely in command of the situation. For all his intensity, his words had both content and style. He was saying that he has as much right to be mediocre as the scholarly student had the right to be brilliant. He was also saying that he has a right to be taught, and to be taught in a different way. And he was saying that administrators will need far more than scored brows and glib rhetoric to provide for his needs and for the needs of other students like him.

The administrator must see the marginal student as being indistinguishable from other students when the student is involved in sports, or the student government, or simply walking across the campus. In this way, the student is a part of the masses—safe from ridicule. This is preferred anonymity that the student has a right to enjoy. On the other hand, the administrator must understand that the student's learning style is significantly different from the typical college student. Because he recognizes this difference, the efforts made by him to improve the instruction for the high-risk student ought to be clearly identifiable. The faculty as a whole should be able to see the efforts being made. The administrator must be willing to see some standards changed or adjusted. The concept of a movable standard seems most appropriate. If, for example, a faculty member discovered that all of his students had IQ's of 140-plus and a past record of high achievement, he would not hesitate to adjust his standards and his teaching techniques for the class. To do less would probably mean that he was insensitive to the needs of and necessary challenges required by his students. Similarly, if his students had IQ scores ranging from 90 to 110 and a past record of low achievement, it is reasonable to expect that he would also adjust his standards and his teaching. This, however, is not usually done. In higher education

[3] "There are different strokes for different folks" is an expression current among college-age people.

the student is required to make the adjustment. Since most of the students enrolled in community colleges are not eggheads, the fussing and fidgeting about quality in a few students seems unwarranted. It is important to concentrate on stimulating the full range of students. It follows, then, that quality must mean different things for different students, that is, each student can achieve quality within his level of proficiency. The student from California said it well when he said, "There are different strokes for different folks."

Beware of the administrator who says, "Familiarity breeds contempt." Aloofness also breeds poor communication. The detached and aloof administrator is frequently not people-oriented. This type of "leader" is deadly to a remedial program. He will probably measure the effectiveness of the developmental project by the number of students who go into English 101 or college algebra. Too often he will be more concerned about the records and reports of his staff members than about their creativity. There are many cases where he is willing to sacrifice a creative teacher, department head, or division chairman for one who is an expert on getting in the reports. In like manner, he will be more sensitive to the way his institution looks to him on paper than the quality of the education carried on in the school. One expects him to do that which is administratively expedient more often than that which is educationally sound. He will be more concerned about how smoothly the organizational structure works than the quality and relevance of the instructional program, its content, and the goal-seeking behavior of the students. When a new educational venture, change, or innovation is proposed, he will turn to the budget and the calculating machine first. He will make decisions which affect others without consultation, then announce the decision. Whether these allegations are excessive or true, and it is obvious that they cannot apply to all administrators who are reserved, unsocial, and reticent, the aloof administrator and the marginal student have a long history of barely noticing one another. Such mutual detachment blights the present and threatens the future communication between the leader and the led.

The detached administrator belongs to what is becoming

a vanishing breed. Neither faculty nor student will tolerate the
old detachment of school leaders or their arbitrary decisions.
It is especially important that the administrator be approach-
able. The whole area of administration has a new rhetoric and
a new style. The new vocabulary is stated well in the Biennial
Report (1966–1968) of Chicago State College:

> The new administration . . . must offer a new kind of
> leadership. Receptive, flexible, and patient, without
> secrets and subterfuge, it must encourage the involve-
> ment of the faculty and the student body and find con-
> sensus for new policy. It must not become obsessed with
> the virtue of its own thinking and its own plans. It must
> cull wisdom from the concerns of all on campus. But
> also the new administration must have the courage to
> call upon the campus to meet its commitments and to
> fulfill its mission.

Kiernan (1967) wrote:

> Trends in administrative practices are similar to styles
> or fashion in clothing, cars, and even household pets.
> Like other styles of living, they can be linked to eco-
> nomic, political, and social forces and are interrelated
> with each other. Styles of management change as social
> changes occur. For example, when corporations and the
> general economy are prosperous, administrators can af-
> ford to experiment with a variety of expensive educa-
> tional conferences for upper- and middle-level managers,
> held at exclusive resorts or at the corporation's own
> retreat, and they may employ high-priced consultants.
> One of the problems of styles in administration in cor-
> porations, colleges, and all other institutions is that, like
> other styles and fashions, administrators and nonadmin-
> istrators alike are often forced against their wills or
> better judgment to adopt the current mode.

Later in the same article she wrote:

> The college administrator who doesn't know that a
> "style" of management exists, or doesn't accept the new
> administrative techniques at the same rate as his faculty,
> may be faced with a serious morale problem, a high rate

of turnover, and a lower quality of teaching practice.
This can happen even when faculty acceptance of a style
is unreasoned and emotional. The effective administrator often would like to predict a trend, to adapt it early
in its inception to the needs of his college, its students,
and its faculty or to educate his faculty on its uses and
abuses before they "buy" it.

REMEDIAL PROGRAM ADMINISTRATOR

Every developmental program should be directed by
someone whose primary charge is to be responsible for the program. Administratively, he should have a position high enough
in the college hierarchy to have some influence on the decisions
which affect the program. His job should be a full-time assignment and, for the best results, it is proposed that the project he
directs be a regular department or division of the college. It is
expected that the director of the remedial program will report
directly to the same administrator as other academic leaders in
the institution and that he in no way will be subject to the
whims of other department heads. The credentials of the administrator who is responsible for the education of the high-risk
student should be as academically sound as the head of a physics
department. Although such credentials are not necessary to do
an excellent job in developmental education, they do keep the
subject-matter specialists and other "academic natives" quiet.

It is expected that the administrator chosen to head a
remedial program will be more than a subject-matter specialist
who casts the content in the role of hero or villain. Rather, he
should be a person who makes subject matter a servant, not a
master; an instrument, not an end. In other words, he would
not be expected to vulgarize further the subject matter that
twelve years of previous schooling had made more wry than
practical for the high-risk student. The leader in the program
should be a person who has knowledge about the psychology of
learning and motivation, techniques of teaching, classroom
management, audio-visual education, mental hygiene, and some
curricular instruction. In short, the administrator of a program
for high-risk students should have the knowledge and pure
teaching skill of a teacher in the elementary school. At the same

time, he must understand adolescence and young adult behavior. It is preferred that the leader in the program have some teaching experience and some prior experience in working with low-achieving students. Since it is typical for the developmental program to be under harassment from faculty and others in the institution, the project administrator should quickly learn the vulnerable areas of other divisions. As a result of this knowledge, he can be cunning enough to attack when he is being attacked. He can never become the object of much of the scapegoating that takes place in educational institutions. Yet, he should be sensitive enough to recognize and accept suggestions about his program and be ready to cooperate with the other divisions in the college in articulating the programs between divisions.

The administrator of the remedial department must, in essence, speak the language of the marginal students, connect himself with their experiences, address himself to their interests, illuminate their problems, listen to their points of view, respond to their relevancies, eliminate the cloak-and-dagger tactics of their teachers, and suffer the consequences of their sponsorship. This is rarely done for any college student. It is almost never done for high-risk students.

In terms of personality, the administrator should be able to verify the cliche that he can win friends and influence people. He is more effective when he remains detached from the campus politics. Although it will be necessary for him to listen to all sentiments at one time or another, he should remain essentially neutral. The practical consequences of his taking sides may be reflected in what happens to his students or in faculty resistance to the developmental program. These latter consequences represent real losses and real losers. On the other hand, the leader of the developmental program must have convictions; and he must believe in his program and his people. He can only be slightly less than able to walk on the water. In every way, the program director should make every effort to be cooperative, affable, concerned, open, congenial, flexible, and knowledgeable. It helps if he is very articulate and charismatic. It may seem impossible to find all of the qualities suggested in one man. In like manner, if he possessed all of these attributes, he would be more like God than man. The fact is, the man who has one or two of the qualities listed usually has most of the others; none of the traits above which are desirable for the project leader indicate that he will be either omnipotent or omniscient. Rather, they tend to stimulate a positive response from others.

The administrator in the remedial program has to be better known by high school counselors, neighborhood workers and agencies, PTA groups and other such persons, agencies and organizations than other administrators in the college, because these are the sources from which he must locate and recruit students who would not normally come to the college. These are the people and places where the students who have been overlooked or ignored are known and can be found. It will be necessary for the director of the program to spend a great deal of his time in serving the community. He can make speeches, serve on panels and advisory boards, take part in local church programs, and involve himself in many other such activities which demonstrate to the community that he is a part of that community, that he will work for it, and that he is concerned about what happens to it. Although the administrator must, by his very presence, set an example in some of the communities where he finds himself, he should not be abstract, refined, and artificial.

Should the leader of the program be white or black (or Mexican, American-Indian, or Puerto Rican)? The question is a fair one and one that many chief administrators and deans must ask or, at least, contemplate. The race of the developmental program's administrator should be an inadmissible criterion for his selection to supervise an educational venture. That is an ideal. The fact is the race of the project administrator is an unmistakable variable. The observer who is willing to venture beyond the many obvious and specific exceptions will readily see the pervasiveness of the race variable. All things being equal (credentials, experience, training, and so on), a white face gets its possessor in the door many times when a black face will not. Even when all things are not equal, on the whole, a white face is a more effective calling card than a black face both inside and outside of the institution. Repeatedly, college leaders claim that they cannot locate minority group personnel. How often we have heard the statement, "We can't find any 'qualified' blacks." This statement is true only because the wrong person is sent to look for them; the recruiter does not know where to look; and the searcher is not always aware of how he must look to the applicants. There is also a great deal of concern about what is meant by *qualified*. Actually, education is the one observable discipline where there are many qualified blacks. These blacks have come from the same colleges and universities, hold the same degrees, and have been certified by the same local and state agencies as their white counterparts. Blacks teach in the same city school systems, come from the same branches of military services, and other areas as whites. The above statement would be more accurate if it read: "We can't find *enough* 'qualified' blacks."

The pattern is rather well documented that a black applicant must be outstanding to be equal. He must also bear burdens having little relevance to his contracted job description. In an eastern community college, one black staff member puts it this way: "I was among the top ten in my class, but that's not the point. I have as much right to be black, mediocre, and employed as 'Charlie' has to be white, mediocre, and employed. I need the prowess of a Moses. I am expected to be like Caesar's wife—a paragon. When 'Charlie' comes, he gets groomed. They take him out and help him search for a house to live in. He is only expected to learn his job. Me? I become the black in residence—the instant expert on everything black." On the whole, a black director, regardless of his level of competence, in a rural area where there are virtually no other minority group members cannot expect to get enthusiastic support from such a community. It is probable that he would not have the support of his co-workers beyond lip service. In like manner, he would probably not be supported in many middle-class communities where he would be peripheral and add only a touch of color to the community. Here, too, he can expect polite acceptance or, even worse, toleration from his academic peers. There are many other insular communities, suburban and urban, composed of specific ethnic, national, religious, and special interest groups where a black director would not be welcome. In fact, some of these subcultures would be hostile toward him. One finds that such communities are polarized and they are becoming more solidified. Only a few people migrate to them unless they are people who are of the same ethnic, national, religious, philosophical, and political persuasion. Only a few blacks live in or near such communities. In these areas the whites choose each other. The blacks do not have a choice.

On the other hand, there are many areas where a white administrator of a remedial program would have as much difficulty as a black administrator. In cases where the majority of the students in the developmental program are black and when the college is located in or near a black or some other minority group ghetto, a white administrator would not be a realistic choice. Caucasians are almost always suspect in communities where there are minority group members because their attitudes and behavior are too often thought to smack of paternalism. Indigent whites, as well as other minority group members, are no longer willing to respond to a "Great White Father" image. They want the man who represents their youth to know their problems, appreciate their adversities, and applaud their success. In the hard core black ghettos, there is no need to play a game of semantics. The residents tell it straight: "Black people want to see black people representing them, especially in their own neighborhood" (PTA President, Chicago). "I can't see why it is so hard for them [whites] to see why we want to control our own schools—they control theirs" (Neighborhood worker, Milwaukee). "I have never seen a fruit stand in a white neighborhood owned by a black man" (Rent striker, St. Louis).

It is obvious that a white administrator can serve better in some communities and a black administrator can serve best in others. There are some locations where the race of the administrator is of less interest. In the large metropolitan areas where the colleges have a diversified student body, for example, the race of the remedial project administrator is probably less important. On the other hand, if the college district is a multi-campus operation and serving a multi-racial community, it

seems good judgment to reflect the enrollment pattern in all
assignments, including administrative assignments. In spite of
the foregoing, there are individuals from both the majority and
the minority group who by the sheer magnetism of their per-
sonalities and their overwhelming level of competency can
function well in most situations regardless of the location of
the institution and regardless of whether or not the local bigots
are black or white.

It is important that the administrator be chosen jointly
by members of the remedial faculty, other administrators on
the staff, students, and finally approved by the board of trustees.
When these people have satisfied themselves that they have
found an acceptable candidate who holds the right credentials,
has had relevant experience, and who exhibits a personality acceptable to all persons concerned, he should be hired.

Once hired, he must be supported. No more should be
expected of him and his division than any other division in
the college. Unless the program he guides has been in operation for some time, immediate evaluation and the expectancy
of instant positive results are unfair, unrealistic, and plain
ridiculous. The project administrator must have some opportunity to try new approaches, to discontinue those approaches
when they are judged to be ineffective and start over, to create,
to innovate, and to fail. Especially to fail. Just as the neglect
of high-risk students by educators and the educative process
with regard to research, curriculum development, and teaching
methodology has a long tenure, the problems of educating these
students will not be solved over a weekend. Once the project
administrator is selected, let him do the job. Most of the other
persons in the college will have already agreed that they are
not knowledgeable about remedial education.

HIRING FACULTY

Choosing a teacher for a developmental program is a
time-consuming task. It has been stated earlier that teacher
training institutions do not turn out graduates with expertise
in this area. As a consequence, a prospective teacher must be
selected and then taught to teach developmental students. Some-

times it is necessary to interview two or three dozen candidates to find the right person. If one is found, it is still probably an accident. Not infrequently, a satisfactory person is found but he has the wrong credentials or not enough of the right ones according to the college's regulations. The common requirement is a master's degree in the subject-matter field, or at least thirty hours beyond the baccalaureate. When an acceptable person is found, that is, one with the right attitude and commitment, who may not have the right credentials, he should be hired; his credentials can always be improved.

Bakersfield Junior College seriously considered the idea of hiring an outstanding elementary schoolteacher to work in the remedial program but abandoned the idea because it was felt that the teacher would have a "maternalistic view" of the developmental program and disregard or overlook the screening and selecting function envisioned (Luke, 1966). It is to be regretted that this institution did not have enough knowledge about elementary teachers, the foresight to innovate, or the guts to be different. An outstanding teacher, elementary or otherwise, is not maternalistic even with primary children. Roueche (1968) writes:

> Institutions may want to consider the possibility of employing qualified elementary teachers to teach students in remedial courses. Elementary teachers are experienced with the level of subject matter commonly taught in remedial courses. They are not subject matter specialists and the terms "college material" and "college level" may have little meaning or value to them when discussing a teaching assignment. One thing is quite clear: if subject matter specialists are not willing to instruct students enrolled in remedial courses, then other teachers must be found who will enthusiastically and competently provide instruction in the remedial programs.

It is implicit in all of the foregoing in this volume that one of the most essential considerations for a developmental program is the choice of staff. Selecting the best faculty member is part intuition, part experience, and part luck. There is a kind of sensitivity, shrewdness, and charisma a good interviewer has, and that cannot be taught. A good interrogator can often spot this quality in the teacher he is interviewing.

Since the educationally disadvantaged student tends to be unique and candid, those who teach him, counsel him, and attempt to direct him should also be unique. Teachers who are hostile, traditional, or incompetent should never be a part of a developmental program, or any program for that matter. The instructors should be flexible, understanding, and able to establish rapport with students. If there are black students in the school, a part of the faculty, counseling staff, and so on, should also be black. High-risk students (black or white) resent teachers, counselors, and others who cannot relate to them, at some time, from their own frame of reference. The teacher should be a creative and flexible rebel, one who is not afraid to rock the boat or to attempt to do what others say cannot be done. The credentials of the teacher need not always be a master's degree (although this has become an almost universal requirement) or a Ph.D. in the subject-matter area. It does not take a Ph.D. to teach a student to multiply fractions. Sometimes the rapport between a student-tutor and a high-risk student is far more effective. The student-tutor will know the prevailing attitudes, motives, slang expressions, verbal shortcuts, student hangups, gripes, and so on. He will not be frustrated by the other communication and age barriers or adult biases which sometimes exist between student and teacher. To illustrate this point, the following is a taped dialogue between a marginal student and his tutor (who was also his peer) as they worked in a tutoring session at a midwest community college:

"Baby—you need *Scope*."

"Aw man—I brush by teeth."

"You didn't this morning."

The beauty of this was that the student and his student-tutor never stopped working. The above dialogue would not have taken place if a Ph.D. had been the tutor. The student would have endured the good doctor's bad breath; consequently, he probably would have been unable to concentrate on his study and would not have expressed his displeasure.

There are some guidelines which an interviewer can use as he talks to the candidate. As any skillful interviewer knows, a few "off-the-cuff" questions can frequently reveal more about a person than hours of interacting with him in professional jargon. Such an innocuous and seemingly unrelated question as, "What do you think about welfare?" can tell the interrogator much about an interviewee's attitude. If, for example, the candidate responds by attacking the antiquated welfare *system,* he is probably sensitive to the needs of people. On the other hand, if he responds by saying poor people should get some help but they should get out and "pick themselves up by their bootstraps," so they can hold their heads up, he is suspect. If he immediately talks about paying taxes or how hard his parents worked, he probably belongs to what I call the bootstrap school of sociology. When a prospective teacher voluntarily tells of his great love of minority groups, or if he states that some of his best friends are Negroes or Jews and so forth, again, he is suspect. Members from these minority groups know all of the stereotyped statements which reveal insincerity. The implication here is that a person who is to work with high-risk students should be socially conscious. Perhaps, this is one of the reasons why former Peace Corps and VISTA workers are ideal candidates to work with remedial students.

Every attempt must be made to determine whether or not the candidate's assignment in the community college is just a stopover or a way station before he follows many of his predecessors to a four-year or university position. This type of candidate is probably not interested in the students. If the prospective teacher is interested in vocational training for the students, but to him vocational training means that he will seek to make the enrollees waiters and waitresses, cooks, kitchen helpers, groundsmen, nurses' aides, and custodians, then he is not the teacher to choose to work in the remedial program. The reasons are simple: The average man (or woman) can learn more about hotel work (with the exception of management skills) in a month on the job than he can in a year in a college classroom. Most of the landscaping is currently done by men who have minimum schooling. Finally, it does not take special training as a nurses' aide to empty bedpans. "Servants were the only things the schools that I went to turned out. Poor people have been working in kitchens since the Mayflower. They don't have to go to college to learn that. And I mean that just like I said it," states Mattie T. If the person seeking the teaching position expects the program to be an academy for the training of domestics, then, he should not be considered a serious applicant for the position. Teachers who reject students whose demeanor and other characteristics suggest certain kinds of dissent are obviously not ones that would be readily acceptable. A teacher should be chosen who is student-centered.

As the skillful interviewer continues to probe the teacher he hopes to select for the remedial program, he must be keenly sensitive to the loaded words, phrases, and assumptions used by that teacher. *Those people,* for example, is a loaded phrase. It is a phrase that immediately sets the teacher apart from the student. If the interviewee makes the assumption (and many do) that the marginal student is synonymous with minority groups, be sure to talk to him a little longer. This is almost a natural mistake. It is, however, a mistake. The teacher should know it.

The staff member who talks to the prospective faculty member must make sure that he meets every other member of the staff serving in the developmental program on at least three occasions. The first may well be in the normal course of activity as faculty people come and go in the department. The second may be a visit to a classroom in session that has been prearranged with the instructor. The third meeting of staff members may be at the lunch hour in the school cafeteria or some other place equally undesirable where the antics of students can get on one's nerves. The candidate should talk to many people, and should be encouraged to visit the faculty lounge and other places where the total faculty meets and be on his own to inter-act with them. It is often revealing to see the persons he is attracted to. An interviewee's attitude toward the so-called hippies, yippies, and black militants must be discerned early. In the past, remedial students, especially those who have been disadvantaged, were, by and large, the only dissenters. Their dissent came at a time when punishment of some kind was the means of effectively dealing with such behavior. This behavior cannot be turned off now with punishment of expulsion. The teacher to be hired must understand that many remedial students have had unpleasant experiences with teachers during much of their lives and he will probably have to make most of the adjustments; he will have to prove himself to his students.

At this point, nothing has really been said about the academic needs of the teacher. To be hired in the first place implies that the teacher will have a mastery of his subject matter. It is more important, however, that the instructor's techniques of instruction be most outstanding, innovative, fresh, and dynamic. And the instructor must be willing to change the ongoing curriculum or ignore it. In reality, the scholarship of the prospective teacher may be a liability in teaching remedial students. All too often the academically talented teacher cannot relate well with students who learn slowly or in a different way than he himself learned. One remedial student, speaking at a junior college "bitch-in," puts it this way: "That stud is so busy stumbling over all them degrees and rattling all of those keys around his vest buttons that he can't wait long enough for you to understand what he is talking about. Even if he waits, you can't hear over the damn noise from them keys."

Dress, poise, speech, voice quality (whatever that means), the number of "A's" on the transcript, and other such superficialities that have so preoccupied evaluation of personnel in the past, are not, in my view, relevant indices of a teacher's ability to teach. Let us take voice quality for example. If a person talks too loudly, he could be asked to speak softly or vice versa; or if he speaks too rapidly, he could be asked to speak more slowly. Beyond that it is difficult to see what could be done about a teacher's voice quality. It would seem important, however, that the teacher's voice exude confidence, security, sympathy, joy, reassurance, and other such feelings.

It is not to be implied that credentials are unimportant. Such a position is not tenable. But as Betty L. Pollard, Chairman of the Programmed Materials Learning Laboratory at

Forest Park Community College in St. Louis says, "We do get
hung up about degrees. Sometimes I think Jesus Christ couldn't
teach philosophy now because he doesn't have thirty hours beyond the B.A. and Euclid would not be allowed to teach math
because he would not have a master's degree in the subject-
matter field. Seriously, some of the worst people I have had in
the lab looked best on paper. I guess what I am saying is that
I look for the right person first. Then I check his pedigree."

Once a teacher is chosen, make absolutely sure that he
knows the objectives of the program and of the course he is
supposed to teach. It is fairly common to find in remedial
courses instructors who verbalize every item on the brochures
and who are thoroughly familiar with the course outlines but
who do not indicate any knowledge or real understanding of
the basic objectives of their courses or the overall objectives
of the developmental program in their institution.

Too often deans and department heads are so happy to
find people who will work in the developmental program that
the question of competence or lack of competence is not one
of the main considerations when a teacher is chosen. There is,
however, a growing demand that new and potentially fruitful
ways of thinking about the teaching of the high-risk student
be considered and new demands that competent persons to work
with him be found. New models are being called for and explored for their methodological and practical implications.

Methods of choosing teachers currently used in education have evolved from practices of many years ago. Historically,
supervisors have made the judgments relative to hiring new
personnel without the concern, opinion or involvement of the
people who must work with the new teacher. This absurdity
should be ended. It is of particular significance that the instructors in the developmental program have some say about those
new members who are to work on their team. In short, the
hiring of a teacher in the developmental program should be
a joint venture between administration and faculty. The author
would not be opposed to the students making judgments about
the prospective staff member's candidacy for employment. Finally, there are numerous ways for choosing teachers, providing

them with status, eliminating the disparity in their training, answering the critics, providing them with more sophisticated diagnostic techniques, and attempting to change their attitudes. None of the measures used will guarantee the effectiveness of the practitioner. His efficiency and quality will be determined ultimately by the students. Since no one has neatly identified the competent teacher in remedial education at the post high school level, and perhaps no one can, the community college will probably have to assume a part of this responsibility for describing and concretizing those skills, abilities, motives, and so on, which appear to be the criteria for a competent instructor. This must be done to meet the large numbers of students who come from variant backgrounds and who have been low achievers. The college must be able to adapt to these students, to the times, and to the demand for change.

The community college serves a large and diversified student body; it cannot be today what it was yesterday, because it is confronted with problems whose only solution is change. Traditionally, the education of the academically marginal student is a problem that higher education has either overlooked, has not had to face, or to "tell it like it is," has refused to look at. Therefore, there are few persons in the community college movement, or in higher education as a whole, who are experts in dealing with marginal students. Yet, it is becoming increasingly clear that concern with the high-risk student is a dimension that colleges must face.

Obviously, community colleges are attended—and every sign indicates the trend is increasing—by many students who cannot succeed in a traditional college curriculum using the traditional methods of instruction and evaluation. These students need special attention and it has already been stated that there is little expertise in higher education as a whole, and in the community college in particular, to handle such students. What is needed is some blueprint or some structure that will assist community college personnel in developing programs for high-risk students.

The efforts of teachers will probably be the determining factors in how effective the comprehensive community college can be in making available a bona fide education for high-risk students, providing that they (teachers) are trained while they are in school or they have an opportunity to get in-service training in dealing with remedial students.

Whenever an administrator begins talking about his commitment to working with the educationally disadvantaged, minority group members, the culturally different, high-risk students, and other such persons who represent "the problem," you can determine his degree of commitment by looking at his budget. The fact is, programs for high-risk students in the community college get "welfare funding." That is, there is never enough funds to meet the needs of the recipients. The applicants are without sufficient facilities, resources, and expertise, while at the same time they are required to demonstrate need; the receivers are under constant scrutiny, and assistance may be withdrawn without notice.

It is typical to have developmental programs funded by agencies and other sources outside the college (the government, foundations, and so on) and when the funding stops the program is discontinued. Consequently, the administrator working in such a program spends a considerable amount of his time writing proposals to apply for specific grants to assist in providing for the education of students who are characterized as high-risk. Local boards of trustees who, supposedly, are charged with providing for *all* of the students in a given district sometimes give "special" funding for a program that should be an ongoing budgetary item. States sometimes also follow this process of "special" funding. If administrators did their jobs properly, recommendations would include funding for all segments of the college populations. In short, when we really address ourselves to the problem with integrity, we find that money is not spent in an equitable way with regard to the high-risk student. He is cheated. He pays a part of the tab for others.

More specifically, regardless of how the college is financed (state, local, tuition, or a combination of these methods) there is as much money allocated for each high-risk student as there is for each student who is low-risk. The students from both groups are a part of the total enrollment. Funding for colleges is based upon this enrollment and all students pay the same tuition. It is to be noted further that more than 60 per cent of all the students who enroll in the community college are at the 30 percentile or below. Technically, then, the majority of the students in the two-year school are high-risk. It would appear that a portion of the money which should be spent on students at the 15 percentile or below is allocated for students above this level.

The administrator's great challenge is to convince his faculty, board, and others of the necessity of financing all community college students without regard to risk. Thus the remedial program will be just one of the programs in the whole funding process.

FACULTY MORALE AND ATTITUDES

Faculty morale can be another problem for the administrator. It is not so much a problem in the remedial program as it is in other programs if the staff assigned to it is there by their own choice and receive the necessary support. It is appropriate in this discussion, nonetheless, to address the need for good group spirit. Morale in a developmental program, or any other program for that matter, is not the elusive giant that we claim it to be. Most of the things that faculty want, things that keep morale high, can be provided without cost. Members of a faculty want first to understand clearly the goals of the program and the institution. They should have a clear conception of their roles in the developmental program (or any program) and the institution. Work assignments must be realistic, equitable, and fitted to the talents and capabilities of the faculty. Working conditions and rewards, when possible, in the remedial program should compare with those in other programs. Faculty members work best when they can participate in the making of decisions which affect them, such as identifying unmet needs, developing policy proposals, and formulating recommended procedures. Personal and institutional gains must be equally distributed; and, like any human beings, faculty members deserve to be appreciated for their efforts and accomplishments.

Too many community college administrators fail to exhibit the maturity, competency, or desire to fulfill all of the wants of the faculty. Faculty participation in decisions is an area where the administrator frequently falls short of fulfilling faculty desires. Yet, faculty members are entitled to the foregoing conditions and they have a right to expect them.

There are some faculty whose desires, however, can affect morale in an adverse way. They are the staff members whose desires project the university syndrome. They know that the university rewards the researcher, not the teacher; promotes the Ph.D.'s, not the teachers (teaching assistants and other holders of the B.A. or M.A. degree) who really carry on the instruction in the institution; they are aware that the awarding of tenure and other fringe benefits goes to the people who give the least amount of time and attention to freshman and sophomore students, not to the teacher who teaches them; and it is well known that the university system honors faculty members who write books and present scholarly (if not relevant) papers— not the teacher who advises and gives his time to his undergraduate students. Faculty members in an increasing number of community colleges attempt to mimic the practices of university faculty. They want the same privileges as the four-year faculty without the responsibility of writing, research, and advance study. This faculty attitude should be aborted early. The administrator must make it perfectly clear that in the community college teaching—not research, publications, and credentials—will be rewarded. The community college might do itself a big service if it did not seek nor hire holders of the Ph.D. The staff should always know the administrative philosophy. The implication here is that no area of the faculty should be singled out for special consideration.

Never provide the college transfer faculty with any benefits, promotions, titles, and other kinds of recognition that cannot be equally provided for the vocational and community service (continuing education) faculty. More specifically, the administrator should never indicate in any way that the college's vocational and community service faculties are less competent or academically less "pure" than the college transfer faculty. It would seem that the latter statement would be unnecessary; but the conditions show that it *is* necessary.

The vocational faculty is no less competent than the liberal arts faculty. It is a fact that if we measure faculty competence on the basis of student success in the courses and subsequent job placement, the vocational instructors are more competent than the college transfer faculty. The apprenticeship programs (building trades and so on) in Seattle Central Community College, for example, have a 90 per cent retention of students, and 65 to 70 per cent of the students in all other vocational programs complete their work and find employment. Find a college transfer program in a community college anywhere that can match the retention rate success of the vocational program. This assumes that all things are equal. Vocational teachers appear to spend much more time with their students.

In like manner, the community service faculty members also demonstrate this student-centeredness. This faculty, perhaps more than either of the other two, exemplifies what the community college is all about. It makes the abstract platitudes and philosophy about the "open-door" character of the community college a concrete reality. The members of this staff work with an entire community—go where they are invited, get involved, and make education relate to what the people in the community say their needs are. They do not prescribe a course, curriculum, or program and say to a community, "These are your needs." This faculty does not set up criteria to select certain students and exclude others. And one never finds the punitive items in the community service catalog or brochure that he finds in the transfer and vocational sections of the college handbook or catalog, namely, all the ways he can fail (lack of attendance, withdrawal penalties, rules of conduct, dress, and so on).

Summarily, vocational and community service teachers take more time with their students and do not appear to have the same academic "hangups" on credentials and other superficial indices of competence. For this reason, in my view, aca-

demic rank is probably unwise in a community college unless
all of the faculties in the college (transfer, vocational, community service) are awarded academic rank. Actually, the term
instructor is the only term necessary for the members of all
these faculties. This applies with equal emphasis to all administrators. Why have a president, a dean of instruction, and
an assortment of assistant and associate deans who "dean" all
over the place and no one is quite sure what they really do. It
would be much simpler and much less snobbish to address all
of these persons as *Mr.* and note their area of responsibility
when necessary.

　　This whole area of special titles for certain faculty is a
constant source of morale problems for the administrator—not
so much, however, in developmental or remedial programs as
it appears to be in other programs. The administrator would
do well to eliminate or not award special titles to staff members
if such a policy can be initiated. One rarely finds a student who
could care about what his teacher is called. One can always
find a student who cares about what his instructor does—or
fails to do. In fact, it is probably the student who builds the
instructor's or faculty's morale if that instructor or that faculty
is doing its job.

　　In spite of faculty desires, they can live with adversities
and have an outstanding spirit if their leaders (administrators)
are strong, dependable, loyal, and committed. Faculty like to
see their leader take a stand on issues regardless of his persuasion. They want to know his personal feelings as well as his
professional position. To illustrate, in a northwestern community college the president issued the following memorandum
just prior to the October 15, 1969, War Moratorium:

MEMORANDUM
                                                    October 13, 1969

To:　　Students, Faculty, Staff
　　　　Northwestern Community College
From:　James D. Pruitt, President
Re:　　Vietnam War Moratorium, October 15, 1969

Some interested students and faculty members have requested that this college abstain from "business as usual" on Wednesday, October 15. I must respond in two ways to this request:

1. As an *individual* I am against the war in Vietnam. I am against any war. I plan to demonstrate my view and feelings toward the war by wearing a black armband on Wednesday, October 15, and I encourage those faculty and students who choose to please join in this protest by doing the same.

2. As *president* of the college, I must respond as an administrator. Classes will be open on Wednesday, October 15. The school cannot withhold instruction from those students who wish to attend classes.

However:
(a) Students of this college who wish to absent themselves from classes on Wednesday, October 15, in observation of the National Vietnam Moratorium have the option of doing so. I am, by this memo, requesting that they be excused from those classes and that their absence not be counted against their attendance record or reflected in their grade.
(b) Those instructors who wish are encouraged to conduct meaningful discussions in their classes on the subject of the Vietnam War.
I have been asked by the Student Board of Control, in support of the Northwestern Community College Student Mobilization Committee, to extend an invitation to all students to attend a rally and protest of the war to be held at the Elm Street Branch (south side of the building), 8–10 A.M. on that day.

The author of the memorandum first addressed himself to the problem. Second, he took a personal position—one that was not exactly popular with everyone. Third, he gave options to the persons concerned. Finally, he provided a service. The second step—the fact that he was willing to stand up and be for or against something—had great impact on the faculty and student body.

Faculty morale is improved when the administrator does not vacillate and refuses to play the politics of education. The faculty members want him to keep them informed when he is going to make a move. They want him to make sure that his objectives are clear. Staff members need to know that the administrator will contact everyone who has expertise or can shed some light on the situation. Once convinced that he is moving in the right direction, they do not want to guess or wonder about what is going on.

In short, they want him to make a decision. The decision should be firm, whether popular or not. The administrator should not refuse or hesitate to make a decision because he wants to avoid all conflict on an issue or problem, or because he yields to pressure. He should not take a circuitous route to a goal when a direct approach is more frugal. First, a direct approach avoids the games people play. Secondly, it eliminates much of the politics. Once the decision is made, he should stick by it. They do not want to see their administrator get "up tight" and start switching his decision when he is criticized or confronted or panic because the news media, some individual citizen, or student group put pressure on him. His decision is, hopefully, based upon his knowledge of the situation, his training, experience, and objectivity. Faculty members abhor decisions based on sheer emotions, intuition, and friendship. These can be elements, however, in every decision; when they are, the administrator ought to say it.

There are other things that an administrator can do to improve morale. He can ask his public information officer to write personal and human interest stories about faculty members for the local newspaper each week. This is particularly effective when a faculty member lives in a specific section of a city or in a suburb around the city that has a newspaper. This gives an opportunity for other people in the instructor's local community to know more about him and the college.

A file of the birthdays of the faculty member, his wife and children, especially his wife and children, should be on the administrator's desk. Each day he or his secretary should check this file and send his special card in his own handwriting to the faculty member or a member of his household. Even when the card is belated, it will still be appreciated. By the same token, he can call two or three instructors each evening after dinner, taking only five or ten minutes of each person's time to say, "Hi, I just wanted you to know that I know you're around. I haven't had a chance to get by lately, but I will. How are the kids? What did you get on your last fishing trip?" When an administrator does this, the word gets around.

The administrator should make it a point to visit classes (with the instructor's permission) and to return and acknowledge his visit in a note. For the administrator to say that he is too busy to visit is an excuse—not a reason. If a member of the staff is to be brought on the carpet, try to avoid always handling the problem in the office, which is official and authoritative. A good lunch or cup of coffee, or a beer at the end of a previously arranged day, may help.

Early morning breakfast meetings with division or department staff and other staff members is another good activity. It gives the administrators and the staff an opportunity to meet, visit, and do some of the college committee work and other such work before the harassment of the day begins. It also allows the food service division of the college to display their service and products. Or he can invite members of the college family (faculty, students, secretaries) as individuals and in groups to share no-host luncheons with him.

If the school is in the process of new construction and the architect is working on a specific part of the building, for example, the humanities division, the administrator should ask the architect to set up his job near that humanities division or department. As instructors come and go, the architect can ask them their advice, stating that the administrator had requested that they be consulted at every step.

With a new problem or situation, the administrator should not assume that the faculty will automatically be against it. A better way to approach and challenge the members of a faculty is to request from them, "Tell me all the positive reasons why you think this will work." Experience shows that there are members on every staff who will not think of positive rea-

sons for approaching a problem and will choose not to think
of any. In this latter case, those faculty members involved
should have the opportunity of refusing to take part. The administrator should attempt in every way to get the assurance of
those not taking part that they will do nothing to abort the
project. He should also solicit their area of expertise when and
if it is needed. Beyond this, those faculty with the positive attitude toward the project should be given the opportunity to
complete the job and be given the reward. Those who refused
to take part should have the same opportunity when the next
idea is presented.

Many administrators will say, "Well, all of that is fine—
but." It is what follows that but that keeps education in the
last century. Lazy, uninvolved administrators always say but.
Other administrators will say, "No matter what is done, you're
damned if you do—damned if you don't." A good administrator
would rather be damned for doing. The best administrator
seems always to have time—he listens, and he is people-oriented.

Finally, after the administrator has done all of these
things to improve the morale of the staff, if the steps are successful and the morale of the faculty improves, it is still probably an accident.

Closely related to faculty morale is the problem of
negative faculty attitudes. Teachers who work in the developmental program of their own volition do not normally exhibit
the negative attitudes toward their students that teachers who
are assigned such work against their will exhibit. There are,
however, other faculty who will not have any direct responsibility for developmental programs but who will have definite
ideas about who should come to college or may have some re-
jection of students from the remedial program moving into
certain programs in the college. The question is always posed
in conferences, in workshops, in articles, "How do you change
faculty attitudes? What kinds of in-service things can we do?"

Under the present policies of hiring, awarding tenure,
salary advancement, and little or no evaluation of community
college staffs, little can be done to change the typical faculty
attitudes. Students have been "tearing down" the campuses for

several years now and still have not changed faculty attitudes significantly. The students unfortunately always attacked the wrong authority (the administration). The administration does not develop the curriculum, give the grades, give the lectures, or award tenure. Hearing this, the student leader of one activist group shouted, "We have been fighting the wrong enemy!" The implication is that there are certain needed changes for which the administrator has very little leverage. It is becoming more and more apparent that he will not be able to change attitudes. He can, however, provided with the right support, modify some of the behavior of his faculty. He may also ask faculty to demonstrate that their actions match their words.

In spite of their verbal pronouncements to the contrary, the negative attitudes of teachers toward their students are well documented. The data indicate that their adverse attitudes affect their expectancies, the quality of their instruction, the feelings students have about them, and many other factors. The research further reveals that more teachers than we would expect are ethnocentric, provincial, and bigoted in their attitudes. It is no exaggeration that we know a great deal more about how to identify the negative attitudes in teachers than what to do about these attitudes once they are uncovered. The problem is that the public has not been informed about faculty attitudes.

The nation's taxpayers would be appalled to discover how they pick up the tab for many community college teachers who have negative feelings about the students they teach. They would find it difficult to understand that—in the wake of higher salaries, more extensive fringe benefits, and the right to participate in the governance of the college— there are increasing numbers of teachers who refuse to be held accountable for the work they do or to share the power and influence they have with the students.

Students, on the other hand, have been familiar with these phenomena for a long time. *The City Collegian,* the student newspaper of Seattle Central Community College, carried an article which called attention to this situation under the caption, "Who Am I?" The article read:

> I don't have a lot of credentials; I don't have tenure; I
> don't have fringe benefits. I don't get automatic in-
> creases in salary each year. I don't have anyone to repre-
> sent me in negotiations. I have nothing to say about the
> curriculum that is taught me, the teachers who teach
> me, the grades I get, the kind of counseling I get, the
> library I must use. I don't get professional leave or sick
> leave, or bereavement leave, or maternity leave, jury
> duty leave, or any of the rest of those leaves. I can't
> make claims against loss of time. My work day is more
> than seven hours. I can even be found on campus before
> 9:00 a.m. and after 3:00 p.m. I don't get time off or
> pay for professional development. I don't have any of-
> fice hours to ignore. I don't even distrust the adminis-
> tration. As a matter of fact, the administrators are the
> only people that will talk to me—after 3:00 p.m. any-
> way. I'm not very important. I'm just a student.

After reading the article one student asked, "What do I get?
It's like a kid having a birthday party given for him and not
being able to invite the friends he wants, having all of the
presents given to someone else, all of the cake passed out before he gets a piece, and if he refuses to be a good boy—denied
admission to his own party." A black student answered, "The
brothers have been blowing their minds on that one a long
time. What we ought to start doing is changing it *by any means
necessary.*" [4]

The reasons are legion which describe why teachers have
negative attitudes toward students. The psychological and sociological techniques for determining this have been around
since the 1920s and have been applied to teachers at all educational levels. There are two consistent findings observable all
along the educational continuum, from the elementary school
child to the graduate student: the students identify the same
characteristics with regard to negative attitudes in their teachers; and the majority of students who dislike their teachers,
dislike them for the same reasons. Teachers who are well liked
are positive in their attitudes.

Combs (1965) cites evidence indicating that good teachers

[4] Black Panther slogan.

have positive attitudes primarily about themselves; he notes that good teachers see themselves as identified with people rather than withdrawn, removed, apart from, or alienated from others. They feel basically adequate rather than inadequate. They do not see themselves as generally unable to cope with problems. They feel trustworthy rather than untrustworthy. They see themselves as reliable, dependable individuals with the potential for coping with events as they happen. They see themselves as wanted rather than unwanted. They see themselves as likable and attractive (in a personal not a physical sense) as opposed to feeling ignored and rejected. They see themselves as worthy rather than unworthy. They see themselves as people of consequence, dignity, and integrity as opposed to feeling they matter little, can be overlooked and discounted. In a word, they are not afraid.

If teachers are insecure, bitter because of past experiences with administrators, are having marital problems, have poor backgrounds, were unhappy as children, find themselves with one foot in poverty and one foot in affluence, and the whole cadre of other problems, there is really little that the administrator can do about it by using an in-service technique. He may be able to make the teaching environment better (facilities, materials, working conditions, and so on). Workshops, sensitivity or T-group encounters may be utilized, all of the available information about the students whom teachers teach may be provided, the philosophy of the institution may be explored, and in-service courses may be conducted. The results show, however, that none of these techniques are even minimally successful in changing faculty attitudes. This is particularly true if the attitudes are based on personal philosophies and deep-seated bigotry.

The administrator is not a psychiatrist, cannot change the past childhood, background, unhappiness, poverty, or the illness of the teacher, and, therefore, will probably be unable to influence to any significant degree a change in his attitude. Sooner or later we are going to have to face this truth and discontinue many of the educational and administrative charades and benevolent coercions we now employ to appeal to educators to perform better. In short, the taxpayer, I predict, through boards of trustees, administrators, students, and the withdrawal of his dollars, will force us to stop the academic, social, and economic bribing and pacifying of teachers to change their attitudes and to get them to do what they are already getting paid to do. When this is done, administrators will be forced (with the aid of the faculty, students, and others) to reward those people who perform and withhold rewards from those who do not show satisfactory performance. Many reject these ideas. They constantly ask, "What criterion will be used, and who will apply it?"

It is the collective attitude of teachers that students and others are not qualified to evaluate them. It should be suggested, however, that a student can observe whether or not the instructor comes to class and on time; see whether he keeps his office hours; know whether his instructor gave him a copy of the course and lecture objectives; note that the instructor's examination was confined to the materials he covered in class; see how many students fail; listen to or tape lectures to see if the instructor speaks clearly enough to be understood; and there are many other things that any person who knows absolutely nothing about the subject-matter field can tell about the effectiveness of the teacher. If the 125,000-plus academically prepared people who staff more than a thousand community colleges across the country cannot come up with criteria, then perhaps the next step will be to pay some outside agency to do the job and then proceed with the business of educating students. Already, the city of San Diego has brought in a profit-making organization to teach students that the schools have failed to teach. Incidentally, the organization advertises guaranteed results. Accountability keeps coming up. The editors of the *Saturday Review* (December, 1969) wrote in the "Schools Make News" column the following on one city's demand for accountability:

> With the public growing more concerned and skeptical about the results it is getting for its tax dollars spent on education, there is a rising demand to apply performance criteria to education and to hold school systems publicly accountable for student academic achievement.

The people who finance education are rapidly becoming selective consumers. They will not continue to pay teachers a guaranteed annual wage who are indifferent to the students they serve and who refuse to have their performance audited. The citizens are growing increasingly resistant to intimidation by threats of strikes and other abrupt confrontations. One Ohio citizen has said, "I would imagine that their [teachers'] attitudes would change if they went on strike for six months." Many others are also saying that perhaps the way to change faculty attitudes is through their pocketbooks. A ghetto resident in Chicago remarked to his neighbor: "Half of the black kids don't get nothing when that college is open; and the other half can get it by themselves. Let them [teachers] strike. Since they don't worry about students no way, let them worry about money like the rest of us."

His neighbor answered, "Right on!"

Chapter Six

The Curriculum

Curriculum is a tool of instruction. It is a body of knowledge, an experience activity, a performance opportunity, and a response to societal needs. It is designed to assist the student in coping effectively with his environment. For the marginal student, it is much more. It is actually a prescription for his success or failure. In short, a curriculum is a means to an end. It is outstanding when it is flexible, goal-related, motivational, challenging, and relevant. Few, if any, educational interpreters would protest these characteristics of an impressive curriculum. They would also agree that the course of study should fit the needs of each individual student. There is the rub. Much of what is taught in the community college as a whole was not designed for the student with minimal skills. The disparity between the available curricula and the learning style or academic characteristics of high-risk students is all but convulsive. It is a problem of immense magnitude. It is also quite remarkable that the two-year college with its open-door policy and its education-for-everybody pronouncements still accommodates this disparity without much hard evidence that a change is imminent. The statements concerning curriculum which follow are limited to the educationally disadvantaged student.

It is a fair statement that the marginal students are deficient in the traditional language arts (reading, writing, listening, spelling, speaking, grammar) and mathematics. The average high-risk student, after more than a decade of experience in the elementary and secondary schools, has not mastered these skills. He cannot read well enough to handle the traditional complexities of college bibliographies. He has not come to terms with the comprehensive and manipulatory skills in mathematics. And he has a blind spot when he is requested to write a theme or term paper. In fact, in the area of English, the high-risk student becomes immediately confused in the academic cross-breeding of intransitive verbs, direct objects, and possessive pronouns. The failure of the marginal student to master the basic skills has added frustration to his many past semesters of discontent. This failure has also provided his teachers with evidence which they have used to judge the student as academically incompetent. The improvement of basic skills, then, should be a part of any curriculum for the academically slow student. These skills are fundamental. They are prerequisites to most learning in the formal classroom. Mastery of them will open the door to many intellectual, vocational, and economic alternatives. Without them, few opportunities are available.

The professional literature neglects curricula for the marginal student. Even from those sources which are available, the curricula are nebulous. The whole collection of labels used in different colleges to describe the course of study for high-risk students is confusing. Some of the more common designations are: Fundamental Courses, General Education, General Studies, College Preparatory, Basic Studies, Prerequisite Curriculum, and General Curriculum. The label *General Education,* as it has been defined in the past, is a bona fide curriculum. However, this curriculum title is rarely thought of in the same way when it is used to label and describe a curriculum for the marginally educated. Just as the labels are confusing, the characteristics of programs for the academically slow student are contradictory: The same course that is offered for credit in one college is a non-credit course in another; the course may be required of students in some schools and voluntary in others. Many schools make a distinction between developmental and remedial courses while evaluating both types of courses in the same way. Under the guise of prerequisite courses, remedial subjects are frequently isolated parts of other curricula. In fact, it is indeed common to find a remedial curriculum being used specifically as a screening device for other curricula rather than as a tool and technique for providing learning experiences for marginal students commensurate with their needs, abilities, and aspirations. There are some community colleges where the basic academic skills are only a part of the general studies curriculum; in others, these fundamental skills constitute the entire general studies program. There are also many examples where the curriculum for the high-risk student is only a crash summer program each year and not an ongoing program in the college. Such are the inconsistencies which abound with regard to the course of study for low-achieving students. While the labels and characteristics of remedial curricula are confusing and contradictory, two distinct types of curricula are discernible.

The first, and by far the most frequently observed, curriculum is the traditional Three-R's course of study. The second is the Three-R's plus General Education plus Group Guidance configuration. The premise used to support the traditional Three-R's curriculum is that the program for the high-risk student must be simplified and that the emphasis should be on the basic skills. The premise used to support the Three-R's plus General Education plus Group Guidance format is that the student must develop other useful skills, acquire knowledge, know and understand himself, deal with others, and make practical and useful decisions while he remediates his level of proficiency in the basic skills.

THREE-R'S CURRICULUM

The Three-R's curriculum has many critics. Students say that it is "Mickey Mouse." Some modern educational innovators point out that it is sterile, diluted and seriously deficient in content. Loretan and Umans (1966) suggest that the marginal student "needs just the opposite of a bland, dull curriculum. He (the educationally disadvantaged student) is one who lives for today, settles his problems as they come, who seldom plans. He is one who needs stimulation, motivation, challenging content. He needs exposure, not enclosure."

The Three-R's pattern, as it is implemented in the community colleges I have seen, rarely offers content that is current, sophisticated, challenging, important, and interesting. Rather, the content, by its very nature, is boring, burdened with the rules of grammar and spelling, the mechanics of reading and writing, and the accumulation of arithmetic facts. These characteristics turn the student off and deprive him of his imaginative and active participation in the learning process. It is understandable, therefore, why the community college student who is having difficulty with basic skills is not motivated to learn them.

The grammar, for example, is repetitive. The student has been studying it since he was in the fourth grade. There are too many rules of grammar he must memorize. Once the student commits the rules to memory, he must then memorize the exceptions to the rules. Moreover, except for what is taught in the primary and elementary grades where activity units, games, rewards, and other types of reinforcement are used in instruction, it is difficult to find grammar taught with much creativity and originality.

Reading is as burdensome as grammar to the high-risk student. In the first place, several techniques may have been used to teach the student to read. It is not inconceivable that the methods themselves confused the learner. The student's first-grade teacher may have used the sight method; his second-grade teacher may have used the phonetic approach; his third-grade teacher may have used both; and so on. Regardless of the techniques used in the instruction of reading, much of the content deals with such subjects as adventure, sports, patriotism, morality, and other such concepts. These subjects may excite the young child or the preadolescent, but they do not excite an

impressive number of young adults. Many students who are
currently on the college scene reject these subjects entirely.
More specifically, much of the material in remedial reading
classes is considered contrived trivia by the high-risk student
because the information does not offer him any direct relationship to his life and the world that he can readily see, and, in
fact, contradicts much of what he experiences in the real world.
Rather, the information tends only to accumulate.

Finally, the student is confronted with remedial arithmetic. By the time he reaches the community college he has
traveled the full circle in mathematics. If the student started
kindergarten in 1956, he studied the "old math" of adding
apples and oranges. The "old math" was replete with its multiplication tables, addition and subtraction facts, drill, and traditional vocabulary. When the student reached the seventh
grade he was exposed to the "new math" with its abstract
sophistication, its intricate formulas and a new vocabulary dealing with communative, associative, and distributive properties.
The student went on to high school. There he often found half
of his teachers taught the "old math" and the other half (probably the younger teachers) taught the "new math." The marginal student did not learn either. Finally, the student reaches
the community college and evaluative instruments indicate that
he is deficient in mathematics and needs remedial instruction.
He is right back to adding apples and oranges, multiplying them
by pears, and dividing them by the other fruit that has always
characterized the content used to study the "old math."

There is no question that the mastery of the basic skills
is important; yet, the high-risk student at the college level is
"turned off" by them. His reasons for rejecting them are both
realistic and psychological. In the real order, he knows he can
actually get along without them. He is impatient with the drill,
drudgery, and time that it takes to learn them. He is aware that
there are few shortcuts to learning the fundamentals of the
Three-R's; and he quickly accepts the idea that much of the
media (audio-visual and other teaching tools) used to give him
instruction in the basic skills are really gimmicks which require

as much routine as any other drill. The gimmicks are, in fact, repetitive, non-changing, and inflexible unless a unique and creative human being programs them. This does not mean that media as instructional devices are not effective or should not be used. The point emphasized here is that even media have some built-in monotony, and the student recognizes it. One student says it well: "When you start out using tape recorders and all them audio-visuals, they are pretty interesting. But as soon as you learn how to work with them, they are no longer interesting. You can't ever ask one of them machines a question. And it sure don't say good morning to you when you walk in. About the only thing that tape recorder can do is say the same thing, the same way, every time. Sometimes I slow the speed down so it will sound different."

It is obvious that this student is one whose learning style, emotional needs, and perceptions require a live teacher to support him through the drudgery of basic academic skills. His view of media may be colored by his own specific needs. Another reason why students are "turned off" when the basic skills are taught is because the skills are usually taught in isolation from other subject-matter materials. High-risk students do not live in a basic skill vacuum. In like manner, learning does not take place in a vacuum. The same student who is having difficulty with the so-called basic skills is also having difficulty with social studies, science, and the humanities. In spite of the fact that a high-risk student may not be proficient in the fundamental skills, as a consumer, he borrows money, buys clothing, purchases entertainment, secures insurance, pays rent, and pays for many other goods and services. As a citizen, he votes, pays taxes, obeys the laws, supports schools, and assumes other responsibilities which make a contribution to society. As a husband, father, comrade, friend, and co-worker, he earns a living, takes a temperature, applies a tourniquet, offers his services, and is cooperative.

It cannot be denied that mastery of basic skills is not a prerequisite to life: Students in their day-to-day life do not walk around conjugating verbs, reading about what a marigold thinks of spring, and adding fruit. Yet, it must be agreed that the student can carry on the above functions with much greater proficiency if he has learned to accommodate and communicate the fundamental skills effectively. It is understandable, therefore, why a curriculum for marginal students must provide for the basic skills. It must also provide much more. Such skills can only be antecedents or supplementary to other parts of the curriculum.

THREE-R'S-PLUS CURRICULUM

In the second pattern of curriculum for the academically slow student, the Three R's are linked to the so-called general education group of courses, and it is not too unusual to find the basic skills courses further linked to group guidance classes. With the exception of group guidance courses, this course pattern is hardly unique. Typically, one finds in this configuration courses in natural science, social science, humanities, communications, and sometimes courses or classes in orientation. Macomb Community College's Division of Basic Education, Warren, Michigan, has developed the Educational and Cultural Development Program, which is an example of this general education course configuration:

EDUCATIONAL AND CULTURAL DEVELOPMENT PROGRAM

First Semester	Credit Hours	Second Semester	Credit Hours
Social Science 150	4	Social Science 160	4
Natural Science 150	4	Natural Science 160	4
Communications 150	4	Communications 160	4
Humanities 150	3	Humanities 160	3
Orientation 150	1		
	16		15

A considerable number of community colleges with programs for the marginal student have the same general pattern as Macomb County Community College. Chicago City College is another example:

THE BASIC PROGRAM [1]

First Trisemester	Credit Hours	Second Trisemester	Credit Hours
Social Science 088	3	Social Science 089	3
Natural Science 088	3	Natural Science 089	3
English 088	3	English 089	3
Speech (Alternate) 088	3	Speech (Alternate) 089	3
Reading (Alternate) 088	2	Reading (Alternate) 089	2
	14		14

There is nothing wrong with a general education curriculum. In the truest sense, it is a valid curriculum. Almost two decades ago, Johnson (1952) listed the principles or assumptions supporting the need for general education: "(1) General education must be based on the characteristics of students and of society. (2) All areas of experience, at home and in the community, as well as in the college, interact to affect the student's growth. (3) The junior college will not complete the student's general education; rather, it will aim to equip and encourage him to pursue the goals of general education throughout his life. (4) Students in California junior colleges differ greatly in experiences, needs, capacities, interests, and aspirations. (5) The general education program must promote the growth and development of each individual student on the basis of his particular abilities, interests, and other characteristics. (6) The final test of a program of general education is changed student behavior, motivated by the student's desire to improve himself and society." Although the fourth assumption applies specifically to the state of California, the reader has but to substitute the name of his own state.

The problem with the general education curriculum is that it is always suspect. From at least two points of view, one observes this problem. First, the vocationalists, specialists, and other opponents of general education are contemptuous of such a curriculum. Faculties hasten to point out that general education does not give the student competencies in any one area.

[1] As listed in the Chicago City College Catalog, 1966–1967.

An eastern dean calls general education a "shotgun approach to a college education." A chemistry professor in Michigan charges, "Whenever a student is enrolled in general education I know that he is not very bright." Similarly, a physics teacher in California says, "Most of the content of general education is hypothetical and is artificially contrived to prove its need for existence." Perhaps these teachers are right. Yet, while the chemistry professor's bright students developed cosmetics to make people appear more beautiful; produced the wonderful artificial fabrics to make clothes more comfortable and easy to care for; compounded many of the wonder drugs to help fight disease; and raised the octane of premium gasoline, they also created the atomic bomb to destroy whole cities; they dumped their chemical waste into the rivers and streams of America and have polluted these waters; they have seen the fumes from the premium gas they perfected pollute the air we breathe; and they developed the napalm bomb which puts entire villages to the torch. In short, the bright students in chemistry or physics or any of the other specialties and technologies have indeed developed those specialties. It is obvious that the bright student has helped to provide for both the pleasures and the miseries of mankind. Yet, his knowledge of his specialty has done little to help correct the social maladies of society. The divorce rate continues to rise; the relationship between the races continues to deteriorate; many people in America are hungry; crime is on the increase; the poor, the unemployed, and the blacks still do not receive an equitable share of America's rewards. For these reasons and for other reasons which are too numerous to list here, a curriculum in general education is justified. To put it more succinctly, the specialists have had a considerable amount of time to create a better world (of people—not things) and they have not succeeded. Perhaps the generalists deserve a chance. The Harvard Committee on Education in the book *General Education in a Free Society* notes that education is divided into general and special dimensions and that the two kinds of education are not mutually exclusive:

> Education is broadly divided into general and special education; our topic now is the difference and the rela-

tionship between the two. The term, general education, is somewhat vague and colorless; it does not mean some airy education in knowledge in general (if there be such knowledge), nor does it mean education for all in the sense of universal education. It is used to indicate that part of a student's whole education which looks first of all to his life as a responsible human being and citizen; while the term, special education, indicates that part which looks to the student's competence in some occupation. These two sides of life are not entirely separable, and it would be false to imagine education for the one as quite distinct from education for the other.

The second point of view from which one observes the problem of general education is in the confusion of it with liberal education. The Harvard Committee also attempts to clarify the confusion between liberal and general education:

Clearly, general education has somewhat the meaning of liberal education, except that, by applying to high school as well as to college, it envisages immensely greater numbers of students and thus escapes the invidium which, rightly or wrongly, attaches to liberal education in the minds of some people. But if one clings to the root meaning of liberal as that which befits or helps to make free men, then general and liberal education have identical goals. The one may be thought of as an earlier stage of the other, similar in nature but less advanced in degree.

The opposition to liberal education—both to the phrase and to the fact—stems largely from historical causes. The concept of liberal education first appeared in a slave-owning society, like that of Athens, in which the community was divided into free men and slaves, rulers and subjects. While the slaves carried on the specialized occupations of menial work, the free men were primarily concerned with the rights and duties of citizenship. The training of the former was purely vocational; but as the free men were not only a ruling but also a leisure class, their education was exclusively in the liberal arts, without any utilitarian tinge. The free men were trained in the reflective pursuit of the good life; their education was unspecialized as well as unvocational; its aim was to produce a rounded person with a full understanding

of himself and of his place in society and in the cosmos.
Modern democratic society clearly does not regard labor
as odious or disgraceful; on the contrary, in this country
at least, it regards leisure with suspicion and expects its
"gentlemen" to engage in work. Thus we attach no
odium to vocational instruction. Moreover, insofar as
we surely reject the idea of freemen who are free insofar
as they have slaves or subjects, we are apt strongly to
deprecate the liberal education which went with the
structure of the aristocratic idea. Herein our society
runs the risk of committing a serious fallacy. Democracy
is the view that not only the few but that all are free, in
that everyone governs his own life and shares in the
responsibility for the management of the community.
This being the case, it follows that all human beings
stand in need of an ampler and rounded education.
. . . Our conclusion, then, is that the aim of education
should be to prepare an individual to become an expert
both in some particular vocation or art and in the general art of the free man and the citizen. Thus the two
kinds of education once given separately to different
social classes must be given together to all alike.

Morse (1964) removes liberal and general education from
the historical frame of reference and looks at them in a more
current and practical application. In two succinct statements
he compares them:

Liberal education is considered to be subject-centered,
with a fairly fixed body of content material, logically
organized. Its goal is also the stimulation of reflective
thinking, with less emphasis on behavior, and it draws
its clientele from the intellectual elite. It implies a concentration in depth with frequently a more intensive
cultivation of one or two special fields of knowledge. It
clings closely to tradition in the kinds of learnings it
sanctions. General education, on the other hand, is more
concerned with the learner than with the content, which
may be organized or reshuffled with regard to traditional
fields. Its goals are individual development in its various
aspects, and it places emphasis upon behavior and social
usefulness as well as upon intellectual development as
an outcome of learning. It is a manifestation of the
democratic spirit in higher education, for it admits a
wider scope of abilities and a far broader clientele.

It is rather clear, therefore, by the above definition, that a liberal education curriculum is a "knowing" curriculum—rigid, traditional, with a subject matter designed to serve a narrow and selected group of students who have demonstrated academic competence, and who are expected to do well in the four-year college or university setting. Since the community college serves a wider clientele with broader short-term goals, the curriculum must be a "knowing" and a "doing" curriculum. While it cannot be stripped of its intellectual components, it has to be flexible, practical, and oriented more toward individual differences in the students than toward academic conformity to the subject matter.

It must be admitted that while general education has been more people-oriented in philosophy and more practical in application, it is still traditional in the course patterns and in the way the courses are taught. Even a cursory observation of the course groupings is enough to convince the least sophisticated observer that he is considering a traditional curriculum pattern. In like manner, the goals in general education have appeared to be idealistic and remote. Traditional teaching and indistinct and remote goals are two danger signs in a curriculum for low achievers. Marginal students are idealistic but they are also practical. They want their means (instruction) to be dramatic, interesting, and relevant; and their ends (knowledge and skill to perform the job they are preparing themselves to execute) to be well defined and immediate.

Group guidance is another component of the second pattern. The function of group guidance is to provide a process through which students will be enabled to make good choices, improve their interrelationship with people and the world, and to develop to the optimum of their ability. Group guidance is probably a framework in which most of the things that counselors are doing can be fitted; however, it has special significance to a program which is composed of students who are considered poor scholastic risks.

There are students in the community college whose transfer or two-year degree aspirations are unrealistic in view of their very low academic skills. There are others who know their pattern of abilities and have some information about occupations in which such abilities are most applicable and yet are unable to accept this knowledge because of ambition, family expectations, and self-rejection. Still others are deficient in study skills and habits, they are uncertain in their goals and have little knowledge of how to obtain either educational or vocational objectives. Many of the students have had traumatic experiences in the past which have given them a sense of failure, distrust of authority, and a severe lack of self-confidence.

These students in group guidance have both the problems common to their state of development as college freshmen and the problems of being high-risk students. Group guidance attempts to make the student aware of his abilities and talents, social assets and liabilities, values, and aspirations so that he can make choices that will influence his subsequent development.

Through group guidance sessions the following specific objectives are sought: (1) orient the student to a college environment, for example, the college presents so many new freedoms and responsibilities that the new student becomes overwhelmed by all the new experiences; (2) orient the new student to the general curriculum program, its purposes, its operations, and its goals; (3) assist students in learning how to project suitable, long-range educational plans; (4) assist individuals in learning how to project suitable, long-range vocational plans; (5) study and application of efficient methods in study skills and habits; (6) help the student satisfy his need for acceptance, security, affection, and a sense of service at a time when such help is needed through the interaction of the group; (7) provide a sense of belonging to a specific group with the security and acceptance of group membership; (8) provide release of emotional tension by having group study of common human problems in a permissive atmosphere; (9) make individual counseling more effective by establishing rapport through the group; (10) increase the student's self-insight and self-understanding; (11) help the student learn how to communicate through listening, self-expression, and critical evaluation of ideas; (12) provide standardized test service to give students insight into interest and points of strengths and weaknesses in study skills; (13) provide a laboratory of human relations in which the student works cooperatively with others on problems of common interest; (14) coordinate all phases of the remedial program for the student.

The main goal of group guidance is that the student who leaves the remedial program will be better adjusted, a more mature person emotionally, and have a more wholesome outlook. It attempts to prepare each student so that he will be able to make his contribution to society at the level of his ability.

THE GENERAL CURRICULUM

Forest Park Community College of the St. Louis–St. Louis County Junior College District combines both curriculum patterns into a third pattern: the General Curriculum. Although the General Curriculum is similar in part to the curricula implemented in many community colleges, it is much more comprehensive than most and has a well-defined theoretical framework. The remainder of this chapter focuses on this curriculum—its rationale, objectives, structure, operations, and so on. First, however, a word about the selection of students seems appropriate. Students assigned to the General Curriculum are assigned on the basis of two criteria: high school rank at graduation and percentile rank on the School and College Ability Test (SCAT). These ranks must be in the lower third and the tenth percentile or below, respectively. Both criteria must be met. The program, however, is not a dead-end. If the student makes satisfactory progress (grade point average of B) after a semester or a year in the program, he may move into the transfer, technical, or career programs.

A full-time General Curriculum student would take all of the fifteen hours each semester. However, part-time students can take one or all of the PMLL (and Application Lab) courses and repeat them at will. The courses (PMLL and Application Lab) may be taken without time limit until the work is satisfactorily completed.

The General Curriculum is an experimental curriculum designed for the marginal student. It was developed on the premise that the high-risk student who has this program pre-

GENERAL CURRICULUM COURSE FORMAT

Academic:

	Team I (1 semester)	Credits		Team II (1 semester)	Credits
1.	Sociology	3	Consumer Economics		3
2.	Science	3	Society and Science		3
3.	Humanities	3	Humanities		3
4.	Group Guidance	1	Group Guidance		1

Basic Skills: (No time limit)

	Team I	Credits	Team II	Credits
5.	PMLL[2]	2	PMLL[2]	2
	Writing Lab	1	Writing Lab	1
	Math Lab	1	Math Lab	1
	Reading Lab	1	Reading Lab	1

Total credit hours: 15 per semester

scribed for him will need simultaneous assistance in the basic
academic skills (reading, mathematics, grammar, and composition), personal enrichment, and adjustment to self and society.
The program provides this assistance through programmed
learning, general education classes, and guidance techniques.

There are two classifications of objectives for the General Curriculum. The first is concerned with the ultimate
assignment of the student and was originally summarized by
a single term, *placement*. Placement as an objective was conceived to take any of the following forms: (1) placement in a
specific curriculum offered by the college (transfer, career, certified); (2) placement in a training program offered within the
community but not under the auspices of the college (this
program might be in Manpower Development Training
Courses, apprenticeship programs, area vocational school offerings or other training opportunities); (3) placement directly
on a job that offers possibilities of advancement and appears to
be consistent with the student's interests and aptitudes; and
(4) placement from the standpoint of reassignment or upgrading
an existing job. This may mean providing the student with
enough supplementary skills so he can qualify by test or some
other criterion for the job.

2 Programmed Materials Learning Laboratory.

The fourth objective was not one of the original objectives. Yet, it has proved to be an important function in the curriculum.

It should be noted that one type of placement would not be given preference over another except as it might better meet the needs of a given student. Further, there would be a maximum attempt to utilize and mobilize all the services in the community to improve the opportunities for the disadvantaged. Retention in formal classes for a predetermined length of time would not be considered as a criterion of success. Instead, the program would emphasize the identification by the student of a specific vocational goal followed by acceptance of a rational procedure for attainment of that goal. Since many students enter junior colleges with unclear vocational objectives, the General Curriculum could serve as a specially controlled holding program to permit students of uncertain abilities and objectives to experience college without the threat of immediate dismissal. Through this approach a major source of technical trainees could be developed.

A part of the General Curriculum is a second classification of objectives which have national application for community colleges and other institutions serving educationally disadvantaged students. This classification of objectives includes: (1) the development of a model program for educationally disadvantaged students with a consistent theoretical rationale that could serve as a guide for the administrators and staff personnel of other institutions confronted by similar conditions; (2) the establishment of an active program of community involvement seeking to provide leadership and direction to a multitude of community, state, and federal organizations having an interest or a responsibility in this program—such a blueprint for community mobilization should have far-reaching consequences; (3) the offering of an internship experience for present and prospective instructors interested in teaching the disadvantaged student; (4) the development of curriculum materials and instructional aids specifically designed with the needs of this group of students in mind; (5) the evaluation of the effectiveness of materials and techniques developed for the disadvantaged student; and (6) the development and dissemination of information concerning the characteristics of disadvantaged students and successful methods of teaching them.

The General Curriculum is organized around three areas of the student's academic and individual needs. The areas of need are basic skills, personal enrichment, and adjustment to self and society. The vehicles for solving the problems of basic skills are achieved through the use of programmed instruction in the Programmed Materials Learning Laboratory (PMLL). The method by which the personal enrichment of high-risk students is achieved is a one-year program of general education. Finally, the adjustment facet of the program is achieved through group and individual guidance counseling and human relations.

BASIC SKILLS

The Programmed Materials Learning Laboratory [3] handles the basic skills component of the General Curriculum. PMLL is a self-help or a self-study lab that provides for students whose verbal and mathematical skills are at or below the tenth percentile on the SCAT Test. It accommodates a large number of students (primarily college freshmen) who are low achievers and have been generally considered high-risk students academically. The primary purpose of the Programmed Materials Learning Laboratory is to provide each student with an individualized curriculum based on the diagnosis, prescription, and remediation of his educational deficiencies. Instruction is primarily through a study of programmed textbooks supplemented by tutoring in basic skills—English grammar and basic math through first-year algebra. PMLL has three supplementary application labs (Writing Lab, Reading Lab, and Mathematics Lab).

The objective of the Educational Laboratory [4] is to enable students to improve basic academic skills by utilizing individualized multi-media programmed instruction. The Edu-

[3] The label *Programmed Materials Learning Laboratory* (PMLL) is used interchangeably with the label *Educational Laboratory*.

[4] The objectives of the PMLL were developed by selected members of the General Curriculum staff: Claire Brew, Charles B. Gilbert, William Moore, Jr., Betty Pollard, and Alice Thelen.

cational Laboratory is a diagnostic and remediation center which is housed in a part of the college facility now called the Programmed Materials Learning Laboratory, Reading Laboratory, and the classrooms which are used for Mathematics and Writing Application Laboratories. Basic academic skills include reading, basic arithmetic, algebra, English grammar, and composition. The term *improve* refers to a positive increase to a predetermined degree in terms of the minimum needs of a program of his choice (transfer or career) in the difference between the student's pre-test and post-test scores. Programmed instruction is a technique of presenting a body of subject-matter content which has been especially designed and organized for self-study. Programmed instruction utilizes the specification of objectives, concepts of repetition, immediate reinforcement, and progression from the simple to the more complex. *Multimedia* refers to those tools of instruction which may appeal to a specific student's learning style. These tools may be audio, visual, or a combination of both, which may be under the individual control of the student or under a central control. *Individualized* refers to diagnosis of the student's content deficiencies as well as diagnosis of his learning style; prescription of appropriate curricula; the student's use of prescribed remedial material; and evaluation of the student's progress.

The specific objectives of the Educational Laboratory are as follows:

A. *For the student*

   1. To improve basic skills
      a. To diagnose individual educational deficiencies.
      b. To investigate the student's learning style as it applies to achievement.
      c. To give to the student appropriate multi-media materials commensurate with his learning style.
      d. To evaluate the student's progress.

B. *For the Educational Laboratory*

   1. To investigate, develop, and use a multi-media approach to instruction.
   2. To develop approaches and techniques for self-instruc-

tion of large groups of students in the lower ability
spectrum.

3. To serve as a diagnostic and remediation center for General Curriculum students and any other Forest Park Community College student who is restricted from taking a course because he is deficient in basic skills.
4. To provide a resource center for the referral of students who are experiencing difficulty in a basic skill while they are enrolled in math or English courses.
5. To make the Learning Laboratory a vehicle for articulation between the General Curriculum and other areas of the college.

The basic skills [5] have two types of class organization: a large-group pattern and a small-group pattern. The large-group segment is organized as a kind of study hall (PMLL) with individual study carrels and is supervised by instructor-tutors. Students have access to a wide variety of printed matter, audio-visual materials, and fully trained subject-matter personnel are available fourteen hours each day as tutors. There is an area for testing and an area for consultation. The student works in a self-help role. Students actually receive individual attention and instruction when it is needed. The small-group segment (Reading Lab, Math Lab, Writing Lab) is set up in classrooms with an instructor-tutor in charge and with specially prepared materials. These problem-solving materials are used in a series of drills and exercises to supplement and solidify the skills (ideas, concepts) learned through self-study in the large study hall. The small groups are called *Application Labs*.

Students write in the Writing Laboratory. They do their composition under the supervision of English instructors. The pattern of errors made by the writer is spotted and corrected immediately. After the pattern of error has been diagnosed, the writer then rewrites with specific attention given to the area of composition where he shows deficiency. Particular attention is given to the student's work to see whether he incorporates

[5] Much of the basic skill information included was collected and interpreted by Charles Gilbert of the General Curriculum staff.

the skills he has learned in the large-group PMLL. The Writing Laboratory content that the student is asked to master is correlated with the programmed texts used in the PMLL. If the student is progressing successfully and completes all of his assignments at any time during the semester, he may be recommended out of the Writing Lab.

The student who works in the PMLL and Writing Lab has many options when he completes his assignments. Obviously, the aim of the English grammar (PMLL) and composition (Writing Lab) training is to teach the student to write better. The student who completes the Writing Lab exercises is assured the opportunity of transferring into regular college English courses. The student is not, however, released from the entire English part of the basic skills curriculum until he completes the grammar part of PMLL.

In like manner, the students who are assigned to Math Labs are provided with a great deal of comprehension and computational exercises. The content in Math Lab—like the content in Writing Lab—is correlated with the basic programmed texts used in PMLL. Just as the student who completes Writing Laboratory has alternatives, so does the student who completes his assignments in Mathematics Laboratory. He has at least two alternatives: If he removes his deficiencies in basic mathematics (fractions, decimals, per cent, and ratio) he is assured entrance into a program which does not require algebra. Or, on the other hand, if the student fulfills the requirements equivalent to one-year high school algebra, he may transfer into the regular college course, Intermediate Algebra. Intermediate Algebra is a prerequisite for college Algebra. In addition to individual and unit tests, a specific instrument is used to measure competency and to establish completion criteria of the algebra work in PMLL.

The Reading Laboratory is a separate self-contained operation. It is actually a part of the English department and is run as a remedial reading clinic with specially trained clinicians. Several specific groups of students use the Reading Laboratory: students who are extremely deficient in reading and need remedial assistance, students who have mild deficiencies (they are encouraged but are not required to enroll in a reading class), and students who are proficient (even highly skilled) but who wish to improve even more. Sometimes this latter group studies reading oriented toward a special subject area such as scientific reading. Completion of remedial Reading Lab work assures transfer into Developmental Reading, a regular college course which is taken under most circumstances at the same time as Developmental English. The latter is the preparation course for regular English Composition or for Communications.

A variety of arrangements are worked out on an individual basis in Writing, Mathematics, and Reading Laboratory which try to assure a student the opportunity to start regular college work as soon as some part of his educational deficiencies has been alleviated.

As is apparent, the Educational Laboratory is a learning laboratory, a center for diagnosis and remediation of education deficiencies of community college freshmen who have been identified superficially as low performers, at least in the subject-matter areas of English and mathematics. As such, the PMLL has been removed from the plebeian function of a mere supervised study hall. Rather, it has developed into a more sophisticated diagnostic center for the study and treatment of learning problems of young adults.

Treatment is seen as a three-step process: identification, diagnosis, and remediation. For the first step, identification, students are identified in three ways: by the college, by the counselor, by personal choice. The college administers the Scholastic and College Aptitude Test (SCAT) to all entering freshmen as a placement device. Those students whose cut-off scores on verbal and mathematical subjects are in the lower tenth percentile and whose rank in their high school graduating class was in the lower third are notified directly by the admissions office that they have been assigned to the General Curriculum.

The counselor meets with students who are above the tenth percentile, who were not in the lower third of their high school graduating class, but who did have low scores on the SCAT. The counselees are advised to enter PMLL for specific remedial work. These students are called non-General Curriculum students. Many students, for example, are assigned to PMLL to study high school algebra because they never took the course and because the educational lab is the only place in the college where this course is available.

Any student in the college may choose to sign up for PMLL and take work in either mathematics or English whether or not he is a student who has been advised to enroll in the course. The student may also come to the PMLL to study programmed texts in other subject-matter areas which are available in the lab. He need not be an enrollee to use programmed materials in areas other than mathematics and English.

Instructors also may refer the student to the PMLL. Frequently, teachers will discover a good student who has a minor academic deficiency in some area of his field of study. This student is then referred to the PMLL on the basis of his teacher's diagnosis and recommendation.

For the second step, diagnosis, during the first week of classes each semester, diagnostic tests in English grammar, basic mathematics, and a writing sample are administered in the small-group section of the Writing and Mathematics Laboratories. The following is an outline of the procedure used to diagnose specific areas of deficiency:

1. *Math*
   A. Educational Laboratory
      (1) Arithmetic
          a. Give arithmetic pre-test (locally prepared) to all PMLL math students.
          b. Patterns of error indicate student's math assignment to Speed program and/or Seventh Grade Math (whole numbers only). Scoring and analysis of error patterns are done by computer.
          c. No additional media have been used at this time.
          d. Student success in programs is determined by a test administered after each unit. A score of 85 per cent is passing.
          e. Arithmetic post-test is administered following completion of units assigned.

(2) Algebra
  a. Lankton test is administered for diagnosis.
  b. Each student is assigned on the basis of score,
     previous algebra courses taken, and teacher's judg-
     ment.
     1. Student without high school algebra or with
        minimal retention (below 35 percentile on the
        Lankton) is usually assigned Fundamentals.
     2. Student with high school algebra may be as-
        signed to Refresher if his score on the Lankton
        is high enough (50 percentile).
B. Math Lab (ML)
  (1) All students are assigned to ML if they have PMLL
      math assignments.
  (2) Each student is assigned to specific units in a math
      workbook for follow-up application and drill corre-
      sponding to PMLL placement in both basic math
      and algebra. A single workbook is used with the basic
      math program while three workbooks are used in
      algebra—one for each algebra program.
  (3) Workbook and tutoring are the only available media
      and techniques.
  (4) Student success is based upon 70 per cent of problems
      completed correctly in each unit assigned in the math
      workbook.

Prescription of the appropriate remedial work is possible
because of the close correlation between the test and the textbook. Topics (or units) of work are assigned on the basis of
items missed on the test. Worksheets and progress tests are maintained.

2. *English*
  A. Educational Laboratory
    (1) *2600* pre-test (and faculty designed tests) are admin-
        istered to all PMLL English grammar students
        (Blumenthal, 1962a).

(2) Assignment into units of *2600* (grammar) based on patterns of errors.

(3) Student success in programs is determined by a test administered after each unit. A score of 85 per cent is passing.

(4) Following completion of the assigned units, chapters or series of frames in the *2600* book, a *2600* post-test is administered.

(5) A *3200* pre-test is administered (Blumenthal, 1962b). Assignment into units of *3200* (grammar) is based on patterns of errors.

B. Writing Lab

(1) All students write an entry essay to determine if any student has been incorrectly placed. If a student's essay demonstrates a level of competence which would enable him to perform adequately in a higher level English class, the English department chairman reads and evaluates the essay. Then he makes a recommendation about student placement.

(2) Initial placement is in Lesson I of Writing Lab series which emphasizes composition skills (organization, arrangement, presentation of ideas).

(3) Tutor has individual conference with each student on each lesson. A tape recorder is sometimes used for evaluating themes.

(4) No other instructional media are used for correction of themes.

(5) At the end of the semester, each student writes an essay which is evaluated to determine placement in composition courses. Each essay is evaluated by his Writing Lab instructor and a committee of instructors in the English Department makes a recommendation to the English Department.

Programmed materials are used in the third step, the remediation process. The premise which supports the use of programmed materials—not machines—is that programmed in-

struction is based on specific objectives. It is systematic; it is
presented in small sequential steps; students can work at their
own rate; there are many opportunities for try-out and revision
of the materials available; there is immediate knowledge on the
part of the student and teacher of just how much of the program has been learned; and it has long been thought that high-
risk students need the specification and structure inherent in
programmed instruction. Some say that programmed instruction is more effective for bright students who read well than
for slow students because the learning situation is so complex.
Fry (1964), for example, lists twenty-six classifications of variables involved in a programmed-learning situation:

1. Step-presentation media (sensory input)
2. Type of symbols used in steps
3. Step characteristics
4. Mediating activity (be-tween stimulus and re-sponse elements)
5. Response mode (form of response)
6. Response ideational con-tent
7. Knowledge of results
8. Reward or reinforcement type
9. Reward variations
10. Presentation rate
11. Branching patterns
12. Branching control
13. Repetition or practice
14. Discrimination and gen-eralization
15. Program length
16. Programming techniques
17. Subject-matter organiza-tion
18. Subject-matter character-istics
19. Coordinate or supplemen-tary presentation
20. Motivational factors
21. Environmental influence
22. Individual differences
23. Measurement of outcome
24. Training efficiency
25. Quality of program
26. Educational objectives

Under each heading there are many subpoints.
If, for example, we change the sensory input from visual
to auditory, or we change the type of symbol from a
word to a numeral, we have pretty completely changed
the learner's situation. Or, for example, if we change
a class of learners from bright to dull, or the motivation
from high to low, or the measurement of learning outcome from recall (essay test) to recognition (multiple-
choice test) we have again substantially changed the
learning situation. . . . We might keep some of these

factors in mind, and in trying to compare programmed learning with traditional instruction any one of these factors can influence the outcome. In spite of the complexities inherent in programmed curriculum, it can be effective.

All texts in the educational laboratory are self-help programmed materials. Student achievement is followed by unit (or progress) tests which must be passed with a score of 85 before proceeding to the next unit. Four alternate forms of each unit test are available. Tests are taken only on student demand. The bulk of the teaching assistant's time is spent following a student's progress, providing tutoring when requested, and insuring continuity of study habits while in class (there is no homework). Learning problems, when they arise, engage the staff in evaluative techniques which will provide students with alternate routes based specifically on extremes of ability (for example, reading grade level), differences in learning style (written versus oral, graphic, or other modes of learning), and levels of anxiety (pre-college failure pattern, test anxiety, terminal hysteria, distractibility, boredom, and resentment).

One of the problems of remediation is to get the student to handle the material effectively. Students who study programmed materials require a special kind of tenacity. When a student studies a programmed text three things are necessary: self-discipline, self-confidence, and anxiety control. The area of self-discipline is observable in PMLL when the student uses his textbooks. The student knows the answers to the questions and problems he is attempting to solve are in his programmed texts. He is fully aware that he has but to turn the page to find the correct answer to the problem or exercise on the page he is studying. Obviously, the student is tempted and tantalized by this knowledge and the next page is his mentor. Although the solution to the problem the student is attempting to solve is never farther away than the turn of a page, his real problem is the frustration of wanting to look for the answer and the need to resist his desire to look. This is an outstanding dilemma for the marginal student. In short, the student must make the decision not to look. He must have the self-discipline to work a problem before he turns the page to find out if his answer is correct. On the other hand, there is some thought that it is all right for him to turn the page. The premise which supports this thought is that it is the process which is important.

The student must also be self-confident. He must have— or develop—some definite feelings of certainty that he can execute various academic tasks. Somehow, he must find the arrogance and belief in his own abilities to attack an unfamiliar concept and know that if he studies the idea (with or without assistance) he will learn. The programmed books are designed to help the student develop this confidence by providing many small successes in every lesson he encounters. The student does not know that he is working with content which reinforces, rewards, and almost assures success through the operant conditioning format of the programmed materials.

Finally, the student must be able to control some of his anxiety. He must learn that the presence of a blank space in a sentence—as in a unit test—is a mere academic confrontation which is not totally unlike many other encounters he has in his day-by-day living. Since the student already knows where the answers are, that he will not be punished or ridiculed for not knowing the right responses, and that he is tested only when he is ready, he is expected to develop the anxiety control not to give up as he works with his materials and look ahead at the answers.

The student that does not have or does not develop self-discipline, self-confidence, and some control of his own anxiety, and looks ahead at the right answer, often places an unfamiliar word into a blank in an unfamiliar sentence or gives up and goes on without understanding what he has read or attempted to read. This is circuitous behavior. It is no different from reading a traditional text full of unfamiliar concepts, information, and experiences which have not, in the past, produced learning for him. How in fact to get students to study programmed textual material and to learn from it is always a serious PMLL problem. The answer does not seem to lie in simply substituting an instructor-classroom or a face-to-face tutoring situation. These only reinforce the dependency feeling inherited from previous unsuccessful educational experiences. So acute is the problem, occasionally, that students present what seems to be a defiant attitude of "Teach me—if you can." This latter attitude can be overcome with a series of immediately successful learning experiences. The answer, therefore, seems to lie in the creation of situations of learning which are far more structured and rewarding than are sometimes thought necessary. It does appear that when a student uses a programmed text effectively he gets, as a side effect, the first clear picture of what it means to study. For high-risk students this is a most important insight into college work. Programmed texts, then, have unusual potential for helping low achievers. Community college people may do well to give attention to this mode of instruction.

ADMINISTRATION

The administrative set-up for educational laboratory is illustrated in Figure 1. It need only be noted that the operation is divided equally between the day and night programs, although the day program is larger. *WL* and *ML* refer to Writing Labs and Math Labs. In actual practice, the department chairman and the two assistant chairmen work as a team, with team decisions. The associate dean of the General Curriculum participates actively in the team discussions. It should be recognized that the team structure is not a formal pattern and extends no further down than the assistant chairman level; however, staff members at all levels take part in the meetings. Staff meetings are frequent but are a problem because of the schedules of part-time teaching assistants and because the basic academic skills classes are in session from 8:00 A.M. to 9:30 P.M., requiring continuous staff coverage. Further development of the educational laboratory as a learning laboratory requires an administrative set-up expanded with additional research and diagnostic personnel. The left side of the chart is representative of the relationship of the educational laboratory to the entire General Curriculum.

Although content of the Writing Labs and the Math Labs was originally the responsibility of the division chairman for the College Humanities Division and the Physical Science Division, respectively, the administration of the labs is now the responsibility of the PMLL. Full responsibility, including hiring of application lab staff, now rests with the PMLL Chairman. Content and administration responsibility are divided between the two assistant chairmen, cutting across the normal division of day and night supervision in the direct line of authority. Thus both the Writing Lab assistant chairman and the Math Lab assistant chairman are directly responsible to the PMLL department chairman.

This is a crucial administrative point since the orientation and in-service training of the part-time applications lab personnel and the coordination of the labs with the practices

FIGURE 1

GENERAL CURRICULUM
ORGANIZATIONAL STRUCTURE

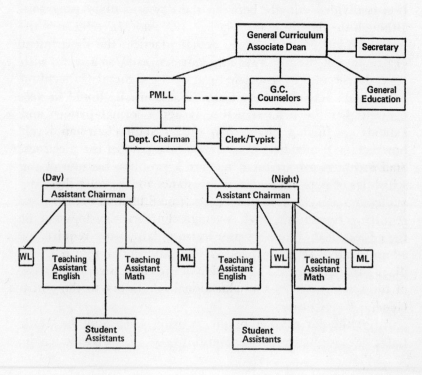

FIGURE 2

EDUCATIONAL LABORATORY

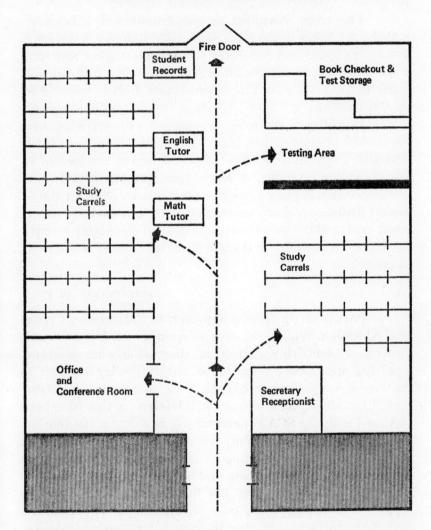

and requirements of related courses in the regular college are considered the least developed aspect of the PMLL operation. The staff agree that the centering of authority over all math decisions in the hands of one assistant coordinator who is a math specialist and all English in the hands of the other assistant coordinator facilitates the coordination. It also helps to integrate the applications labs with the related regular college programs.

The room identified as the Educational Laboratory, called *PMLL,* is a single, large study hall, as shown in Figure 2. It contains individual carrels for 100 students. Classes vary from a dozen to eighty students on regular schedules. Students may come in extra time on their own during PMLL hours, 8:00 A.M. to 9:30 P.M.

In addition, the room is arranged with a testing area, supervised by student assistants. Next to the testing area is the textbook checkout area. Two desks for tutors are located in clearly visible positions. A secretary-receptionist desk is near the main door. A glassed-in corner serves as an office for the assistant chairmen and as a conference room. The students' assignment cards and the time-clock racks (for self attendance records) are located on easy-to-travel traffic lanes. The center of the room is open.

INSTRUCTION IN PMLL

PMLL uses a systems approach to instruction in remedial education. What is the systems approach? It is a systematic process of identifying a problem, diagnosing what is wrong, applying appropriate remediation, and following through to be sure it works. In the PMLL, it means further identifying and diagnosing specific educational deficiencies that have been detected with the SCAT, determining as much as possible the learning style of the student, assigning specific remedial work utilizing the mode of learning commensurate with the student's learning style, and evaluating success with progress checks leading to post-test competence. The limiting aspect of the systems approach in PMLL is that remedial teaching is, at present, restricted to programmed texts in written form and to tutoring.

A programmed text, unlike many teaching tools, has a high degree of correlation between what is taught and what is tested. Tests in programmed material are carefully organized statements of what is expected. The material contains pre-tests and post-tests which are virtually identical. It follows, therefore, that the pre-test serves both as a diagnostic instrument of student deficiency as well as a statement of what the student should know.

The systems approach offers a realistic basis on which to plan for poor student achievement. The student knows immediately what he needs to know, what he needs to do, how, and why. There is no attempt to obscure or hide information from the student. He knows, for example, what to expect on each test. This aspect of the systems approach is unusual. The approach assumes that if achievement does not take place, the responsibility is on instruction, rather than the student. At this point in time, this idea is somewhat foreign, almost heretical, to college-level instruction. Under this concept, the teacher assumes a new responsibility. It is to devise new or additional learning experiences for students. These new or additional learning experiences or approaches are geared to particular student abilities and individual learning styles.

The systems approach makes a strong point that the instructor is responsible for student failure. It is in this spirit that the PMLL staff applies pressure to themselves to find ways to teach students with long histories of chronic failure in the basic skills. This assumption of responsibility by the PMLL staff stems from the open-door policy of the community college and from personal moral commitment. It is from this frame of reference that the staffers point out that progress for the lower ability student can be measured in direct relation to the accuracy of the diagnosis, the appropriateness of the remedy, the time spent in follow-through, and the commitment and hard work of the teacher.

The new role, to quote Don Stewart, director of SLATE (Systems for Learning by Application of Technology to Education) places the teacher in the position of "diagnostician and a prescriber of appropriate and necessary learning experiences," rather than "presenter of information and course content. . . . Students would only contact teachers when they have problems, or for tests, diagnosis or direction in seeking new learning experiences. . . . From time to time, learning experiences would include planned interaction with the teacher and/or other students in small group or 'class' sessions."

The greatest diagnostic problem facing PMLL is not

what to assign a student on the basis of a pre-test. Rather, the problem is to recognize, from the three factors of attendance, test failures, and passed tests, as these variables are spread out over a period of time, what learning problems exist. The problem must be spotted quickly and the remediation applied immediately before the student drops out, ceases to apply himself, starts to cheat, or allows anxiety levels to rise to that point at which he ceases to function or malfunctions academically.

Aside from the problem of spotting learning problems on the basis of student records, the teacher's main role as diagnostician and prescriber hinges on the role of tutor. The tutor is available at all times to answer questions, to listen, to act as confidant, to demonstrate how a problem may be solved or an exercise completed. In addition, all students are required to talk to a tutor if they fail any of the unit (or progress) tests twice. It is obvious that tutoring in the PMLL is not just a dispensing of knowledge. Tutoring has three other functions: supportive teaching, crisis teaching, and diagnostic teaching.

Supportive teaching takes place after a moment of failure. The failure may be as simple as uncertainty in recalling (from previous education) how to cancel in the multiplication of fractions or how to locate a decimal point in long division. It may mean some forgotten or never-learned step. It frequently means that the student is not quite sure when to use the comma. The teacher finds that in supportive teaching of slow learners, the simple and obvious are only simple and obvious to those, like the teacher, who already know. For high-risk students, the apparent may have to be repeated many times. Supportive teaching takes place more often in the early weeks of the semester before the student learns his resources (tutor, available audio-visual materials, and so on) and under the impact of the loss of support known in high school.

Crisis teaching takes place when anxiety over failure or slow achievement reaches high levels. Drastic liberties with the immediate demands of the curriculum sometimes have to be taken to reassure a student of success and make it at all possible for him to get over hurdles created primarily by anxiety. Yet this is not considered prostitution of the subject matter. Rather, the needs of the student receive primary consideration. Although anxiety is motivational for some "good" students, it is almost always a disastrous inhibitor for low achievers. Much of the talk between instructor and student in crisis teaching may involve the kinds of subjects normally discussed with a counselor—personal problems seemingly irrelevant to the course work at hand. Crisis teaching takes place before mid-term examinations and in exaggerated form before final examinations. Since many of the students must achieve in PMLL before being allowed to enter regular college programs, their anxiety is understandable.

Diagnostic teaching takes place when a situation of repeated failure or when observation indicates the presence of learning problems more serious than the student (or the teacher through repeated tutoring) can overcome. Since there is available to PMLL at present too few resources of psychological testing services and basic performance evaluation, it would be, for example, of considerable value to have the reading grade level (comprehension, vocabulary, and so on) on all PMLL students when they come to PMLL. Since this information is not readily available, the diagnostic teaching function of a PMLL instructor consists of trying several different approaches and noting student performance. It would correspond to that part of a diagnostic workup concerned with statements of student behavior as the student reacts to a series of easy-to-simulate teaching situations. Perhaps the diagnostic teaching is the least developed but a most crucial area of the PMLL operation.

As unique as some aspects of the PMLL may appear to administrators, instructors, or students, no one aspect is more unusual than the basic assumption that student failure is a responsibility of instruction. When a student fails, the burden of responsibility is on the instructor and the administration, not on the student.

This assumption of responsibility has the effect of focusing instructor attention on the slow learner. At the same time few college instructors have had training or experience in remedial work. Even though they may accept the new responsibility willingly, there soon appears such a lack of professional information, techniques, diagnostic tests, and appropriate curriculum that the full exercise of the responsibility seems impossible.

The standard clinical approach of psychological and aptitude tests is difficult to apply to such large numbers of students. In its place the PMLL staff is developing a group of performance criteria which will spot learning problems as they arise. These we call *error signals*. Error signals depend on what a student says as well as what he does. We have divided the error signals into two arbitrary classifications: behavior signals and test signals.

Test signals are those patterns of errors associated with passing and failing tests. For example, in the pre-test, errors occurring in the following areas may be taken as test signals: total math or English assignment; wide discrepancy in error pattern on test; repetition of a particular error in the taxonomy analysis of the math test (whole numbers through per cent); per cent and ratio only (Math); and punctuation and capitalization only (English). And in the unit test: failing two tests one after the other; failing several in rapid succession; no recourse to tutor; failure to take at least one test per week; failure to take one test by end of second week; and failure to make positive progress after tutoring. Once an error signal is recognized, the student is flagged down for special tutorial immediately. The form of this help is outlined in the following section.

We recognize, also, a relationship between three factors: time spent in PMLL (hours per day or week), tests failed, and tests passed. These three factors can be charted in the following way to indicate the presence of serious learning problems.

Example	Time	Test Failed	Test Passed	Time Span
1.	+	0	0	any 2-week period
2.	+	+	0	any 2-week period
3.	+	0	+	any 4-week period

Originally, a time-clock was used in the PMLL to serve two functions: to record attendance and to indicate the amount of time the student spent in the lab. The use of the clock has always been a subject of discussion because of the ease with which the students can falsify the time. With the above chart, however, the very fact that they have falsified their time (and completed no work, that is, taken no tests or passed no tests) is now an indication of a learning problem and can be treated as such. Formerly it was treated simply as a disciplinary problem.

On the next few pages are a series of behavior error signals. They are the kind of things students say which give us an immediate clue that learning problems exist—rather than problems of a disciplinary counseling or administrative nature.

Error Signal 1
Identification:
Student failed Unit Test completely on first try. Argues with Student Assistant that the answer key is wrong.
Diagnosis:
1. Ask if student read the unit.
   A. If answer is yes,
      (1) Check on reading comprehension; ask to read a page silently; discuss for comprehension; ask to work sample question on test.
      (2) If he replies, "I don't understand," or fails to work the question correctly, determine what kind of explanation works:
         a. Rote learning (give sample rule), be sure a problem is worked successfully, or
         b. Concept learning (give insight), if appears to respond, give problem and explain transfer from general to specific—be sure a problem is worked successfully.
      (3) Require brief demonstration of skill until student says: "I see" or "I'll try it."
   B. If answer is no, ask, "Why not?" If student replies, "Thought I could do problems without studying unit —they looked easy," dismiss student to study on own. If student says yes, but protests that he does not understand, that our problems were not like problems taught in book, or appears belligerent about inadequacy of books, check for evidence of very low

reading ability. Have him read a page out loud. If level is low (fourth to fifth grade) by ear, be sure student is in reading lab. But even if student is in reading lab, the change will be slow, and tutor can expect to spend much time tutoring student with words, diagrams and simple rules. Expect to say the same thing over and over before student gets it.

Remediation:

1. Send student to restudy on own and for retest, and advise tutoring is available after two failures only.
2. Prescribe alternate media approaches:
    A. Tape-slide unit on Comma splice (example)
    B. Experimental all-oral English sentence pattern class
    C. Instant film-strip units (on Per Cent only) on overhead projector
    D. Tape record difficult section and listen back while reading book.

Error Signal 2

Identification:

Student is virtually uncommunicative in tutoring session.

Diagnosis:

Anxiety and/or shyness negates rapport with tutor.

Remediation:

1. Change tutors.

    Suggest: a. the youngest tutor if student is very shy
    b. student tutor if no contact is made by adult teacher

    Caution: Don't send to tutor who is known by students to be primarily responsible for grades—that is, Department Assistants.

2. Reduce explanation to minimum, pose simplest of problems, be sure student can succeed in any way before session ends.

Error Signal 3

Identification:

"I took a test the first time and failed, but I got an 80. The next time my grade got worse. I got a 60."

Diagnosis:
   Probable reason: High test anxiety plus the fact that studying grammar or math for some students confuses them to
   the extent they no longer are sure of what they already
   know.
Remediation:
   1. Require of student that he retake only problems missed
      on the test with the highest grade (80). Assign alternate
      problems from an unfamiliar alternate test (any one
      of the two alternates remaining he hasn't seen). Score
      and require to get enough correct to raise score from
      80 to passing of 85. Give pages in text which are directly
      related to problems missed on original test.
   2. If problem on original test was missed through simple
      mathematical (computational) error and the procedure
      is correct, give half credit (5 points) and pass student to
      next unit.
   3. Check to see if student read problem carefully. If not,
      have student rework problem on the spot.

Error Signal 4
   Identification:
      Student says: "I need an instructor. I can't learn this from
      the book. I've got to take it as a class."
   Diagnosis:
      1. Student learns better orally and graphically than
         through the written word alone.
      2. Student's high anxiety level requires constant personal
         support from instructor. When support is removed and
         student is forced to study on his own, he simply mal-
         functions.
         A. Anxiety can be fear of repeated failure
         B. Anxiety can be carry-over of high school support
            teaching.
   Remediation:
      1. Some success has been experienced (in Algebra) by
         switching student to different text (Grolier Funda-
         mentals instead of Temac).
      2. You can get student through basic math material under

FIGURE 3

FLOW CHART: IDENTIFICATION, DIAGNOSIS, AND REMEDIATION

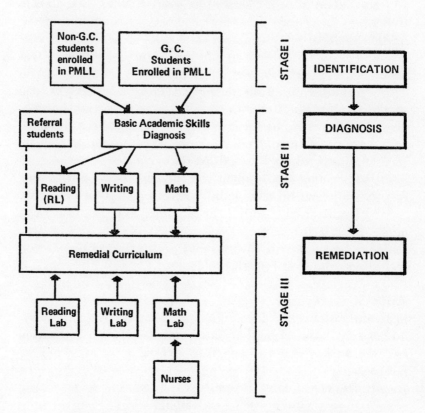

these conditions, if you expect and apply constant tutoring.

3. If subject is Algebra—only remedy is to advise student to sign up for high school Algebra somewhere in the community.

CASE HISTORIES

Case 1. Identification: "I'm going to drop PMLL."

Diagnosis: Student has been here several semesters, is not through required work in English or math. It is four weeks from the end of the semester. If student fails to complete, will have to return next semester. This is called *terminal hysteria*. Facts show student has completed all of *2600* and has two units to do in *3200*. Also, student has unit 11 (per cents) and unit 13 (ratio) to do in math. Four units in four weeks (three-credit student) is faster pace than this student can possibly achieve. Additional facts: Student has taken Developmental English and received grade of C. Is now enrolled in a psychology course which is giving her trouble.

Remediation: Relieve the anxiety with assurances that success is possible. How? On tests that are failed require student to repeat only test items missed (on alternate test). Discuss with PMLL chairman releasing student from last two units of *3200* (Punctuation and Capitalization) since both were studied in Developmental English and both were introduced in simplified form (junior high level) in *2600* and passed.

Case 2. Identification: Student says to a teaching assistant, "There must be something wrong with the answer key. I keep failing these tests." Assistant goes and gets a math tutor and brings him to the student.

Diagnosis: Math tutor discovers from student assistant card that student has taken fifteen tests covering four separate units and failed all of them with grades ranging from 10 to 60. Student has been advised to see a math tutor seven times, but has seen a tutor only twice even though tutoring every second failure is required. Student has been given, in writing, the exact pages to study as remediation for the problems missed. Student is well dressed, speaks well, is an older student (approximately thirty). Math tutor spends twenty minutes explaining how to work the problems missed, in this case four problems on the addition, multiplication, and subtraction of decimals. Raises the following alternatives for student's failures: (1) Does not know how to work the problems—although student claims to have read the text. (2) Too anxious about math (student is a woman). In working sample problems in the presence of the tutor student is very anxious to conceal ignorance. Also subtracts 4 from 7 and gets 5, multiples 5 times 2 and gets 12, says, "Oh, of course," when tutor explains mistakes. (3) Cheating. Test questions answered correctly are exact duplicates of test

questions answered incorrectly. Lack of knowledge indicates inability to have answered any questions correctly.

Remediation: First step is to ask student to retake just
those problems missed—using an alternate test with new figures in familiar problems. The result: student fails all problems
on extra test and leaves room before tutor can see or talk to
her. The second step is to plan for next meeting with student
and relieve the anxiety with verbal reassurance, emphasizing
that student will not fail—that she can take time to learn, or,
since student is here voluntarily, assure a WP grade at end of
semester if student wishes to withdraw—but not until the end
of semester. An alternative for this next meeting is to admit
that there is obviously a problem. If student wishes to continue
and if it can be identified we can work it out. Or the instructor
can take first chapter of unit studied, assign the two pages
which deal with the first problem, have student study them
and discuss it with tutor. Determine reading comprehension.
The result of this second step: *on reading*—reads slowly when
reading aloud, pronounced minuend as minus. Was unable to
sound out the unfamiliar word, minuend, or pronounce it even
when it was repeated aloud. Understood written text, about a
paragraph, only when material was paraphrased in simple
terms—"straight up and down" for "in a vertical line." *On rate
of learning*—the full hour was spent by the instructor at the
blackboard and at the desk taking student through the procedure for lining up decimals for addition and subtraction. On
final practice problem student could not do it without help.
Student does not appear to be below 10. Her uncertainty is so
great however, that when you ask her for an answer she will
hesitantly suggest an answer and then watch your face to see it
light up or cloud over. As the explanation was repeated and the
practice problems attempted unsuccessfully her anxiety rose.
She was unable to tell me that she didn't understand or that a
problem existed.

For the third step in remediation, a second diagnostic
teaching session was arranged and the student came. The subject was the problems missed on a test and concerned changing
fractional per cents (½%) into decimal and fractional form.

Result: (1) student cannot begin to work a problem based on material studied or explained previously; (2) student cannot learn a simple mathematical procedure repeated orally and demonstrated graphically; (3) student is so unsure of own answers as to make it impossible for her to work problems. Referred student to counselor again when student asked to accept instructor's offer of a Withdrawal Passing.

PERSONAL ENRICHMENT

The personal enrichment component of the General Curriculum is met by general education courses. *General education* is defined here as a series of educational experiences and subjects chosen in terms of their relevance, timeliness, practical application, and intellectual matter to develop the individual student into a sensitive, concerned, involved, and productive member of society.

The content of general education as it is applied in the General Curriculum is expected to supplement the basic skills. It is designed to touch the student in a direct way by avoiding many of the circuitous routes of traditional college content and to distill what is to be learned from the excessive abstract academic snobbery normally prescribed for students as a part of their college experience. The courses are organized to stimulate interest and meet the needs and abilities of high-risk students. While the general education courses maintain a centrality of subject-matter areas, the General Curriculum approach has been to organize them around practical, everyday problems, functional living, and around those other types of vital problems of personal and social concerns. Considerable attention is given to the necessary competencies common to youth and adults in the community and in society.

The program has utilized a wide range of informational sources, materials and other suitable enterprises which are fundamental for the solution of the vital problems and the mastery of certain skills. The curriculum further guarantees the development of the competencies through the use of effective "classroom leadership" (instruction). The courses start with the total environment for the elements which will contribute to the solution of these problems. They involve a complete disregard of existing subject-matter lines or subject-matter emphasis when necessary.

General education courses are structured to involve and provide for the full range of faculty participation and cooperation in the planning of the curriculum. The academic specialties of the faculty are subordinate to the curriculum as a whole. In fact, the individual faculty member in the general education program is a part of a professional team whose collective skills are designed to help students develop their skill for competent living. In sum, general education as it is applied in the General Curriculum is freed from much of the traditional and historical frame of reference of liberal education and emerges as a more contemporary and relevant useful curriculum for high-risk students.

The general education component does not have as complex and sophisticated a structure as that of the basic skills component. The courses can be taught in a regular classroom. The teachers are subject-matter specialists who are housed with other members in the college who work in the same discipline as their own. Class loads, class sections, conference hours, and all of the other characteristics normally associated with college, except the method of instruction, are apparent.

The general education faculty are divided into two teams according to the following assignment. Team I teaches Basic Sociology, Basic Science, Basic Humanities, and Group Guidance. Team II teaches Consumer Economics, Society and Science, Basic Humanities, and Group Guidance. Each member of the team is a subject-matter specialist. The team leaders are the counselors, who teach group guidance. One hundred and twenty-five students are assigned to each team in classes of twenty-five members or fewer.

Individual teams hold separate weekly meetings. In these meetings a given member may discuss a teaching technique that he has found to be effective—one that another instructor on the team may wish to try. Another person in the group may wish to explore the habits, learning style, and problems of a specific student. Since each faculty member in the group teaches and counsels the same student, it is not difficult to use a collective approach to appraise a student's behavior and academic performance. The selection and placement of a student into other programs in the college once he has completed the General Curriculum is another team function, as is evaluation (grading). The weekly meetings also provide an opportunity for the general education staff to gripe, reexamine the curriculum content and reevaluate instruction.

General education courses and content are organized around five broad concepts: orientation, the self, the self and society, human relations, and values. Each subject-matter discipline is brought to bear on each of these broad concepts. To the concept of the self, for example, the disciplines bring these understandings: as an aesthetic, moral, and rational being (Basic Humanities); as a social being (Basic Sociology); as a physical being, conqueror of the environment (Basic Science); as a consumer and producer (Consumer Economics); as a builder, discoverer, and historical being (Society and Science); and as a psychological, adjusting, and emoting being (Group Guidance).

No single method of instruction is used by the general education staff. The instruction is devised so that the learning takes place in seminars, through the assignment of projects, through the use and manipulation of media, through field visits for practical observation and through contrived hypothetical conditions. The lecture as a method of instruction is discouraged. The lecture is considered a supplemental technique reserved for businessmen, managers, labor leaders, and others who are invited in to give instruction (make a presentation, serve as resource person, demonstrate some method, some material, and so on). The intent of the mode of instruction is always to make the learning climate as real, as practical, and as relevant as possible. For example, mock trials are held using real lawyers. Students are then asked to visit real trials to observe the differences and similarities between the game and the reality. A specific technique of instruction is chosen because it seems appropriate for the learning situation. Sometimes several different methods are used within the same class to complement the varied learning styles within the class. Each mode of instruction has value.

The seminar is generally used with graduate students who read and write well, have the toleration and skill to handle the traditional academic abstractions, know how to study, and who have the discipline, independence, and confidence to take on academic work. Those who work with remedial students suggest that the seminar can be put to even better use with these students.

The general education teams use the seminar approach because it has proven to be effective in teaching the General Curriculum student. The reasons are numerous: The small group pattern of the seminar provides for flexibility and mobility, that is, the seminarians are not confined to any one facility, time, or set of rules. The seminar has a psychological affect on General Curriculum students because they feel it is a more sophisticated form of learning, it is oral in nature, everyone has an opportunity to be an active participant, the instructor is a member of the group and there is more opportunity to interact with him; absence of the instructor is not as great a handicap as it is with his absence in a normal classroom situation, and the seminar provides a learning climate that tolerates a diversity of ideas while providing opportunities for leadership.

The General Curriculum student is impressed by the relaxed "nonacademic" character of the seminar. He notes that the instructor does not rely exclusively on paper and pencil tests to evaluate the members of the group. This student is also aware that he does not have to wait for the periodic examinations to know his progress because he has an opportunity to evaluate himself in relation to the group each day. There are two other characteristics of the seminar that General Curriculum students frequently cite: namely, that there is more opportunity to handle concepts rather than isolated facts, and that this method of instruction is not predicated on completing a given body of knowledge within a specific designated time interval. Finally, the General Curriculum student feels the climate of the seminar is relaxed without much of the pressure of competition found in other forms of instruction. He has an opportunity to do some independent projects and he has the proximity to his instructor and others necessary for group interaction.

The student enrolled in general education courses who prefers to work alone or in committee on some specific problems has the option of doing so with the approval of his instructor. He is able to work on his own time, at his own rate, and on that part of the subject matter which is of interest to him. The project method of instruction has a tolerance for many approaches and it challenges the initiative of the student. General Curriculum students involve themselves in many projects because this technique permits them to supplement the "normal" classroom practices with nontraditional approaches and resources.

The general education instruction staff utilizes the project method whenever it is possible to do so. For one reason, the learning experience is focused on the learner where it should be and not the ability of the teacher to produce information. Another reason this method is used is because instructors have found that a variety of things may be investigated simultaneously. Most important, however, the faculty has noted that the assignment to, or the selection by, students of a special project has a positive and motivating affect on the student. The student has an opportunity to use his talent. He has an opportunity to learn and report his findings in a way appropriate to him. The recognition that he has a responsibility to the group gives him a sense of worth. This is of particular significance when he knows that if he does not function others cannot. The student learns to use the knowledge of others in the group and can more honestly evaluate himself. Specific instructors in the General Curriculum—not all of them—prefer the assignment of special projects as a method of instruction. Some faculty members feel that this mode of instruction is better suited for a student who demonstrates a more traditional way of learning. Nonetheless, the individual, small group, or class project is a definite method of teaching in the General Curriculum.

Forest Park Community College is well equipped with

media. The hardware includes such things as language laboratories, a responder system, closed circuit television, and other
sophisticated technological innovations to assist in instruction.
It is not surprising, therefore, that media have been used effectively with General Curriculum students. However, the staff
members have concentrated on using media more as a method
than as a tool of teaching. The use of programmed materials—
explained earlier in this chapter—is a case in point. It was
quite apparent in the explanation that the media were not only
tools of learning but also a prescription for learning. It contained the procedures to guide, control, and direct the student's
learning. Thus the apparatus (programmed textbooks) and the
technique (programmed instruction) were operative within the
same medium. Each was inextricably pinioned to the other.
Moreover, the tools were supplemented with human effort
(tutors).

In short, the general education staff uses media as one of
the many techniques of instruction. When they are used, the
media themselves become the tools, sometimes the content, and
—with increasing regularity—the method. No specific medium
is used more than any other; and no faculty member is required
to use a specific medium. He is asked, however, to become
familiar with all of the available instructional resources and
devise some of his own. He is also asked to observe a specific
medium being used by another faculty member who demonstrates its successful use. In this way, he not only shares his own
ideas but also supplements them with the thoughts and expertise of his fellow instructors.

It was discovered early in the General Curriculum program that the convening of large numbers of students with
varying interests—or no interest—in a given alternative was not
fruitful. Students are rarely requested to take field visits en
masse. They are asked to participate only in those field visits
commensurate with their goals, interests, and aspirations. For
example, one of the students interested in nursing may wish to
go on a field trip to a hospital while the student interested in
business may choose a bank. The needs of both students are
usually met. In cases where a single student wishes to take a

field visit where no other student in the class indicates an interest, his request is also met. Actually, it is frequently easier to set up an interview and a field visit with one student than it is to schedule a group visit. Field experiences are scheduled months in advance, and they are coordinated through the counselors.

Through the use of interest inventories and other such instruments early in the semester, counselors gain some preliminary knowledge of those students who have specific interest in certain occupations, professions, and firms. This knowledge is supplemented by suggestions of places to visit from the students. The firm acting as host is provided with information about the class, a bibliography, those students who may be interested in employment after completing their schooling, and so on. The firm in turn is asked to assign a special guide to the class who will devote all of his time to the group. Finally, there is extensive evaluation and follow-up after the field trip.

Every conceivable technique of teaching that an instructor can conjure up is used in the General Curriculum. In a consumer economic class, for example, students planned the learning experience—and thereby the teaching technique—to show the differential treatment shown certain economic groups of people in credit buying. The students sent members of their class to three different furniture stores to purchase a television set on the installment plan. The first contract was made with a store in the ghetto; the second was with a downtown department store; and the third contract was with a store which specializes in appliances located in a suburban shopping center. Once the contracts had been prepared by the credit representative, the students would "suddenly discover" that they had not brought their money with them for the down payment or some other such pretense which made the contract null and void.

Back in the classroom the class members evaluated the contracts. Interest was computed and, of course, was expected to be one of the legitimate charges. The students noted, however, that there were carrying charges, service fees, charges for running credit checks, late fees, and even insurance on the life of the purchaser hidden in the contract and prorated in such a way that over a period of time the buyer is unaware of what he is spending. The students also learned that the hidden charges are highest in the communities where the poor live. The class quickly concluded that no matter where you make a purchase on credit you will get taken. The group also learned that one can minimize the degree to which one is "taken" by selecting the "right part of town" to make his purchase. The class members then invited a lawyer in to explain the tyranny of the fine print.

Having been presented with the facts, if the student later decides to make a purchase on credit in one of the stores in the "wrong part of town," at least he would know what he is doing. Derivation of the above procedure has also been used with loan companies.

Finally, there are many other teaching methods used. The teaching technique is limited only by the imagination and creativity of the instructor and the climate within which he works.

A few people have asked, "Isn't the General Curriculum simply a watered-down curriculum?" A few others suggest, by inference at least, that it is really a "lowering of standards." Still others ask, "Is it really college level?" These questions and suggestions couch the academic paranoia which the author feels besets far too many educators who either cannot or will not teach the high-risk student and who delude themselves into thinking that to make information available in terms so that the student can understand it is "watering down." The whole "watering-down" argument in many areas of education (certainly not all) is a rationale used by some educators to cover up the fact that they are lazy, more subject-matter oriented than need, change, learning, education, and indeed people oriented.

Let us take a look at this "watering-down" charge. A student taking, for example, basic science in the General Curriculum finds that one of the units in the course deals with the human body. The teacher can approach this unit from one of two obvious alternatives. He can treat the students as though he is teaching anatomy to a medical student or he can teach the student the basic information which is commensurate with the goals, needs, and demonstrated ability of the student. For example, there is a muscle between the knee and the hip which is called the *sartorius* muscle. The teacher can locate the muscle on a chart and could attempt to explain to the student in this way:

> The *sartorius* muscle has its origin at the greater tuberosity of the *ischium* and extends laterally to its insertion at the crest of the *patella*. It is an important muscle.

or the teacher could say:

> The *sartorius* muscle starts at the outer hip and extends downward at an angle to the inner knee. It is an important muscle.

How does the teacher know which of the definitions to give to the student? Here is where the program makes use of the counselor and individualized instruction. If a student in the General Curriculum expects to be placed in the nursing or para-medical field the counselor knows it and informs the instructor of the student's goals. Accordingly, the student receives more individual attention to make sure that the student learns the information including the terminology such as that used in the first example above.

On the other hand, if the student's goals are such that a specific proficiency in anatomy and physiology is not needed, the counselor knows this also, and works with the instructor to prescribe a more generalized approach to the subject such as the one explained in the second example above.

As to college level—what is college level? Nobody gives a definitive description of what is meant by *college level*. There is hardly any doubt that quality can exist at any level. Many of those who espouse the "college level" and "high standards" argument would never have been admitted to college themselves if they had had to meet the same admissions requirements that they demand of students today.

Regardless of the course taught in the general education department of the General Curriculum, five criteria are used.

The content and material must be: directly related to the problem; contemporary, speaking to students "in their own language"; not exceedingly difficult to read or understand, yet not demeaning; relatively short, not defeating the student "by volume"; and primarily prose, being the most immediate and accessible of written forms for low-ability students. The student whose goal is college parallel receives additional assistance from the counselor and teachers in conferences and from tutoring to prepare him for the pattern of study needed if he succeeds in going to the four-year college.

To add flexibility in meeting the above criteria, use of the traditional textbooks has been discouraged. Through the use of release-time, general education faculty developed their own teaching materials. Each instructor has chosen readings from magazines, newspapers, and other sources used in lieu of textbooks.

One member of the staff gathered all of the readings that he used in his course in humanities, edited them, secured permission to reprint them, and had them published in the form of a book (Kraus, 1968). The reprints and other handouts are still in use and are the exact same material found in the book. The instructor and the student have an option: the instructor has the flexibility to use a handout or a book; and the student who feels more comfortable or wants to look the part of "Joe College" may choose to purchase a book. On the other hand, the student who is poor or does not care about a textbook continues to use a free handout. Instructors also use well-chosen paperback books to supplement the reprints and handouts.

Every course in the General Curriculum, the objectives of the course, the means for reaching those objectives, the methodology of instruction, and so on, could be recorded here. At best, we would have only one curriculum which has been applied to teach marginal students and which has had a surprising degree of success. What is it in the curriculum that makes it work—or worthless? Is it the goals of the college, the books used, the instructor, the hard- and soft-ware, the prevailing attitude of the educational community, or all of these factors? The questions remain unanswered. Hundreds of books have been written on curriculum and even more theories are espoused. Most are redundant. It is still difficult—if not impossible—to find a curriculum written with specific application to the high-risk student in the open-door college. The above curriculum is one that works. There should be others. Perhaps there are. General Curriculum can boast that in 1968–1969, 47–50 per cent of the students who have been assigned to the program were able to move into some program (college transfer, technical, vocational, and so forth) in the college.

Regardless of the curriculum used, in the final analysis it is the people who make a curriculum work. The essence of the program at Forest Park cannot be captured in writing. It is more than an educational program; it is people—creative people who have endured the frustrations, conflicts, dilemmas, dynamics, and myriad struggles of human interaction. It is the long hours, coffee-stained tables, overflowing ashtrays, skipped lunches, forgotten dinners, and foregone nights of sleep; the endless meetings, conferences, memos, reports, and deadlines. It is the persistent challenge of doing what we did not know could not be done. And it is also the conversion of an English teacher into a programmed-learning expert by trial and error, the small successes, the blundering into a new technique or procedure that worked, and unsolicited letters from students who said they were helped. All these are the human ingredients.

Epilogue

The Prospects

*C*hange is a part of our current society, and the college should be an integral guiding and participating partner in this process. Although educators may speak in terms of the "open-door, changeability, flexibility, adaptability, emerging concepts" and the myriad other descriptive terms easily stated but largely misused and not understood, their words are primarily philosophical constructs and seldom apply to the marginal student. What, then, is the prospect?

Though their numbers have increased, the problems of the high-risk students have not changed significantly. It is no exaggeration that the entrance to the "open door" college is open, but once inside the student finds the English and mathematics departments are locked tight and guarded by a department head, he cannot get permission to enter the social science department because a division chairman is acting as a sentry, and the door to the technical program is barricaded with a dean posted as a lookout. These administrative sentinels are a part of the college bureaucracy who work in concert to prerequisite the marginal student out of technical education and evaluate him out of the college parallel curriculum. With no door to the A.A. degree discernible and few certified programs available, the student wanders aimlessly until he reaches the entrance of the student union. There he finds the door open with warm people inside who are just like himself. They spend their time playing pool, ping-pong, and cards, and watching television. At last he is among friends. Toward getting an education, his counselor will restrict him to traditional remedial work and a few other isolated courses leading to nowhere but the back door. In fact, counselors in the community college continue the process started in the high school—they are the "con artists" who counsel the high-risk on to the remedial treadmill and out of attempting to try for a meaningful education.

The deliberate and systematic exclusion of the marginal student from a quality education can be seen everywhere in the community college—though not in each community college everywhere. Curriculum committees conclude their task before developing a course of study designed to meet the specific education needs of the low achiever (Schenz, 1963, 1964). Planners of facilities submit their reports without reference to space allocations for him. Administrators continue to recruit faculty members who demonstrate that they are more subject-matter oriented than people oriented. Budgets are prepared disregarding financial commitment to the high-risk student. Poor instruction is legitimized for the student who desperately needs the best possible instruction. And the question has been asked, "What is the prospect?" The students are angry—as they should be.

It is not enough to say community college people are becoming aware of the problem. People have been aware of the inequities in education since Dickens wrote *David Copperfield* over a hundred years ago. More recently Cross (1968), Knoell (1966), Mack (1967), Rogers (1968), and myself (Moore, 1969) are authors who have repeatedly called attention to the unequal opportunity for high-risk students to get an adequate education. The enactments of the Higher Education Act of 1965, The Upward Bound Program of the Office of Economic Opportunity, the Educational Opportunity Act of 1968, the Vocational Education Act of 1963, the Report of the National Advisory Commission on Civil Disorders (1968), the Coleman Report (The

Equality of Educational Opportunity) are all clear and vivid indications that educators should be aware of the problem. Certainly everyone else is. Edmund Gordon and his associates at Columbia are currently developing a complete accounting of the developmental programs or programs for the high-risk student across the country. The American Association of Junior Colleges prepared a matrix as a part of a proposal for Association Programs for the Educationally Handicapped which chronicles the professional involvement of the AAJC staff, the needs and programs currently in progress, and future needs. Yet, too many two-year college educators are still pondering what to do. Dare we consider the question yet—that is, "What is the prospect?"

Although it is true that more than 200 community colleges (Gordon and Wilkerson, 1966; Roueche, 1968) can identify some compensatory or remedial courses being taught, it is difficult to locate a significant number which have developmental or remedial departments as an integral part of the total college program. Even where one finds this integration, it is correspondingly more formidable to find it reflected in qualified staff, appropriate curriculum and sufficient budget commensurate with other programs in the college.

Community college people seem to think that the problem is developing a way to provide an education for high-risk or disadvantaged students who are black and who live in the inner city. Their conjecture is only a small part of the problem. There is no definite evidence to show that the vast majority of high-risk students are either disadvantaged, black, or live in the inner city. Numerically, we know they are not black, although the education of black youth requires special kinds of attention. Just as there are black students who are marginal in their achievement, there are many times more whites; and there are, of course, Mexicans and Puerto Ricans. The problem is more one of commitment to a quality educational program than of the specific ethnic group to which the program is addressed. The problem requires teachers with know-how, who do not consider teaching slow achievers the same as instructing students in some remote outpost. It requires

curriculum with a rationale and a budget with teeth in it. The
problem calls for making the community college a clinic; it
necessitates correlating the academics with the vocational and
practical; and it demands complete knowledge and understanding of the learner. Fantini and Weinstein (1967) say it well:

> Indeed career-oriented education is really the most
> humanistic education if we acknowledge that education
> in a free society should enable an individual to pursue
> these satisfying, effective careers in the world of work,
> as a parent, and as a citizen, and to sense that he is
> something of value, that he is growing positively, and
> that he is cultivating—and being helped by society to
> cultivate—his potential.
> Diagnosis: To make education relevant we must also
> regard understanding of learners as more than a means
> of motivating or making contact with them. The results
> of diagnosing learners must be a central factor in plan-
> ning all phases of what is taught and how it is taught.

Most important, the plight of the slow-achiever in the
community college requires a sense of urgency on the part of
college personnel. For the first time high-risk students are asking
questions about their education, but are not getting answers;
members of the community are making inquiries but fail to get
adequate information; the federal government has invested
millions of dollars in marginal and disadvantaged students with
too few tangible results or explanations about what has happened to the investment. It is not only naive but also inconceivable to think that the public will continue to permit the
lack of audit from the education profession. The non-explana-
tory insulation this profession maintains from its constituency
—that is, students and their supporters, taxpayers—and from
city, state, and federal departments and officials is another area of
impending scrutiny. "No comment" can no longer be considered a conclusive report, and "We are researching the problem"
is no longer an acceptable excuse. The time of evasiveness in
public information about education is past.

One need take only a cursory look to see that the magnitude of the disparity between the number of high-risk students

who move into the open-door college and the number who finally leave (with either an Associate in Arts degree, a certificate, a vocational skill or simply the correction of the academic deficiencies they had when they came) are all but convulsive. There is little reason to think that this disparity will change. Only 20 per cent of the community colleges have developed or attempted to develop a special curriculum for low-achieving students (Schenz, 1963, 1964). The evidence does not support a significant change in this pattern. Three hundred and seven community colleges sent representatives to observe the General Curriculum at Forest Park Community College in St. Louis, Missouri. Only fifteen of the colleges' representatives expressed any intention of developing a curricula for marginal students beyond simple remedial courses. It is rather well understood that simply providing equal educational opportunity to remedial students is not enough. Frequently these students must be aggressively recruited. Moreover, once these students are in college they should receive preferential treatment if they are to compensate for past failures and negative experience. Many question giving preferential treatment to high-risk students. The question should be: Why not? We have always given the brilliant students, athletes, musicians, and other students who have unique talents but who are, nonetheless, marginal, special treatment. One professor suggested that preferential treatment was placing the student on the academic dole. One could legitimately ask: who gets more welfare than the professor himself who gets paid for not working; who has one class to teach and assigns that class to a teaching assistant; who writes books that only a few can read (or care to); who claims he does research, to add to man's knowledge, that helps no one? It is, perhaps, unfair to compare the remedial student with the professor because the student always ends up on the wrong side of the comparison. Therefore, we cannot expect high-risk students to get preferential treatment.

It will be an expensive undertaking to reverse the cumulative effects of long-term educational deprivation on the marginal student. Funds will be needed to train special teachers, buy unique kinds of hardware, underwrite exhaustive tutoring, maintain effective counseling and design and develop appropriate curricula. Financial aid should also be provided for these students in the form of scholarships. A Seattle Community College instructor asked that such aid be given to "qualified" deserving students. The best response I have heard to this request came from a low achiever: "I kept his qualified and deserving ass out of the army while I spent two years in Vietnam. That should qualify me for something I deserve." The respondent's words were well taken and his argument had personal investment; the fact remains, however, that only a very small number of scholarships go to the educationally handicapped. The federal government subsidizes more students than any other source.

CONFRONTATION

Confrontation! Merritt—San Mateo—Seattle—Compton —Laney—all sound like the names of places we have read about in history books where great military battles have taken place. Battles *have* been fought on these campuses. These scrimmages, however, have been for change, not conquest; to take part in the decision-making process, not to make the decision; to bring others (Chicanos, blacks, orientals, Indians, and the poor) into the educational mainstream, not to keep them out. The unique character of the confrontations in the junior college stems from the fact that many of the student participants are not among the academically talented. They are high-risk students—they are more concerned about poor teaching, teacher attitude, equitable sharing of financial aid, grades, and black studies than the kinds of political concerns which appear to dominate the Students for a Democratic Society. To be sure, there are students representing the SDS on two-year college campuses, confronting administration and making demands. They are not by any means the intellectuals we find on the campuses of four-year institutions, nor are they buffoons. They are students who are well known and ones whose activities are well researched as the following memorandum will document.

MEMORANDUM   July 18, 1969

To: Dr. F. S. Dequinn
From: Dean Smithers
Re: *Problem Students: Robert Casmier, Juan Terry,
       Marc Stubblefield* [1]

The following students should be a part of your file on activist students.

Robert Casmier is a bold, dedicated activist who appears to be one of the key people. He is present at all disturbances and seems to generate or relay plans of action. He is fairly articulate, very vocal, and very profane. He is sullen and moody and in my opinion is a committed militant-revolutionary. You can note his 1.54 G.P.A., but also the dissipated schedule (he enrolled Spring quarter, 15 units, and withdrew from 10; he enrolled for 15 Winter quarter and took incompletes in 7 units; he enrolled in 13 Fall quarter and took a D for 5 units). A strong SDS member.

Juan Terry is also a leader and organizer of SDS activities. My concerns for Mr. Juan Terry are as great as those for Mr. Casmier. He also has an erratic enrollment pattern with a recent history of W's and incompletes. His early quarters also reflect enrollment indecisions. The G.P.A. is 1.53, and the load is light. He is peaceful when alone—when with his cadre he can become belligerent and forceful.

Marc Stubblefield is not the leader that we know in the previously mentioned names. He is however, active in literature pass-outs, demonstrations, and for a short period was editor of the student newspaper. He has written much about the workers uniting to control their destiny. There were several student complaints that he threatened persons and defaced posters during student elections. He was responsible for a mocked-up inflammatory article and picture in one issue of the paper where a false situation was actually rigged to confuse the student elections. He is a 1.67 student who has been here three quarters and emassed eight credits (about 2½ units a quarter). Reformist or revolutionary —I do not know. I think he is a believer with a substantial commitment to violent change.

[1] All names have been changed to protect the identity of the actual persons involved.

Student activisim has come to the two-year colleges. The signs are clearly visible. There is the presence on campus of non-registrants and members of militant non-college organizations. Students have been found to be armed and threaten to do bodily harm to security officers, faculty, and administrators. There are periodic attacks on student newspaper editors and others. The publication of underground papers without college control or participation is still another symptom. The increase of student demands is a sign. The demands are for the use of college facilities, the hiring of minority instructors and administrators, and curriculum changes (Afro-Asian, Afro-American, Mexican-American curricula and courses, experimental colleges). There are also numerous demonstrations protesting the war, the draft, censorship, and recruiters from big corporations, replete with strikes, walkouts, and sit-ins. The most dramatic symptom has been the challenge to the administration. Confrontation will not end without some change.

Since a majority of students who previously were enrolled in remedial courses in the four-year institutions are now a part of the community college population (Bossone, 1966), it is reasonable to assume that some of the dissenters are high-risk. A study by the California State Department of Education (1964) revealed three out of four community college students were taking courses offered in the high school. This also indicates that many of the activists are marginal students. The fact that there is a 25 to 75 per cent enrollment of black students in certain urban junior colleges is still further evidence that there are a considerable number of students who are among the educationally disadvantaged. Regardless of the student composition which makes up the dissenters, many of their complaints are legitimate.

It is true. Faculties have been all white in most community colleges. They still are. Curricula have been traditional and not related to real-life situations. For the most part this has not changed. Administration has been inaccessible. This is changing rapidly primarily due to the activity of the students. Apprenticeship programs have remained discriminatory in some community colleges. Students were never on committees, and were excluded from school without adequate hearings. Activist students are changing all of these conditions. A sizeable majority of these students can be classified as high risk. The prospect is that their activity will intensify in the community colleges in the future.

High-risk students are like other students—they are asking the community college to become an instrument of social change. This request invites new dimensions that the two-year school still has time to accomplish. Even the so-called marginal student sees the need for the community college to participate in outreach programs to involve the inner city. In fact, the low achievers, many of whom come from the city, are saying to community college faculty and administrators that the city *is* the classroom; and the streets, agencies, businesses, and industries *are* the laboratories. For these reasons and for many others, high-risk students are saying to educators, get involved and identify with the city. Some colleges are involved. Gleazer (1968) documents the activities of a number of them. There is voluminous evidence that the poor and ghetto residents of the city have a stereotyped image of the college as being cold, detached, and wanting the best of everything—the best students, the best teachers, all the money it can get to spend, academic freedom, the right to punish, and assurance that it does not have to change. The very philosophy of the community college, its existence in time and place, its nonpartisan stature, its cross-bred clientele (that is, of all races, religions, socioeconomic groups), and its expertise are all characteristics which would allow, indeed suggest, that the community college volunteer as an agent of social change. The high-risk students who are the activists are simply making sure that the junior college volunteers.

TRAINING TEACHERS

In spite of the encouragement of the Council of Graduate Schools in America, the American Council on Education, and the American Association of Junior Colleges to the universities and other teacher-training institutions to involve themselves in the development of junior college teachers, little has been done. Fewer than a dozen large institutions have "significant" teacher-training programs for two-year college people. None of them, however, indicates training designed to assist faculty who have an interest in working with the educationally handicapped. Only about 6 per cent of the colleges and universities in the country claim to do something with regard to the training of community college teachers. Again, none of them claim to provide teachers to work with the academically slow student.

A few isolated community colleges offer an institute for the members of the developmental faculty. Occasionally a small group of directors in community colleges meet for short workshops on working with the disadvantaged. Most of the knowledge gained by teachers who work with high-risk students comes from trial-and-error, from "on-the-job-training," and from the informal bull sessions carried on in faculty lounges. These informal bull sessions are rarely recorded or written and the information is simply passed on by word of mouth in much the same way that primitive people passed their folklore to succeeding generations. The expectancy for better trained teachers of high-risk students is dismal with no immediate—or long-range —change in evidence. The prospect, then, is not good. Although more college people are aware of the problem and the challenge, few are attempting to make significant changes. The burden of this commentary is to emphasize that the community college has not changed significantly—and that it needs to— while the community and the students that it serves are undergoing continual modification.

One need remains constant. Always, regardless of the changes, students need instructors dedicated to the duty to make other human beings better than they were—and the high-risk students who make up a considerable part of the community college population need those practitioners more desperately than ever. Providing enough good teachers can help the community college fulfill its mission of a quality education for all. This is because it is at the eyeball-to-eyeball, gut-to-gut level where the high-risk student will really be helped.

To insure that the community college carries out its philosophy, a resolute myriad of educators will find it necessary to move out of the past century into the present one. They will have to listen to housewife and minister, philanthropist and president; they will have to be advised by militants and moderates; they will have to rock the boat and make waves. I do not believe educators are equal to the task. Yet, it is this kind of involvement that will increase the high-risk student's chances against the odds.

Bibliography

ALTSHULER, T. "Classroom Testing Practices in the Junior College," *Junior College Research Review 2,* September 1967.

ATHERTON, J. W. "Who Teaches the Teacher: Expectations and Responsibilities of the Employing Colleges." In C. B. T. Lee (Ed.), *Improving College Teaching.* Washington, D.C.: American Council on Education, 1967.

AUSUBEL, D., and AUSUBEL, P. "Psychological Aspects of Education in Depressed Areas." In A. H. Passow (Ed.), *Education in Depressed Areas.* New York: Bureau of Publications, Teachers College, Columbia University, 1962.

BARD, L., LERNER, L. L., and MORRIS, L. S. "Operation: Collegiate Horizons in Baltimore," *Junior College Journal,* 1967, *28,* 16–21.

BERGER, E. "Vocational Choices in College," *Personnel and Guidance Journal,* 1967, *45,* 888–894.

BLANTON, F. L. "The Results of Two Experiments in Remedial Mathematics for College Freshmen at Abraham Baldwin College," *Research Report Number 64-2.* Tifton, Ga.: Abraham Baldwin College Office of Institutional Research, January 1964.

BLEGEN, T. C., and COOPER, R. M. (Eds.) *The Preparation of Teachers.* Washington, D.C.: American Council on Education, 1950.

BLOCKER, C. E., and RICHARDSON, R. C., JR. "Teaching and Guidance Go Together," *Junior College Journal,* 1968, *39,* 14–16.

BLOOM, B. S. *Stability and Change in Human Characteristics.* New York: Wiley, 1964.

231

BLUMENTHAL, J. C. *English 2600.* Revised Edition. New York: Harcourt, 1962. (a)

BLUMENTHAL, J. C. *English 3200.* Revised Edition. New York: Harcourt, 1962. (b)

BOSSONE, R. M. "Understanding Junior College Students," *Journal of Higher Education,* 1965, *36,* 279–283.

BOSSONE, R. M. *Remedial English Instruction in California Public Junior Colleges: An Analysis and Evaluation of Current Practices.* Sacramento: California State Department of Education, 1966.

BOWLIN, R. L. "An Investigation of the Influence of a Summer Orientation and Counseling Program for Entering Freshmen Whose Predicted GPA at the University of Oregon is Less than 2.0 (C)," *Dissertation Abstracts,* 1965, *25,* 6423.

BOYCE, D. "Toward Innovation: The Golden West College Story." Paper presented at the Seminar on the Experimental Junior College, Palo Alto, Calif., 1967.

BURCK, H. D. "An Experimental Study of Counseling Effects with Low Ability, High Educational Aspiration Level College Freshmen," *Dissertation Abstracts,* 1965, *25,* 6423.

California State Department of Education, Bureau of Junior College Education. *Student Majors by Curriculum Fields and Other Related Data in California Junior Colleges.* Sacramento: Department of Education, 1964.

CARMICHAEL, S., and HAMILTON, C. V. *Black Power.* New York: Vintage Books, 1967.

CLARK, B. R. *The Open-Door College.* New York: McGraw-Hill, 1960.

CLARK, K. B. *Dark Ghetto.* New York: Harper, 1965.

COHEN, A. M. "ERIC and the Junior College," *Junior College Journal,* 1967, *38,* 17–19.

COHEN, A. M., and BRAWER, F. B. *Focus on Learning: Preparing Teachers for the Two-Year College.* Occasional Report No. 11, Junior College Leadership Program. Los Angeles: University of California at Los Angeles, 1968.

COLLINS, J. J. *Meeting the Needs of the Less Able Junior College Student.* Paper presented at the American Personnel and Guidance Association, San Francisco, 1964.

COLVERT, C. C., and BAKER, M. L. *The Status of College and University Offerings and Services in the Area of Junior College Education and Professional Upgrading of Junior College Faculty Members.* Austin, Texas: Research Office, American Association of Junior Colleges, 1955.

COMBS, A. W. *Professional Education of Teachers: A Perceptual View of Teacher Preparation.* Boston: Allyn and Bacon, 1965.

CROSS, K. P. "Higher Education's Newest Student," *Junior College Journal,* 1968, *39,* 9.

CROW, L. D., and CROW, A. *An Introduction to Guidance: Principles and Practices.* New York: American Book, 1951.

DAVIS, A., and DALLARD, J. *Children of Bondage.* Washington, D.C.: American Council on Education, 1940.

DEUTSCH, M. P. "The Disadvantaged Child and the Learning Process." In A. H. Passow (Ed.), *Education in Depressed Areas.* New York: Bureau of Publications, Teachers College, Columbia University, 1968.

DEWEESE, H. L. "The Extent to Which Group Counseling Influenced the Academic Achievement, Academic Potential and Personal Adjustment of Predicted Low Achieving First Semester College Freshmen," *Dissertation Abstracts,* 1959, *20,* 3192.

ESBENSEN, T. *Working with Individual Instruction.* Palo Alto, Calif.: Fearon Publishers, 1968.

FANTINI, M. D., and WEINSTEIN, G. "Taking Advantage of the Disadvantaged," *The Record,* 1967, *69,* 2.

FIELDS, R. R. *The Community College Movement.* New York: McGraw-Hill, 1962.

GARRISON, R. H. *Junior College Faculty: Issues and Answers.* Washington, D.C.: American Association of Junior Colleges, 1968.

GLEAZER, E. J., JR. *This Is the Community College.* New York: Houghton Mifflin, 1968.

GOLD, B. K. "An Experimental Program for 'Low Ability' Students." Los Angeles: Los Angeles City College, 1965. (Mimeographed).

GORDON, E. W., and WILKERSON, D. A. *Compensatory Education for the Disadvantaged: Programs and Practices: Preschool through College.* New York: College Entrance Examination Board, 1966.

HAMRIN, S. A. *Guidance Talks to Teachers.* Bloomington, Ill.: McKnight and McKnight, 1947.

HARRINGTON, M. *The Other America.* New York: Macmillan, 1962.

HARRIS, N. O. *Technical Education in the Junior College/New Programs for New Jobs.* Washington, D.C.: American Association of Junior Colleges, 1964.

Harvard Committee on Education. *General Education in a Free Society.* Cambridge: Harvard University Press, 1945.

HAVIGHURST, R. J., and RODGERS, R. "The Role of Motivation." In

B. S. Hollingshead (Ed.), *Who Shall Go to College?* New York: Columbia University Press, 1952.

JOHNSON, B. L. *General Education in Action.* Washington, D.C.: American Council on Education, 1952.

JOHNSON, B. L. *Islands of Innovation.* Los Angeles: University of California, 1964.

KAGAN, N. "Group Procedures," *Review of Educational Research,* 1966, *36*, 274–287.

KIERNAN, I. R. "The New Style in College Administration," *Junior College Journal,* 1967, *38*, 22–23.

KNOELL, D. M. *Toward Educational Opportunity for All.* New York: State University of New York, 1966.

KNOELL, D. M. "Are Our Colleges Really Accessible to the Poor?" *Junior College Journal,* 1968, *39*, 9–11.

KNOELL, D. M., and MEDSKER, L. L. *Articulation Between Two-year and Four-year Colleges.* Berkeley: Center for the Study of Higher Education, 1964. (a)

KNOELL, D. M., and MEDSKER, L. L. *Factors Affecting Performances of Transfer Students from Two- to Four-year Colleges.* Berkeley: Center for the Study of Higher Education, 1964. (b)

KOOS, L. V. "Preparation for Community College Teaching," *Journal of Higher Education,* 1950, *21*, 309–317.

KRAUS, A. *Basic College Issues.* New York: Random House, 1968.

LOMBARDI, J. *Student Activism in Junior College: An Administrator's View.* Washington, D.C.: American Association of Junior Colleges, 1969.

LORETAN, J. O., and UMANS, S. *Teaching the Disadvantaged.* New York: Teachers College, Columbia University, 1966.

LUKE, O. A. "A Study: Probation at Entrance." Bakersfield, Calif.: Bakersfield College, 1966. (Mimeographed).

MCGEOCH, M., et al. *Learning to Teach in Urban Schools.* New York: Teachers College Press, Teachers College, Columbia University, 1965.

MCINNIS, N. F. "Students Are a Lot Like People," *Junior College Journal,* 1968, *38*, 40–43.

MACK, R. W. *Transforming America: Patterns of Social Change.* New York: Random House, 1967.

MALLAN, J. P. "Some Special Problems of Junior College Faculty." Unpublished paper, 1968.

MARSEE, S. E. "AAJC Approach," *Junior College Journal,* 1968, *39*, 9.

MEDSKER, L. L. *The Junior College: Progress and Prospect.* New York: McGraw-Hill, 1960.

MOORE, W., JR. "A Portrait: The Culturally Disadvantaged Preschool Negro Child." Unpublished dissertation, St. Louis University, 1964.

MOORE, W., JR. "The General Curriculum: A Proposal for the Educationally Disadvantaged." St. Louis: Forest Park Community College, 1965. (Mimeographed).

MOORE, W., JR. "Opportunity for the Disadvantaged." In G. K. Smith (Ed.), *Stress and Campus Response.* San Francisco: Jossey-Bass, 1968. (a)

MOORE, W., JR. "The General Curriculum: A Program for the Educationally Disadvantaged." St. Louis: Forest Park Community College, 1968. (Mimeographed). (b)

MOORE, W., JR. "The Anatomy of a Developmental Program." Paper presented at the Student Personnel Workshop, William Rainey Harper College, November 1968. (c)

MOORE, W., JR. "Opening the College Gates to the Low Achiever," *NEA Journal: Today's Education,* December 1968, 38–40. (d)

MOORE, W., JR. *The Vertical Ghetto: Everyday Life in a Housing Project.* New York: Random House, 1969.

MORSE, H. T. "Liberal and General Education: A Problem of Differentiation." In J. R. Rice (Ed.), *General Education.* Washington, D.C.: NEA Association of Higher Education, 1964.

MUNROE, C. R. "Guiding Principles for the Development of Semitechnical and Vocational Programs in the Chicago City Junior College." Chicago: Chicago City Junior College, Wilson Branch, 1964. (Unpublished).

NELSON, M. O. "Individual Counseling as a Basis for the Counseling of Low Achieving Students," *Personnel and Guidance Journal,* 1967, *46,* 283–287.

O'CONNELL, T. E. *Community Colleges.* Chicago: University of Illinois Press, 1968.

PETERSON, B. N. *Critical Problems and Needs of California Junior Colleges.* Sacramento: California Junior College Association and the California State Department of Education, 1965.

PHAIR, T. S. "California Colleges Look at Their New Faculty," *Junior College Journal,* 1969, *39,* 48–50.

POLLARD, B. L., et al. "Objectives of the Programmed Materials Learning Laboratory." St. Louis: Forest Park Community College, 1967. (Mimeographed).

POWELL, H. M. "Implementing a Curriculum for Provisional Students." Los Angeles: Los Angeles City College, 1966. (Mimeographed).

PYLE, G. B. "Teaching and Teacher Responsibility," *Junior College Journal,* 1968, *38,* 48–54.

RAWITCH, R. "Merritt College's Negro Leader Faces Broad Racial Challenge, *The Los Angeles Times,* Section C, September 8, 1968.

Report of the National Advisory Commission on Civil Disorders. New York: Bantam Books, 1968.

REYNOLDS, J. W. *The Junior College.* New York: Center for Applied Research in Education, 1965.

RICHARDSON, L. H. "Counseling the Ambitious Mediocre Student," *Journal of Counseling Psychology,* 1960, *7,* 265–268.

RIESSMAN, F. *The Culturally Deprived Child.* New York: Bureau of Publications, Teachers College, Columbia University, 1962.

ROGERS, D. *110 Livingston Street.* New York: Random House, 1968.

ROSENTHAL, R., and JACOBSON, L. *Pygmalion in the Classroom.* New York: Holt, 1968.

ROTH, A. J., and ALTSHULER, T. C. "Ending the Teacher-Student Mystery: Structured Assignments," *Junior College Journal,* 1969, *39,* 33–38.

ROUECHE, J. E. *Salvage, Redirection or Custody? Remedial Education in the Community Junior College.* Washington, D.C.: ERIC Clearinghouse for Junior College Information, American Association of Junior Colleges, 1968.

RYAN, D. W., and GAIER, E. L. "Student Socioeconomic Status and Counseling Contact in Junior High School," *Personnel and Guidance Journal,* 1968, *46,* 466–472.

SCHENZ, R. F. "An Investigation of Junior College Courses and Curricula for Students with Low Ability." Unpublished dissertation, University of California at Los Angeles, 1963.

SCHENZ, R. F. "What is Done for Low Ability Students?" *Junior College Journal,* 1964, *34,* 22–28.

SEXTON, P. *Education and Income.* New York: Viking Press, 1961.

SHUEY, A. M. *The Testing of Negro Intelligence.* New York: Social Science Press, 1966.

SIEBEL, D. W. *Testing Practices and Problems in Junior Colleges: A Survey Evaluation and Advisory Service Field Studies Report.* Princeton, N.J.: Educational Testing Service, 1966.

SIEBEL, D. W. "Measurement and Evaluation," *Junior College Journal*, 1967, *38*, 13–15.

SINGER, D. S. "Do We Need a Community College Institute?" *Junior College Journal*, 1969, *39*, 36–40.

SMITH, D. H. "The White Counselor in the Negro Slum School," *The School Counselor*, 1967, *14*, 268–272.

SOBEL, H. W. "The New Wave of Educational Literature," *Phi Delta Kappan*, 1968, *50*, 109–111.

TENNYSON, W. W. "Time, The Counselor's Dilemma," *Personnel and Guidance Journal*, 1958, *38*, 129–135.

THELEN, A. M. "The Effectiveness of Required Individual and Group Guidance Procedures in Promoting Change in Selected Characteristics of High-Risk Junior College Freshmen." Unpublished dissertation, University of Wisconsin, 1968.

THORESON, C. E. "A Behavioral Approach to Encouraging Accomplishment in Disadvantaged Youth: An Exploratory Study," *The Journal of College Student Personnel*, 1967, *8*, 173–175.

THORNTON, J. W., JR. *The Community College.* Second edition. New York: Wiley, 1966.

TRUBOWITZ, S. *A Handbook for Teaching in the Ghetto School.* Chicago: Quadrangle Books, 1968.

WEBER, J. "Recommendations for Better English Instruction," *Junior College Journal*, 1968, *38*, 32–38.

WILSON, L. "Foreword." In C. B. T. Lee (Ed.), *Improving College Teaching.* Washington, D.C.: American Council on Education, 1967.

WILLIAMS, R. L., and COLE, S. "Self-Concept and School Adjustment," *Personnel and Guidance Journal*, 1968, *46*, 478–481.

WILLIS, W. K., and KERR, W. D. "Interest and Ability: Are They Related?" *Vocational Guidance Quarterly*, Spring 1966, 197–200.

WISE, W. M. *They Come for the Best of Reasons—College Students Today.* Washington, D.C.: American Council on Education, 1958.

WITHERSPOON, F. D. "Group Guidance in the Junior College: A Frame of Reference." St. Louis: The Junior College District, 1966. (Unpublished).

ZIEGLER, J. M. *Disadvantaged Youth and the Two-Year College.* New Bedford, Mass.: Rodman Job Corps, n.d.

Index

239